W1D

Victorian Writers and the Image of Empire

Recent Titles in
Contributions to the Study of World Literature

Victorian Writers and the Image of Empire

The Rose-Colored Vision

Laurence Kitzan

Contributions to the Study of World Literature, Number 104

GREENWOOD PRESS
Westport, Connecticut • London

Library of Congress Cataloging-in-Publication Data

Kitzan, Laurence, 1936–
    Victorian writers and the image of empire : the rose-colored vision / by Laurence Kitzan.
       p. cm.—(Contributions to the study of world literature, ISSN 0738–9345 ; no. 104)
    Includes bibliographical references and index.
    ISBN 0–313–31778–X (alk. paper)
    1. English literature—19th century—History and criticism. 2. Imperialism in literature.
    3. Colonies in literature. I. Title. II. Series.
    PR468.I49K58   2001
    820.9′358—dc21   00–061722

British Library Cataloguing in Publication Data is available.

Library of Congress Catalog Card Number: 00–061722
ISBN: 0–313–31778–X
ISSN: 0738–9345

First published in 2001

Greenwood Press, 88 Post Road West, Westport, CT 06881
An imprint of Greenwood Publishing Group, Inc.
www.greenwood.com

Printed in the United States of America

The paper used in this book complies with the
Permanent Paper Standard issued by the National
Information Standards Organization (Z39.48–1984).

10 9 8 7 6 5 4 3 2

For

SONJA, CHRIS, and JENNIFER

Contents

emerged from my own readings and discussions with students in a great many seminar classes on Victorian imperialism. Several of my graduate students have been interested in imperial writers and their impact, and I have benefitted by the extensive discussions, and even arguments, which went into the creation of their theses.

Definitions of imperialism are tricky, because none exist that I find completely satisfactory, or that would meet with universal approval. I give my classes a "working definition," which is that imperialism is the use of power of all types by a political unit to dominate another political unit to cause it to serve its purposes. This still leaves hazy areas, such as the cultural influences that can be viewed as imperialism, even though the imperialistic impact is sometimes unintentional. Victorian writers also tended to be hazy about their own definitions of what constituted the British Empire, and for historical and cultural reasons they included, at times, the United States, Latin America, and most of the South Pacific, little of which at the time of writing were part of either formal or informal empire. For reasons of convenience, I have followed them into this expanded version of empire.

Because I do not favor single-cause explanations, as enticing as they often are, of the impulse to create empires, I tend to emphasize that individual acts of imperialism can have multiple causes, including economic, which can be studied. Individual influences can vary in importance from one event to another, often depending on time and place. It is this variety to be found in imperialism that makes the topic so interesting. Once again, the writers I have used also tend to emphasize individual responsibility for the creation and maintenance of empire.

I have not attempted a literature review of books discussing imperial literature and ideas because this literature is now so extensive that such a review would be a book in itself, and this is not the object of my study. I have also not attempted to indicate fully in the endnotes my debts to the books I have read; this too would be a massive and perhaps not very useful task. Mainly, I have provided references to original sources, and occasionally to secondary sources that I feel should be noted.

There are a great many authors that can be used for a study of this type, and I have found it necessary to be selective. I have chosen not to mine the fictional works of authors who include imperial references on an incidental basis, for example, Dickens, Trollope, Thackeray, and Tennyson, though I have occasionally referred to some of these. I have chosen the obvious writers—Rudyard Kipling, Rider Haggard, John Buchan, and G. A. Henty, the "stars" of the genre. I have made extensive use of Frederick Marryat, Robert Ballantyne, G. M. Fenn, W.H.G. Kingston, and Herbert Strang. I have also found F. S. Brereton, Harry Collingwood, Gilbert Parker, Mayne Reid, and Gordon Stables of substantial value. I have introduced a number of other authors on an occasional basis. The inclusion of Robert Louis Stevenson's irresistible *Treasure Island* in this study points to the anomaly that while this work concerns imperial writers, not all the works used are, strictly speaking, imperial literature. Many of them would be more accurately described as adventure stories; I have included them because they deal with most of the same themes and create images similar to more identifiably imperial stories. Since the latter are also mainly adventure stories, there is often such a close correlation that the two types of books reinforce each other in the impact they make on their readers.

Using writers of imperial and adventure novels in a study of the long-lasting influence of an image of empire is not merely a convenience. Just as a reading of one of these books intensified my interest in Britain and the British Empire in a way that the symbols of empire—king, queen, flags, songs, and prayers in assemblies, and the like—never could, being as they were merely the mundane wallpaper of everyday life, I found in my researches that imperial and adventure novels frequently had caught the attention of many other people, at a young age. These novels appealed to the imaginations of those who had very little contact with those parts of the empire that had the greatest impact on the romantic imagination—namely, somewhere else. Saskatchewan may have been a part of the empire, but this fact scarcely made an impact on our young minds; India, Africa, the South Seas—they seized the mind and brought ordinary, bland Saskatchewan in conjunction with almost inconceivable excitement and glory.

There was, of course, the "real" empire. Britain occupied and administered various parts of the world, and strongly influenced the course of events in others. To what extent did this process create the image of empire? Substantially, of course, in the minds of the people on the receiving end of what occurred. But for the most part, what these people thought about what was happening was not available at that time, and for a long time continued to be unavailable. Those who carried out the process and wrote about the experience tended to write in much the same terms as the novelists, and presented a romanticized version of events. The "real" story, as far as it can ever be known, existed in various archives, or locked away in the minds of the participants, and in the legends that often quickly developed. All of these needed to be deciphered much later by historians and other scholars, at a time when the romantic hues surrounding the British Empire had already faded, or were well on the way to doing so.

The novelists of empire, particularly in the period before 1914, concentrated on presenting a very positive view of the phenomenon they were describing. Already, though there were in this period criticisms of notorious aspects of imperialism—witness the campaign against King Leopold II and his Congo—British writers in the main ignored unsavory aspects of Britain's imperial experience, past and present. None of the heroes of their stories, for example, were slave traders. I have chosen, therefore, in this study, to ignore for the most part the evidence that the images being presented were distorted, or even false, and that the picture was not so rose-colored as it appeared. Interestingly, my current students, who know all about imperial exploitation, injustice, misery, and death, and have been raised on vivid television images of conflicts around the world, when required in a seminar to read a Henty novel, or one of the others from this period, often confess, to their surprise, that they were not able to put it down until they were finished. So the magic is still there, dimly, and students who know that it presents a distorted image, and are in no danger of being captured by it, can feel it.

Many topics can be considered in a study of the images of imperialism and their impact, from the traditional ones of politics, economics, biography, and military activities to topics more in vogue in the last three decades—gender, race, culture, space, and even the impact of lines drawn on maps. I have generally used John

Buchan, discussed in detail in Chapter Four, as my guide, added some topics that pervaded the literature of the time, and emerged with a list of topics that it appears to me engaged contemporaries the most. The writers of imperial fiction in this period were not especially subtle in their approach and it is not often necessary to dig far below the surface to understand what interested them, and the images that resulted from these interests. There is a fascination with space, and adventures often ranged over thousands of miles. There are discussions of the possibility of the utilization of such space, for settlement perhaps, and certainly for the gaining of wealth in some fashion, preferably in a hurry. Not unexpectedly in Victorian writers, there are discussions of humanitarian projects, of religion, and of the manifestations of character. Both implicit and explicit, there were presentations on what was to be expected of empire, and of its peoples. Though Buchan did not talk of something specifically called gender, it quickly becomes obvious in reading Buchan, and most of the other writers of the imperial/adventure genre, that the empire is about manly virtues and manly concerns, and a good deal of this I have noted as helping to form a bold and vivid, almost aggressive, image of empire. My perception of the British Empire had been born in the midst of a world war, and the more I read in imperial literature, both primary and secondary, the more I am aware that the images of the "virtues" of war have persisted in defining the "virtues" of manhood, and of an empire.

I would like to thank my colleagues, J. Michael Hayden and Dale Miquelon, for reading my manuscript and making valuable suggestions, and Dave De Brou, for essential technical help. Linda Dietz and Ingrid McGregor helped greatly in the intricacies of computer operation and in putting the manuscript together, as did Joni Mazer, who, on occasion also saved me from panic when the computer turned erratic, and I am most grateful to all of them. The University of Saskatchewan has helped fund this project through two sabbatical leaves. I would especially like to thank my children, Chris and Jennifer, who, as preteens, read a number of the "boys'" books and gave me an impression of how modern youngsters would react to literature that was so popular among the young a hundred years ago. My wife, Sonja, helped tremendously by tolerating all the time I spent thinking about this project, and by never pressuring me to get those thoughts down on paper until I was ready.

1

The Dreamweavers: An Empire of the Imagination

The British Empire did exist. At the beginning of the twentieth century it covered millions of square miles populated by hundreds of millions of people, all lovingly and in great detail described in multivolumed gazetteers that proudly lined the library shelves of the middle and upper classes of Britain.[1] For some periods of its existence the empire drew a great deal of attention from the British public, and, at times, an enormous amount of approval. It is sometimes necessary to assert this, because in the course of the previous century a partially imaginary empire grew up that was often confused with the real one. For much of Queen Victoria's reign the question of empire was a matter of hard economics and practical politics. Even flights of romantic fantasy, such as Edward Gibbon Wakefield's plans to colonize the empty spaces of the world with cross sections of British society, had to be clothed in substantial analyses of economic and political benefits.[2] Only gradually did the empire penetrate extensively into the realm of imagination—into the kingdom of the fiction writers. By the end of Victoria's reign the fiction writers had to a large extent taken over the image of empire and had succeeded in creating an emotionally driven concept of empire that they, and a considerable portion of their readers, continually confused with the practical imperialism of the earlier period.

The existence of the gazetteers to a certain extent hid the amount of the confusion. A gazetteer can seldom claim to be a vehicle of romance. It is a matter-of-fact tool for practical people—how many square miles, and where, how many people, and how much and what will they buy and sell. A very useful production it is, created by experts who speak knowingly of constitutions and cables, coal deposits and cod fisheries, climates and customs. Gazetteers are books of lists, and the glamour springing from their pages has to be carried there in the eyes of the readers. The writers of imperial fiction helped to provide the glamour.

In the early twentieth century many readers of the gazetteers of the British Empire certainly saw more than bare descriptions of islands and continents. They saw a glorious concoction, "a world whose boundaries no man can define,"[3] an evocation of land and sea that promised fulfillment for an ancient race, a master race that kindly and firmly guided so many peoples of the world. They saw a dream, a dream that over recent decades had taken a form and shape so powerful that it seemed to be as solid as the reams of "fact" that underpinned it. The gazetteer still remained as it had been, a basic celebration of the profit motive by a commercial people, and as such would have taken its place without shame in any previous century when an empire existed, without qualms, for the economic benefit of the British population. The dream superimposed upon the facts of the gazetteer has led later generations to suppose the Victorian imperialist to be a great hypocrite, spouting pious aphorisms of mission, and at the same time pulling in his profits. But the two aspects of imperialism existed side by side, and one did not try to hide the other. They were just clean different things, and the imperialist who celebrated one or the other had no notion that he must consequently abjure one of them. There is even little indication that he seriously confused the dream and the reality of empire, except insofar as he tended to believe that the dream had more substance than it actually did. The confusion came later in the minds of critics, who, because it appeared that the British enjoyed the dreams created by their dreamweavers, thought that they were consequently not aware that the countinghouse was still there, solid and necessary.

Certain "facts" lend themselves to the magic process of dream-making more readily than others. Consequently, at the beginning of the twentieth century there existed a very selective vision of the British Empire, a vision that could be broken down in all its particulars, but which taken together maintained for a time a very powerful hold upon many individuals, and influenced, or attempted to influence, British policy at home and abroad for a time, until the nightmare of twisted and broken bodies in sodden trenches grimly began to push it into the realms of nostalgic fantasy. To match the cold and relentless facts of the gazetteers, the imperial vision created a picture of the British Empire so vivid that for a long time it needed only a mention of key words to be evoked, code words that carried with them without further mention the whole paraphernalia of a detailed description, words such as Kipling's rendering of the British Empire in a phrase, "dominion over palm and pine."[4] To create this picture the dreamweavers often cast their nets over much more than the geographers of empire would allow.

In the magic world the British Empire was in reality Greater Britain written very large. It was far more than a finite number of colonies and dominions over which waved the Union Jack. Greater Britain certainly included the United States—various writers saw the Americans as only slightly aberrant countrymen. It also included virtually any portion of the world not occupied by a western European state. South America was the realm of adventurers where, had history unfolded as it should, the adventurers would have been performing their feats of daring under the British flag, to their benefit and the benefit of all concerned. In Africa, the hunter, the sailor, the trader, and the missionary all went where they so plainly had the right to go. "Primitive" Asian potentates in the natural order of things all needed the world explained by British wanderers. The Pacific islands were set in a British lake where trespassing was deeply resented by right-thinking Englishmen, if not by their government. Germans and Frenchmen should stay out;

Americans just might claim the rights of kin. Even the wastes of the Antarctic seemed to be more British because of the blundering death of Robert Falcon Scott and his British companions—somehow the neat efficiencies of the Norwegians established no claims in the minds of the worshipers of the chivalric and the heroic.

The "Empire" as perceived by the image-makers was largely not urban. Cities carried very few connotations of romance, or of the exotic; to describe an urban area was too often to describe dirt and squalor, and the "idea" of a city not yet seen, an unreached Timbuktu, was far more attractive than the reality of standing in the middle of it. Why describe the rookeries of Calcutta when the rookeries of London and Liverpool and Glasgow embarrassed tender consciences? The fascination with cities is more a function of the twentieth century, a fascination shared by jet-setters and tourists hungry for the culture of older societies. It betokens an interest in nightlife that Victorian writers usually were too delicate to do more than hint at, if at all; the "City of Dreadful Night"[5] did not have too many imitators among the writers of imperial fact or fiction. The reader of imperial stories had no need to vicariously share in the crowded existence of a perhaps all-too-familiar urban existence.

The empire of adventure was full of space, full of the exuberances and the extremes of nature, whether on land or sea. Adventures occurred in deserts, waterless and harshly glaring, on plains swept with snow or overrun with startling herds of game animals, on mountains majestic and mysterious, and in forests and jungles, dark, oppressive, and treacherous. The seas were vast and storm-racked, the rivers fast-flowing and dangerous. Adventure almost always occurred out-of-doors, and when it ventured in, it was often to fortresses, grim and forbidding. But even when the writers moved from adventures to usually brief considerations of "practical" matters, it was a move to fields of waving wheat, to dark, black soil and lush pastures, though occasionally the mining camp, raw, rough, and just barely torn out of a natural landscape, would provide a setting. When nature was in need of miniaturization, then a tiny Pacific island, palm-studded, kissed by warm currents, and framed by coral reefs, was called into being, a little natural paradise even if some things that went on there were less than natural to "civilized" man. It was an empire of space and nature—and the Englishman from his own miniature landscapes, perfectly willing to regard himself as a rural person, was completely at home in all the variations of this setting. It is little wonder that Jules Verne took an Englishman *Around the World in Eighty Days*.[6]

The emphasis on nature very quickly created stereotypes, so that in the second half of the period under discussion much of the literature of empire indulges in few actual descriptions of the locales. Treasure Island or Coral Island once established, from that point on only the barest mention of palms and reefs created the scene, redolent with soft tropic breezes and the smell of frangipani hanging in the air. The Canadian prairies became synonymous with driving snowstorms and biting cold, or an endless tract of grass crossed only occasionally by buffalo hunters and bands of Indians. Africa needed but a tangle of mangrove swamps to create the slave coasts with all their horrors, and the very word "veldt" conjured up migrating hordes of antelope tracked by marauding lions. Creeper-entwined ruins inhabited by monkeys and poisonous snakes soon became almost automatically evocative of

Southeast Asian locales. Anacondas, shrieking parrots, and vast, piranha-haunted rivers served as the necessary codes for so many of the South American settings. These code words provided not only a shorthand for the authors, but also for readers who needed to hurry on to the "action," which was the real stuff of their dreams.

The reason that the codes could serve so effectively is that they were based on fuller descriptions available not only to the authors, and frequently acknowledged in their prefaces, but usually available to the readers in cheap editions, or, more likely, in the libraries. The nineteenth century was a golden age of travel books, tales of "real-life" adventure that usually contained mountains of information on the exotic regions of the world, as well as the more familiar. Younger readers who were reluctant to face the perhaps daunting task of wading through these substantial epics—travelers who did write usually did not stint the flow of their descriptions and passed easily into second volumes—often found extensive summaries in the frankly didactic fictional renderings of Kingston, Reid, and Ballantyne, whose works in the middle of the nineteenth century helped establish the stereotypes of imperial settings. In addition, many travelers were adept at sketching, and in the days before the availability of easy photography, their line drawings, supplemented by occasional watercolors, and usually concentrating on simplified images of the exotic, helped fix the stereotypes into the minds of their readers. Based on their writings and drawings, the periodicals of the time, such as *The Boy's Own Annual*, were replete with illustrations creating a suitable atmosphere in which to set exciting adventures, real and imagined.

In the heyday of the imperial adventure story, the sea became a British element, appropriated with brooding effectiveness by Conrad at the end of the period, but long a part of the imperial ethos of such writers as Marryat, Kingston, and Collingwood, as well as the more matter-of-fact productions of sailors and travelers. There is very little verse more evocative than Masefield's "I must go down to the sea again," or his "Cargoes" poem.[7] So powerful became the image that in a postimperial age—in the depression of the 1930s—an American author featuring a disreputable Scottish engineer on a tramp steamer, who was engaged in often scandalous enterprises, still could not avoid suggestions of the sheer romanticism of these adventures on the seas and in the trading ports around the world.[8] Charles Darwin[9] may have been a poor sailor, and he did not really like the sea, but his voyage on the *Beagle* became the stuff of many adventure tales, and played a role as well in the formulation of his scientific theories which helped color speculations on race and the place in the world of the Anglo-Saxon peoples, and all the "lesser breeds without the Law"[10]—whoever they might be, German militarists or jungle-bound tribesmen.

Just as the literature of empire created an almost automatic evocation of the physical features of the empire, it also performed the same task for the peoples of the empire, be they Britons direct from the home country busily impinging upon the world; colonials, raw, brash, awkward reflections of their more polished cousins from the "mother country;" or the "natives" who in their various guises and methods of living so colorfully inhabited great portions of the earth—cluttering it up one would almost say, except for their usefulness as porters, loyal servants, and even dastardly enemies without whom no imperial tale would be really complete. Stereotypes of physical features and capabilities, moral qualities and characteristics, and intelligence levels soon became commonplace.

There were two types of Britons who were part of the image-making process; the people from "home" who could afford to travel and often did, and the "colonials," born in or raised from youth in the colonies. Strangely enough, it is usually those in the first group, the home group, that emerged from the imperial writings as the best imperial types; they were somehow more "real," perhaps because more familiar to the writers. Both groups, home and colonial, can be divided once again into people who actually existed and the people created by the writers. In imperial writings the created people were the idealized portraits of the real people; they were Britons as they should be.

The "real" people who traveled and wrote at length about their travels did so for a variety of reasons, but curiosity and a sense of adventure predominated. This was true whether they were searching out the agricultural possibilities of the Canadian West or the legendary sources of the Nile. This was true even of the missionaries searching for souls lost in the moral darkness of India or Africa; it might be argued that missionaries at least would have stronger motives than mere curiosity or desire for adventure, but when the state of the churches and churchgoing in the nineteenth century is taken into account along with the evident scope for missionary activity in the darker reaches of industrial British society, then the inescapable conclusion is that a desire for the exotic was at least equally as strong as any purely religious motivations that might have existed.

The real Briton might be a young parliamentarian seeking knowledge and stature, or an old scholar on the trail of well-earned kudos for a lifetime of academic achievement.[11] He might be a wet-behind-the-ears schoolboy thrust by death into a position of daunting responsibility, or a seasoned soldier for whom adventuring was second nature.[12] She might be a wealthy young horsewoman seeking glamorous adventures at the side of her poet husband, or an aging spinster freed suddenly of the responsibility of caring for ailing parents and determined to find identity while studying fetishes in West Africa.[13] The old, the middle-aged, the almost young, produced their journals of pilgrimage, sometimes exciting, almost always informative. Men far outnumbered women—though Thomas Cook was rapidly making it possible for groups of women to engage in something more dashing than a jaunt across the Channel or the Atlantic.[14] When women did travel further afield, they were the equal of men in intrepid adventure.

The characters of the travelers varied; they did not readily reveal themselves, and when they did write about themselves, they tried to create favorable images. Their real personalities often appeared only between the lines. Almost without exception they were courageous, they were capable of a great deal of endurance of discomfort and outright hardship, and they were persistent. Those who were not any of these things seldom completed adventurous journeys or tours of duty in dangerous climes, and they did not write about their adventures, or lack of them. The people who persisted and did write helped create and perpetuate the British view of themselves; hardy, bold, competent, and wandering across the face of the earth by the right given to them by God and Nature. If sometimes they appeared arrogant, the British felt they had a great deal to be arrogant about, though it was not fashionable to allow arrogance to appear too openly. Brutal arrogance was to be downplayed, and was not really necessary when condescension could do just as well and was in keeping with prevailing racial theories. If too often they appeared too serious and even portentous, it must be remembered that the responsibility of being British was very serious indeed; the empire certainly was no laughing matter, and very few imperialists could successfully emulate Mary Kingsley's light touch.[15]

By and large Britons who traveled tended to be imperialists, Wilfrid Blunt[16] to the contrary. People with little or no interest in Greater Britain had enough to occupy their attention in Little England, with perhaps the odd excursion to Calais or Marienbad, or to examine the artistic remnants of a more glorious Italy. Lack of travel of course did not preclude interest in empire, and imagination and romantic indulgence could turn a Ruskin or a Tennyson into sentimental imperialists even though their actual experience of empire was limited.[17] Few people "needed" to travel far abroad, and those who did and chose to see the empire, both formal and informal, tended to have a very positive attitude toward what they saw. Consequently, they had a positive attitude to other Britons whom they met in their travels, and beamed at examples of Anglo-Saxon enterprise that they encountered around the world. They were usually very ready to identify the racial characteristics that produced such impressive results.

The fiction writers also contributed their pictures of the conquering Anglo-Saxons, usually thinly disguised portraits of how the writers regarded themselves. Though their heroes appear to be divided on an age basis, between boys and men, closer examination shows that there were very few real boys in the literature of the period; the boy heroes presented by many writers were really adults artificially made young to appeal to young readers, but bearing all the qualities, including physical strength, at the adult level that alone would make many of their adventures possible. Courage and strength were the prime characteristics of the adventurous heroes of all ages, as well as wisdom and leadership ability. Fictional heroes also shared with their nonfictional counterparts their upper middle-class origins; though a hero might be poor at the beginning of a story, he was never a street arab. Breeding will tell, and honor, virtue, pluck, and chivalric instincts, all assumed to be class as well as racially determined, rapidly surfaced to carry the heroes to fame and fortune. Man or boy, the British hero had a sense of justice, and the touch of ruthlessness that obviously equipped him for success on the imperial stage. Many of the heroes owed a great deal to Sir Richard Burton,[18] though the authors would not dare to associate themselves too closely with the more scandalous elements of Burton's career. Like Burton traveling in secret to the holy places of Islamic society, many of the fictional heroic young Englishmen became adept at disguise and had Burton's absolute genius for learning languages; only a few months' study of culture and language often gave them the facility to pass as natives on very dangerous assignments.

Fiction and nonfiction then came together to create the picture of the Victorian and Edwardian Briton who provided the essential backbone to the British Empire. Not one of the world's great intellectual forces, though often devoted to amateur scholarship on a hobby basis, he was possessed by an overwhelming common sense that was prized so much more highly than mere cleverness. He was sturdy and strong, a rock that could be depended upon by sovereign and subject. If he tended to be unimaginative, this kept him from brooding about the rightness of his actions and of his place in the world—Lord Jims[19] always had in their mental anguish the fatal flaw that weakened their hold as lords of the earth. Above all, he had the natural instinct to win, ultimately if not every time, and to rule successfully in such a manner as would always earn him the eternal gratitude of all subordinates not too perverted in their nature to appreciate true value when they experienced it. This Briton was also hardworking, though in the empire of the imagination his hard work seldom fell in the industrial or commercial fields, and it is because of his hard work as well as his other sterling qualities that the rewards of virtue came flowing.

The imperial Briton was a true gentleman, with all the vague and indefinite qualities that this position entailed. His subordinates recognized this and instinctively acknowledged his right to command. The "natives" also were aware of his quality, and treated him with awe and respect and even love. Steevens's British officers were heroes to their men,[20] Nickel Seyn, the frontier administrator, was a god to his subjects,[21] Sanders was the all-seeing magician who inspired awe as well as respect.[22] Occasionally he might be a "flannelled fool,"[23] but most often he was "the voice of a schoolboy" rallying the ranks,[24] stiff upper lipped, stoic, impervious to all sentiment except for flag and queen.

The colonial Briton on the other hand emerged as somewhat different. A Briton he was, undoubtedly, with many of the characteristics of the Anglo-Saxon homeland, but wind and sun and rain had bleached some of the civilization out of him; he was closer to an earlier form of hero, more brash, but also given to silences and contemplation. His eyes saw further, and nature was a book he easily read; he knew nature must be feared but he had learned to master it. He was more unrestrained in his sense of fun when he relieved his solitude in the company of those who were like-minded; he might even engage in excess. The colonial tended to be harsher, more angular, reflecting the less gentle natural environment from which he had sprung. But he was honest and courageous, full of the wisdom and skills that many writers feared were disappearing from the smoke-laden cities of industrial Britain. He was a natural soldier, if somewhat undisciplined, and upon him surely fell part of the burden of maintaining the British Empire as a force for justice and goodness in the world. As a natural man, especially in his American manifestations, he tended to be more openly interested in material wealth. He was either not quite a gentleman, or he was one of nature's noblemen, with a lot of rough edges that would ultimately be rubbed off by a more intimate association with all that was pure and civilized from England, especially if civilization came at the hands of one of the gentler sex. Perhaps in the back of the minds of the image-makers was the awareness that it had not always been the best and the noblest that had filled the emigrant and convict ships, and had become the parents of the new-sprung colonials. Nature and the homegrown Briton had to act together to make sure that the Anglo-Saxon abroad was suitably aware of his destiny and his obligations not only to the Empire but to humanity. He must certainly be made aware of his purity, for in this dream world of the British Empire the Anglo-Saxon was a champion prude. The image-makers felt that it had been sensuousness that had led to the decline of great empires in the past, and the colonial certainly had to be made fully aware of the need for discipline; he must accept that lack of response to the serpent-lures of sex and luxury was one of the surest signs that the Briton did have the moral right to his great imperial status.

The "natives," whether subjects or potential subjects or mere worshipers at the shrine of British virtue, came in many shapes and sizes and colors. They very obviously had different lifestyles and different scales of values than did the British. Some shared certain characteristics with the British—courage and fighting ability, and a sense of honor, were those that writers most liked to point out—but none were viewed as sharing all characteristics because this would have made them equals. Natives were not equals; they were subordinate and consequently inferior, inferior even to the lower classes of British society, though it was acknowledged that the very best of native society could outshine in many ways the worst of the British. The natives were peoples to be dominated, guided, paternalized, and ultimately to be made fun of in their curious attempts to emulate their superiors.

The dreamweavers created stereotype views of the native populations that were equally as strong and evocative as their views of the physical empire and of the Anglo-Saxon who ruled it. Obviously there could not be a blanket view of all the diverse peoples with whom the British came into contact. Asiatics had different characteristics than Pacific islanders and Africans. The American Indians had special characteristics all their own. But there were some basic things that could be said generally of all native peoples.

First of all, native peoples were exotic; they had customs that differed markedly from the customs of London and Birmingham. They appeared to live more in the open, leaving their customs and their differences accessible to what appeared to be easy analysis; their peculiarities could consequently be more readily explained to a British public that seemed to have an inexhaustible capacity for information. Exotic information about natives filled books of fact and fiction; the emphasis constantly was on difference and not on similarities, because difference was inherently more interesting, but also because too much emphasis on similarities carried with it the danger that wrong conclusions might be reached about the relationship of native peoples to the British. It was already necessary to be very determined to maintain the Irish, especially the Catholic Irish, in proper perspective.

Native peoples were quaint. They were not just different; their difference took on the qualities of daftness, of not being quite natural, of being an illustration that natives were not wholly governed by reason. It was quaint to have "slanted" eyes and pigtails and to write "backwards." It was quaint to believe in seas of milk or in an earth borne on the backs of turtles. It was quaint to eat seal blubber and live in snow houses and share women. It was quaint that people had different notions of private property, though the sense of quaintness soon became strained when Britons met whole populations that exhibited skills that a professional pickpocket might have envied. It was tiresome to constantly guard one's pocket or undertake massive investigations to determine who actually had the right to sell a piece of property. Quaintness quickly became equated with backwardness, the lack of a sense of morality, and most important, the lack of a proper view of progress that would fit native peoples to reside in the modern world. The White Man's Burden was a response to quaintness.

When quaintness was not being troublesome, it was generally humorous. Native peoples who were "behaving themselves," that is, not engaging in sullen, rebellious, or criminal activities, were funny. They provided the comic relief for many works of both fact and fiction. The natives themselves were normally so lighthearted that they gave the impression of being children at play. Even when they were being serious they often acted in such strange, unexpected ways that the natural reaction was laughter. But, of course, the business of life, especially in social Darwinist struggle-for-survival terms, was serious. People not equipped with the proper framework of serious application to survival aroused doubts about their abilities and their right to live unrestrained and unguided. Even serious children who did things wrong were still children. People who were funny, intentionally or unintentionally, created suspicions about their levels of maturity. Consequently, their position within the dream empire was clearly set out. They needed to be guided and set on the proper paths by the strong, silent men who heeded the call of duty to serve these unfortunate, funny people in the same way as a parent, stern and loving, guided his brood of offspring.

The empire consequently carried with it the evocation of values. Most writers stressed the value of the imperial connection to subject peoples. By being ruled and corrected by right-acting Britons, they could absorb the values that motivated their masters, to their own long-term benefit. They could learn how to govern themselves according to proper principles of liberty and justice to all, and honesty. They would learn proper principles of family and community relationships and would create societies of solid citizens, perhaps still worshiping their own gods, but with a worship shorn of all elements of "superstition" and "irrationality." Even if they already possessed codes of personal honor and bravery, they would learn how to harness these for the benefit of the empire and the greater benefit of their own people. Good principles are only really good if acted upon in the proper context. If the natives did not have many desirable values, then perhaps if they were carefully organized and disciplined by British superiors, they would perceive the benefit of developing at least an approximation of these values—though there was a great deal of doubt about whether a sense of personal courage could be developed; Kipling, who gave a great deal of attention to this question, gave arguments on both sides.[25] Missionaries, teachers, and administrators all saw the question of values as being paramount in their relationships with native peoples, and many believed that Christian values should be inculcated even when individuals had doubts as to whether the Christian religion itself would suit the situation. The values of a civilized British middle-class conservative, as distinct from anything this being might owe to his Christian church, were perceived to be of extensive benefit to the less fortunate peoples of the world.

Empire and values had another connection. The pursuing and the carrying out of imperial ideals contributed to the strengthening of the values of the British people; it counterbalanced the acquisitiveness that followers of the dream were beginning to view with almost as much distaste as the critics. Acquisition now had to have a more clearly moral purpose. Related to this, and very strange in a society that prided itself on its modernity, the imperial dream tended to reinforce the imaginary values of feudal society—paternalism, chivalry, honor, reckless courage, and simple faith. The society that conscientiously carried out its imperial mandate was a morally better society, and the improved morality contributed to success in a potentially hostile world. For the individual as well, imperialism served to strengthen personal devotion to doing his duty, enabled him to prove his courage, and, in the contemplation of poor unfortunates lacking his qualifications, enabled him to appreciate and enhance his basic decency, honesty, and sense of what was right. He learned to make decisions quickly and effectively; he practiced his natural talents for command, and earned the confidence that a grateful nation would have in his services in future moments of crisis. Most of all, he would get satisfaction—pleasure would be too strong a word—from a job well-done, British people and native people alike well-served, and the country and the empire upheld, quietly and with dignity. Pomp and circumstance perhaps, but flag waving was unnecessary. There was an overwhelming sense of the rightness of it all—Alfred Austin's sin was not merely that he was a bad poet but that he was too blatant about his imperialism: "Wrong—is it wrong?"[26] Deep in the hearts of all proper-thinking Britons, firmly planted there by the dreamweavers, was the absolute conviction that empire was right. When the conviction was brought out into the open air, it was then exposed to doubts, to ridicule, even to the unenlightened attack of people who had equally strong convictions that pointed in different directions. Actual discussion of values could lead to treacherous grounds; it was better to leave them mutely felt.

The imperial dream was without question an evocation of opportunity. The imperialist held in his hands the key to the "sensible" exploitation of resources; it surely would be a sin to waste the precious resources of the world. Opportunity could exist on a variety of levels. It could be dreamlike, a fantasy gamble, a windfall that needed to be instantly seized; it could be the chance to tear out the riches of natural resources; it could be a steady, unspectacular, respectable living. It could also be a furthering of career, civil or military.

Empire in the widest sense, to include the whole unknown, "uncivilized" world, was in imagination the hiding place for countless hoards of treasure. King Solomon's Mines beckoned, as did The Treasure of the Incas and Montezuma's Gold. Somewhere in a jungle temple was a fabulous jeweled idol. Pirate gold lay beneath the waves of the Caribbean, or was buried on some remote tropical isle—a veritable Treasure Island. In the depths of Africa surely must exist the elephant's graveyard—myths have their bases in facts, do they not? Perhaps even a shiny pebble picked up beside a river might bring with it a tidy little sum of money to ease one's problems.

Tied very closely to treasure hunting was treasure seeking of a different sort. The gold rushes were its most spectacular manifestation, a slightly hysterical not quite respectable manifestation, especially when it was not brought under strong British control and discipline—Sam Steele[27] of the Mounted Police maintaining justice in the boomtowns of the Klondike was much more satisfactory than the vigilante justice of the California goldfields. Apart from the gold fever, temperatures could be sent soaring by great diamond discoveries and emerald and silver finds on various untamed frontiers. Much cooler and slower was the wealth to be found in the exploitation of tin and copper and less precious metals. The prospector was an honored if somewhat eccentric denizen of both the dream empire and the real world. His activities were a magnet for adventuresome souls.

Agricultural resources could be exploited as well, and the successful collaboration of adventure and science helped create the rubber industry of Malaya. Wheat farming on the plains of Western Canada or South Australia carried their own attractions, with wheat the modern equivalent of earlier glamour crops such as sugar and tobacco. Stock raising was much more romantic, thanks to the activities of penny novelists who glorified the activities of the "cowboy" and his equivalents in other parts of the world. Agricultural activity was outdoors, it was healthy, it was hard work, and it was character building, building the kind of character that contributed to the strengthening of the empire. A sense of independence and the ability to cope with all difficulties in the process of taming nature proved that the Anglo-Saxon did not waste his opportunities. The conquest of nature also gave him status, a prestige that he would never have enjoyed at home in Britain; it was not an accident that the rescue societies in England, picking waifs off the streets and out of the slums, preferred to send their charges to new careers in the rural world of the colonies, where they could imbibe all the virtues of the moral life as well as create material benefits for themselves.[28] Among the intangible benefits of the agricultural colony, some of the surplus women of the mother country could find husbands there, and help create new colonials to strengthen the empire.[29]

Empire and the advancement of career seemed to be closely related. To the officers in the army and the navy, the empire not only represented the prospect of adventure, and the possibility of windfall gain, since prizes and bounties, as well as the occasional spot of looting, were still firmly entrenched, but also represented the strong possibilities of promotion and of the winning of honors that not only enhanced one's own personal esteem, but also the likelihood of future employment in desirable enterprises. Young merchants and fledgling entrepreneurs of all types, blocked by lack of sufficient capital or opportunity at home, often found that the wider world deemed their services of great value. Creation of competency and a good retirement income was at least possible, and the achievement of actual wealth was not unknown. In a less regulated society the returns on ingenuity promised great rewards and, as long as one did not sail too far beyond the bounds of propriety, delivered respectability and recognition. For those for whom service appealed, whether because they lacked the acquisitive instincts of their more business-minded brethren, or because they were responding to a genuine call, the imperial services offered careers of eminent respectability, a relatively well-served lifestyle in the colonies, and a comfortable retirement to a perhaps less well-served but substantial lifestyle in England.

A too earnest gazing at maps creates its own illusions. A fond regard for all the red splashed about a world map, a tendency to equate space with strength, created, though to their credit the statesmen knew better,[30] the illusion that was known as Pax Britannica. For dreamweavers and dreamers alike, even otherwise very prosaic dreamers, the empire was an evocation of power. Power past, power present, power future. This was an aspect of mercantile theory that free traders never totally eradicated from the conscious, let alone the subconscious, of the British people. Empire provided the sinews of war. England even under free trade was a commercial nation, and a commercial nation must need rely heavily on naval strength to maintain security and the freedom to trade wherever markets might present themselves. Imperial territories were the strong points that provided naval bases and sometimes troops for those dozens of little colonial conflicts that occurred in the Victorian period.[31] Trade protected was industry saved. Industry saved provided the great economic resources, the funds of capital that government could draw on in times of war.

The empire also gave employment to military forces. This might be much decried by Little Englanders, but the fact remained that a tool to be effective in the long run needed some honing and perfection in the short. Protecting the empire provided the opportunity. That the experience of empire might be less than perfect for preparing Britain for the experience of 1914 was less than evident. That anything that happened in the nineteenth century could have convinced nations about the effects of warfare in the twentieth is unlikely. The British army might be small and the navy might be coming under increasing technological challenge, but the public was usually confident, despite the scaremongers,[32] that British wealth would create the resources to make things right. And even with shortcomings, the empire-based military might of Britain appeared not to be negligible. One of the great nations of Europe, with an army many times the size of the British, carelessly challenged the right of the British to remain protectors of the Nile, debouching a small force of French officers and Senegalese troops at Fashoda. The British, armed with all the righteousness that a Chamberlain[33] could muster, stood firm, and the great nation was forced to back down. It was a lesson, perhaps the wrong lesson, and a powerful stimulant to the imaginations of imperial dreamers.

Still, this imperial strength was based too much on the center, on the blood and iron of Britain itself, to be totally satisfactory to the imperially minded. The best-selling lectures of a university professor[34] had explained to the public what a great many were already beginning to perceive as obvious. The future belonged to large states, and the drift to disintegration that seemed to be inherent in such developments as dominion status and, much worse, home rule for Ireland, must be reversed, and a much more formal organization, an imperial federation, must emerge. This would be a superstate in an age of superstates; it would be the epitome of empire. It would be strong, and its strength would be celebrated. More important, it would be listened to. Splendid Isolation might remain, perhaps, but it would be the isolation that comes of being at the top, arbitrating the world not by force, but through the knowledge that that force existed to be pledged on the side of right and justice wherever it was needed.

The vision of colonial soldiers leaping to the defense of empire was also heartening. The young men of the colonies, bold, strong, and vigorous, would have a heartfelt commitment to the great imperial state, and any tale of imperial strength would have to take the tally of the empire. It might be Canadian boatmen on the Nile, working for the relief of Gordon.[35] It certainly was Canadian, Australian, and New Zealand regiments fighting beside the British on the veldt of South Africa.[36]

Most heartening, it was the response of all the colonies, not just the white dominions, to the call of serving the king, with money, men, and rhetoric, when the guns of August 1914 plunged the empire into a conflict, the causes of which few colonials understood. Just how the empire worked at this point was not clear, and colonial conferences did not seem to make it any clearer, but that it appeared to work as the dreamweavers had postulated was a matter for self-congratulation.

The imperial dream as it existed in Victoria's day and the period immediately following had in all likelihood as many manifestations as there were dreamers. But whatever the details, the common core of these dreams helped to develop a certain frame of mind, partly based on illusion, that had substantial impact in the short run, and sent tendrils of assumption deep into the twentieth century. It took a long time for the dream to shatter, killed partially by external events, and partially by its own lack of reality, but its elements often had to be killed one by one before they disappeared.

NOTES

1. A good example of such a gazetteer is *The British Empire Series* (London: Kegan Paul, Trench, Trubner & Co., 1899–1902), 5 Vols.

2. Edward Gibbon Wakefield, *A View of the Art of Colonization, in Letters Between a Statesman and a Colonist* (Oxford: At the Clarendon Press, 1914 [1849]).

3. John Buchan, *A Lodge in the Wilderness* (London: T. Nelson & Sons, 1916 [1906]), 198.

4. Rudyard Kipling, "Recessional," 1897.

5. Rudyard Kipling, "The City of Dreadful Night," from *Life's Handicap*, 1891.

6. Jules Verne, *Around the World in Eighty Days* (New York: William Morrow & Co., 1988 [1873]).

7. John Masefield, "Sea Fever," from *Salt-Water Ballads*, and "Cargoes," from *Poems and Ballads*, collected in *Selected Poems* (London: William Heinemann, 1922).

8. Guy Gilpatric wrote a series of books starring Colin Glencannon, such as *Scotch and Water, Half-Seas Over*, and *Three Sheets in the Wind*, collected in *The First Glencannon Omnibus* (New York: Dodd, Mead & Co., 1946). See also *The Second Glencannon Omnibus* (New York: Dodd, Mead & Co., 1946).

9. Charles Darwin (1809–1882), scientist and writer on science subjects.

10. Rudyard Kipling, "Recessional."

11. Charles Dilke (1843–1911), Liberal member of Parliament, and J. A. Froude (1818–1894), historian, Regius Professor of History, Oxford.

12. Joseph Thomson (1858–1895), Scottish explorer, and Fred Burnaby (1842–1885), army officer.

13. Lady Anne Blunt (1837–1917), traveler, wife of Wilfrid Scawen Blunt, and Mary Kingsley (1862–1900), traveler in West Africa, writer, and lecturer.

14. Edmund Swinglehurst, *The Romantic Journey* (London: Pica Editions, 1974), 38–40.

15. Most would likely have found her self-deprecating wit too uncomfortable to use to describe themselves. See *Travels in West Africa* (1897) and *West African Studies* (1899).

16. Wilfrid Blunt (1840–1922), who traveled a great deal in the Near East, was strongly anti-imperialist. See Elizabeth Longford, *A Pilgrimage of Passion: The Life of Wilfrid Scawen Blunt* (New York: Alfred A. Knopf, 1980). Kathleen Tidrick suggests that Blunt's anti-imperialism dated from the British occupation of Egypt in 1882; *Heart Beguiling Araby; The English Romance with Arabia* (London: I. B. Taurus & Co., 1989), 129.

17. John Ruskin (1819–1900), art critic and writer, and Alfred Lord Tennyson (1809–1892), Poet Laureate, 1850–1892.

18. Sir Richard Burton (1821–1890), traveler, linguist, orientalist, ethnographer.

19. Joseph Conrad, *Lord Jim* (Oxford: Oxford University Press, 1983 [1900]).

20. G. W. Steevens (1869–1900), a war correspondent who died at the siege of Ladysmith in the Boer War, was most complimentary to British officers and their ability to command native troops in *With Kitchener to Khartum* (New York: Dodd, Mead & Co.,1898), Chapter 6.

21. John Nicolson (1822–1857), British administrator and soldier in the Punjab. Lewis Wurgraft, *The Imperial Imagination: Magic and Myth in Kipling's India* (Middletown, Conn.: Wesleyan University Press, 1983), 92.

22. Edgar Wallace, *Sanders of the River* (London: Ward, Lock & Co., n.d.).

23. Kipling, "The Islanders," 1902.

24. Henry Newbolt, "Vita Lampada."

25. For example, in "His Chance in Life," "The Head of the District," and "Gunga Din," though in the case of Gunga Din, the salient fact was the existence of a high level of courage in someone where it would not normally be expected.

26. Alfred Austin (1835–1913), Poet Laureate when he wrote "Jameson's Ride," published in the *Times*, January 11, 1896.

27. Sam Steele (1849–1919) was at the goldfields in 1898–99 and referred to this period as "trying years." Col. S. B. Steele, *Forty Years in Canada* (Toronto: McLelland, Goodchild & Stewart, n.d. [1915]).

28. Joy Parr, *Labouring Children: British Immigrant Apprentices to Canada, 1869–1924* (London: Croom Helm, 1980), 46.

29. Susan Jackel, ed., *A Flannel Shirt and Liberty: British Emigrant Gentlewomen in the Canadian West, 1880–1914* (Vancouver and London: University of British Columbia Press, 1982).

30. Lord Salisbury informed the House of Lords on June 11, 1877, with regard to yet another Afghan crisis, "I cannot help thinking that, in discussions of this kind, a great deal of apprehension arises from the popular use of maps on a small scale." Quoted in Robert Taylor, *Lord Salisbury* (London: Allen Lane, 1975), 53.

31. Byron Farwell, *Queen Victoria's Little Wars* (New York: W. W. Norton & Co., 1972) has an excellent list of these, 364–371.

32. For example, Gordon Stables, *The Cruise of the "Vengeful": A Story of the Royal Navy* (London: Dean & Son, n.d.) and Erskine Childers, *The Riddle of the Sands* (New York: Penguin Books, 1978 [1903]).

33. Joseph Chamberlain (1836–1914), Colonial Minister in Lord Salisbury's administration from 1895.

34. Sir John Seeley, *The Expansion of England* (Chicago: University of Chicago Press, 1971 [1884]).

35. Roy MacLaren, *Canadians on the Nile, 1882–1898* (Vancouver: University of British Columbia Press, 1978).

36. A recent study of the Canadian involvement is by Carman Miller, *Painting the Map Red: Canada and the South African War, 1899–1902* (Montreal and Kingston: Canadian War Museum and McGill-Queen's University Press, 1993).

2

World Pictures: Travelers and Explorers

In nineteenth-century Britain two substantial groups of people wrote about empire and about worldwide adventures from more personal experience than what was available to most people. One group were travelers of all types,[1] who recorded their adventures, and the second were the fiction writers, who often supplemented their own experiences by references to travel and exploration books. A close relationship between the works of the two groups gradually built up, as they created their images of the different parts of the world and of the people who lived and adventured there. This chapter and the next shall examine this relationship.

There is a long tradition of tourists in English history, people who traveled primarily for the pleasure of traveling, and secondarily to extend their education in some form approved by the society of their age. Such in essence was the Grand Tour of the eighteenth century, some forms of which continued in the nineteenth century and well into the twentieth. But in the nineteenth century, the definition of tourist and the scope of tourism greatly expanded, and in directions that prompted the wealthy to identify themselves as travelers in order to distinguish themselves from the tourists. With the advent of the services of Thomas Cook[2] in the 1840s, travel was facilitated, through organization, for classes lower in the economic and social scale. These tourists traveled in groups, under a leader, and appeared to travel more to satisfy curiosity than to enhance education. Welcomed by the hotel owners and service industries in France, Switzerland, and Italy, and then across seas and oceans, they eventually came in droves. This caused their well-to-do compatriots, who affected seeing countries "as they really were" but who were essentially doing the same thing more expensively and more independently, to resent deeply their activities; their numbers, chatter, and aggressive Britishness were an embarrassment.[3] Both types of tourists tended to enjoy themselves, and to come home thoroughly convinced of the innate superiority of everything British, and of simply being British.

Large-scale tourism coincided with, if it did not contribute to, the growth of "Anglo-Saxonism" and the development of the scientific racism that deepened in the second half of the nineteenth century. To a complacent middle class the evidence for such theories, albeit at a very superficial level, was there for everyone to plainly see. Basically, the attitudes of the tourists were little different than those of the travelers, who might have had greater intellectual preoccupations, but whose observation of everyday life tended to be at the same superficial level. Some travelers of true intellectual ability, such as Sir Richard Burton, who had a deeper understanding of the societies through which they traveled, still emerged with basic judgments about racial superiority that largely coincided with those of the majority. British travelers and tourists went out with their racial concepts already formed, and usually managed to arrive home again with their sense of superiority intact. The fact that this was so suggests that racism and imperialism existed concurrently, but were not necessarily related to each other; it is very likely that neither was the cause nor the result of the other.

Tourists and travelers who traveled in groups seldom wrote books about their experiences; solitary travelers, or travelers who traveled with a purpose, often did. There was a substantial market for their works, and these were popular in the lending libraries, so that the views that they put forward were fairly widespread. Most British travelers traveled in European countries, but enough went to areas around the globe to provide a good coverage of information. They usually traveled in civilized countries, but often ended up on the frontiers of civilization, and many were adventurous enough to travel through areas that were dangerous, either because of a physically difficult terrain, because of disease, or because the country was unsettled enough that law and order did not protect the traveler against banditry or the possibility of murder. Some traveled so far beyond the confines of civilized government that they became explorers, at least as far as European experience was concerned, and brought back to Europe information about these areas that either did not previously exist or was available mainly as vague rumor. These travelers became the heroes of nineteenth-century British adventure, often performing incredible feats of endurance in order to achieve their purposes.

Whatever the state of civilized amenities available in the areas crossed by British travelers, the journeys required a good deal of patience and stamina; even in the age of steam, journeys were relatively slow. Traveling was not for the weak, and certainly not for the timid. The points of view expressed in travel books, therefore, were the points of view of vigorous and adventurous individuals, individuals who would be inclined to a more rigorous judgment of the foibles and perceived weaknesses of the peoples among whom they traveled. They were the type of persons who would be likely to judge others by the standards of their own performance, and consequently would more readily reach the conclusion that the world would be better off being run by leaders full of British pluck, daring, and initiative. Considering the cost of any substantial travel, the travelers were also likely to be at least moderately well-off, though a number of them, such as G. N. Curzon, supplemented their income by contributing articles about their travels to newspapers and journals.[4] Explorers, who faced very high costs, especially in Africa where the most expensive and least efficient means of carrying good—human porterage—frequently had to be adopted, usually were subsidized, by newspapers, by governments, by mission societies, by organizations like the

Royal Geographical Society, or occasionally by public subscription.[5] More modest undertakings, such as journeys across unexplored portions of Australia looking for grass and water, still had to have some outside financial backing.[6] Again, travelers who either personally had funds to travel, or who commanded the type of backing necessary to become explorers, had a distinct and often elitist point of view about the peoples they encountered in their journeys, and the potentialities of the areas through which they had passed.

People who traveled in dangerous areas of the world, whether "civilized" or "uncivilized," often appeared to have something to prove to themselves. Hardships met and pain undergone did not seem to deter them from embarking on new adventures when the urge returned. An individual not renowned as a fire-breather, George Curzon, was willing to put up with an extremely bad back, the pain of which was made worse by riding on horseback, in order to achieve the results that his restless ambition dictated. Inevitably, such recklessness did take its toll, and adventurers such as Arthur Connally and Charles Stoddart, A. R. Margary, and William Henry Shakespear found that their luck ran out as they fell victim to the politics of the regions through which they traveled.[7] African expeditions that started out with several Europeans seldom returned with their full complement intact, and even the survivors arrived back in Britain debilitated from the severe bouts of the tropical diseases that had killed their companions.

Not all the people who traveled, whether as tourists, travelers, or explorers, were imperialists or became imperialists as a result of their activities. Some of them were apolitical, some were too shallow to make any type of serious reflection about the world they lived in, and some were sensitive enough to feel that the peoples of foreign areas not only appreciated their independence, but had the right to continue to enjoy it. But a very large number accepted that the empire was a "good thing," that the expansion of the empire to a new region might also be a "good thing," and that most people of the world would benefit from a closer connection with Britain. Consequently, the accounts of their travels were often an exposition of this point of view, with the bulk of the evidence being marshaled in its favour. Their books were a very good source of information on the world as it existed at that moment, even though their biases are evident and need to be taken into account.

The travelers were also representatives of an expansive community, a community that since the sixteenth century had been operating on a worldwide basis. Technological improvements over the centuries ensured that the contacts of this community with the rest of the world would become more frequent and more intimate in its nature. The travelers were a natural expression of the need to know more about the world, for one of the characteristics of an expansive community is curiosity. Curiosity breeds ambition, not in all, but in enough so that the result is action. In the end, the forces in the European community that the travelers represented would have made sufficient contact with the rest of the world, with or without imperialism, so that the way of life of previously isolated communities, or less technologically advanced communities, would have been irretrievably changed. The stories the travelers brought back with them fed a hunger and provided justifications for certain actions taken by European societies, including the English. The travelers' tales did not of themselves create the hungers and urges of a restless society, but they played a role in helping to feed them.

In the course of feeding the curiosity of a newly developing naval state on the peripheries of Europe, British travelers since at least the sixteenth century had helped to create images of the rest of the world, and these images, in turn, helped propel British sailors and merchants into a search for new trade, fisheries, and ultimately, colonies. Every generation added its own contributions to the building up of the world picture that influenced the adventurous elements of British society. Very naturally, given the position of Britain, every set of images had to begin with the sea and the activities of the British upon the waves.

The great age of seaborne explorations, culminating in the voyages of Anson and Cook, was over by the nineteenth century, though there still remained many areas of the world to be charted, and some unfinished business that refused to relax its grip upon the imagination, such as the perennial search for the Northwest Passage, which lured Sir John Franklin and his crew to their deaths in the mid-nineteenth century. But if the nineteenth century no longer saw the epic maritime explorations, it was the century of the passenger. Charles Darwin took passage in the *Beagle*, as a naturalist, sailed around the world, saw an immense amount, recorded a great deal, and added to the fund of knowledge that fueled his theory of evolution.[8] James Froude and many other passengers described in detail both the delights of passage and the landing at exotic ports.[9] Mary Kingsley's outward-bound ship salon was an intriguing source of information, as "old hands" filled the newcomer with varieties of stories, horrific or delightful, in the manner of "old hands" on ocean voyages.[10]

Many old sailors wrote their memoirs at the end of long careers. To these men, the sea was both benign and wild—a source of employment, and a sudden implacable enemy that punished the slightest error with death and destruction. Service in foreign ports, particularly in Asia and Africa, could be exotically interesting, or destructively dangerous. There was excitement in these ports, with their teeming populations full of peculiar customs, their strange buildings and stranger smells, their drinking shops and tattoo parlors. Foreign stations also brought with them the promise of action; this could mean threatening obstreperous populations in China's treaty ports, chasing pirates through the China Seas and Straits of Malacca, or making swift forays up jungle-lined creeks to blow up the stockades of stubborn, troublesome Malay or Dyak chieftains. To the British, the navy of the nineteenth century was the Pax Britannica, and despite occasional panics about French naval strength and sudden scrambles to catch up to technological developments, it managed to fulfill its functions adequately, and to be perceived as doing so. It kept Britain secure on the wilderness that was the sea. And the sea was the pathway to the empire in its widest sense.

A considerable number of visitors came to Canada in the course of the nineteenth and early twentieth century. Some were there to satisfy a rather limited curiosity, and included a few weeks in Canada as sort of an appendix to a trip to the United States and the superior attractions of New York and Boston.[11] Some came as settlers and described the manner of their coming as a service, or warning, to prospective travelers to British North America.[12] Some came in service, as part of the imperial bureaucracy, or as part of the military.[13] Some came as sportsmen, to taste the vaunted thrills of big-game hunting and fishing in the North American wilds.[14] Some came to gather information to encourage migration to the new lands. They all helped to create a very detailed image of what was to be found there.

In the first half of the nineteenth century most travelers to Canada confined their experiences to the more easily accessible eastern provinces. Travelers were not often impressed with this sleepy frontier, especially if they had previously traveled in the eastern United States. They could not help but contrast the large cities, the extensive transportation networks, and the aggressive business spirit of the American states with what seemed to them the backwoods mentality in the half-developed towns in the British colonies. Vaunted British enterprise, if it ever came to Canada in the first place, appeared to have migrated south as quickly as possible, leaving behind primitive roads and a stagnant economy. Undoubtedly parts of it were picturesque, especially the regions occupied by the French Canadians, but picturesqueness did not make up for what appeared obvious to many travelers, that this part of the population was even more backward than the rest, caught in the time warp of its history, and subjected to the delusions of its religion. Various writers came and judged, and found progress in the Canadas less than satisfactory, as did, more influentially, the radical politician Lord Durham and his entourage.[15] The very best that could be said was that the people were more polite and restrained than the brash Americans.

If development in Eastern Canada was unsatisfactory from the viewpoint of the visitor, civilized development throughout the west, at least until the completion of the great transcontinental railway, the Canadian Pacific Railway, was almost indiscernible. A few farms were laid out along the Red River south of Fort Garry, a number of optimistic villages dotted Vancouver Island and the Fraser Valley, and for the rest, there were mainly fur traders, Indians, Métis, and whisky traders. As long as the buffalo lasted, the prairies were a hunter's paradise, through which big-game hunters such as the Earl of Southesk could wander in amazed contentment.[16] Prairie trails were never-ending; dry, dusty, and windblown in the summer, bleak and blizzardy in the winter. Crossing the prairies was like crossing the uncharted oceans, and at times appeared to be as dangerous, and as boring, though lush grasses and carpets of flowers could call forth paeans of praise for the fertility of this land.[17] Mountains were scenic and wild, lovely to hunt through, but essentially uneconomic and a barrier to transportation. Canoeing along the fur-trading routes, often with French Canadian paddlers and guides, was picturesque, and a link with the great and prosperous days of the Hudson's Bay Company and its Montreal rivals.

The railways brought a great deal of enthusiasm to the west, partly caused by the political completion of Canada's "dominion" from sea to sea. Towns like Winnipeg gained the appearance of boom cities, with frantic speculation in property and the prospect of endless wealth, and as the frontiers moved farther west, this scene was repeated in town after town. The era of the wheat farm was proclaimed, and governments, railways, and land companies outdid themselves in predicting the golden harvests that would flow to the markets of Europe. Coal-mining towns in the foothills promised the beginnings of vast mineral resources that would turn barriers into economic assets.

Still, there was a sense of reality. False-fronted stores, wooden sidewalks, and dusty, potholed streets did not add up to the civilization of Manchester or London. On farms and ranches, isolation was supreme; before the homesteads filled up it could be a long and uncomfortable journey to visit the nearest neighbor. Living accommodations were rough, difficult to keep clean and civilized in appearance, and work was hard, and apparently endless. Farmers had to learn to adjust to the conditions of the prairies, and learn what would produce the best results. And the winter months recalled that the image of Canada as the land of snows had substance behind it. The winds built up huge drifts that obliterated roads and often hid the very fence posts. The ordinary chores of looking after livestock became an ordeal. The cold was unbelievably fierce to emigrants from England, and miscalculation could lead to injury, loss of fingers or toes, or even death.[18] Still, it was noted, almost with surprise, children grew up healthy and strong, seldom suffering from illness.[19] It was a land in which one could survive and prosper; it was not a land that would immediately see a Bloomsbury type of culture established, and presumably those who required it would not come. County culture, complete with cricket matches and fox hunts, could be tried, though with limited success.[20] To succeed, it was necessary to become North American.

In contrast to the fiction of the Canadian west, the travelers knew that they were moving through an essentially law-abiding area. With few exceptions, and these dealing largely with providing liquor to the Indians, the wild west of the United States frontier did not appear on the prairies. A large part of this was due to the appearance of the Northwest Mounted Police in the west in 1873. The "mounties," a substantial minority of whom had experience in other parts of the empire, quickly established their presence, and though there was law-breaking and murder, it was relatively well-contained. The travelers in the west were not reluctant to praise and to help create the legend of the Mounted Police.

Australia and New Zealand also had their agricultural frontiers that aroused the enthusiasms of travelers. Sheep and cattle became the pioneers in creating prosperous agricultural communities, though their profitability fluctuated with world prices. Only gradually could the viability of wheat and sugar be established. Still, the prospect of large spaces that could be opened up to agricultural pursuits was attractive to many.

In Australia these prospects spurred a series of explorations in hopeful searches for enough grass and water to support economic activity. These journeys helped to create the image of Australia as a continent with a fringe of coastal settlement within areas of fertility if not luxuriance, and a vast interior that varied from semidesert to desert. Barren, dusty mountains, broken plains of shale, rivers that appeared and disappeared into nowhere, lakes that were only occasionally in existence, and a tough, scrubby vegetation feeding kangaroos and other weird animals all became part of this image, so different from anything that western Europe had to offer. Central Australia gained a reputation for harshness, a countryside that compelled its travelers to abandon comfort, and at times risk their lives in order to successfully negotiate a journey from one oasis of fertility to another.[21] New Zealand, in contrast, was green, forested, mountainous, and almost luxuriant within its moderate, often wet climate.[22] What it really lacked was size, a factor exasperated by the existence of a native population, the Maori, which was stubbornly attached to its land, especially in North Island. When the land was settled, a variety of occupations, wheat farming, livestock, whaling, and lumbering, promised a moderate prosperity and comfort.

Australia and New Zealand attracted travelers of intellectual and political curiosity, such as Charles Dilke, Anthony Trollope, and James Froude,[23] and they were much more favorably impressed with these colonies than they were with Canada. Life in Australasia might be more primitive than in London, but in all the major cities there seemed to be an attempt to create a reasonable approximation of civilized existence, and certainly the wealthier classes lived at a level that could be compared favorably to the squirearchy. Small town and rural areas appeared almost always to be rough-hewn and raw, dominated by heat, flies, dust, and the smell of dust mingled with the ever present smell of sheep. Australasian colonies had the distinct advantage of not being right next to the United States, which would have invited comparison. Even modest achievements, then, were suitable for the sprinkling of accolades.

There were usually fewer accolades for the southern African colonies. Here the problems of the creation of viable states were so complex that they led to very hesitant and often unsuccessful direction of policy from the Colonial Office. When South Africa was acquired by Britain it had not only a population of European descent, and of a different language and culture, but a Boer culture that proved to be aggressively expansionist. Since expansion, by the time the British arrived, could only be at the expense of a substantial native population itself expanding toward the areas already settled by the Boers, the situation was ripe for tension and conflict.[24] The mixture of communities in southern Africa, with their different lifestyles, ambitions, and attitudes to each other was something that struck travelers to the area forcibly,[25] revealing as it did the almost hopeless diversity of the region that made the evolution of a rational policy almost impossible. When to the mixture were added diamonds and gold, bringing in their wake aggressive entrepreneurs, and when a reviving European imperialism brought the possibilities of international rivalry, the mixture became explosive. It was a situation that created internally a more potent imperialism. Australian statesmen might talk about manifest destiny in the Pacific,[26] but they confined their efforts largely to trying to pressure the British government into annexations of Pacific islands. In southern Africa, Cecil Rhodes brought two colonies under his control into the empire, inspired imperial involvement in several more, and could barely be restrained from making war on Portugal to deprive that country of Mozambique and its ports, which Rhodes felt he could make good use of to base further expansion into the interior of the continent. This was jingoism with a vengeance, and could only occur in an area where the British government had never been totally clear as to its objectives.

Travelers to South Africa were also very mixed in their views. Visitors either found the Boers to be a solid, hospitable, godly people, and admired their virtues, or found them to be a sullen, suspicious, ignorant folk, given to mistreating their

African servants and to complaining in a surly manner about the shortcomings of British rule.[27] English-speaking South Africa was often urban, or it took up areas not occupied by the Boers, such as the Natal abandoned by the Trek Boers upon British annexation. Exploiting the diamond fields and the gold strike was also much more a British occupation than a Boer one. The extensive gold and diamond finds set up shimmering visions of even greater bonanzas, dreams fed by biblical tales of wealthy African kingdoms. Travelers and settlers were also much aware of the native population, as servants, as competitors for the land, as potential hostiles, and as a people with an interesting cultural background; the missionary-minded saw them as multitudes of souls to be saved and protected from the corruptions of the rest of the white population.

To the British traveler southern Africa, even more than North America, meant hunting. For those who still reveled in the slaughter of large numbers of beasts, Africa, particularly in the earlier part of the nineteenth century, appeared to offer unlimited victims to the skilled weapon, though as civilization and commercialism moved in, the game retreated and dwindled. Just the same, throughout the century an adventurous young man could make a career out of hunting in Africa, as did Frederick Selous,[28] and gain thereby a considerable reputation as scout and courageous challenger of the wilderness. Descriptions of hunts became almost mandatory in books on African travel, even in the books of Joseph Thomson, who insisted that he got no special thrill out of the killing of animals.[29] The hunting scenes were designed to attract the reader by providing a description of esoteric adventure; incidentally, they cast the hunter in a heroic light as he dared the wrath of fearsome nature.

British interests in West Africa existed long before those in more southern regions, for it was West Africa that supplied the bulk of the slaves in the British Caribbean colonies, and provided the raw materials for the slave trade that British ships so dominated in the eighteenth century. When qualms of conscience, and the crusades of the Evangelicals, destroyed Britain's participation in the slave trade early in the nineteenth century, British ships of the Royal Navy remained on the West African coast in a desperate, almost futile, attempt to prevent other traders from supplying the still existing transatlantic market for slaves. Even before the slave trade was finally eliminated from the Atlantic, largely because the markets had disappeared, the British were aware of a similar trade from eastern Africa supplying the markets existing mainly among the Arab-speaking peoples. Pressure built up gradually on the British to do something about this trade, and by midcentury, naval units were patrolling the Indian Ocean and chasing Arab dhows suspected of carrying slaves. In the process the British government became grudgingly involved in the politics of East Africa. The long existence of the slave trade on both coasts of Africa, meticulously chronicled and described by visitors, explorers, traders, and missionaries, created an indelible picture in the minds of the British public about the nature of tropical Africa and its people.

Africa was the continent of the slave raider and the slave trader. Though Africans sometimes lived in substantial cities and enjoyed a high degree of civilization, particularly where Islam had penetrated, most Europeans would find it difficult to see beyond the fact that slavery and the slave trade formed an important basis for their economies. Consequently, in the popular image, Africa was the continent of savagery, splendid in its manifestations at times, with colorful ceremonial and hordes of magnificent warriors, and squalid and filthy at other times, dominated by fetish worshipers and noisome execution grounds where bloated vultures tore at the bodies of the victims of human sacrifice.[30] Long lines of slave porters carrying loads of ivory were whipped into line by sadistic guards, or were allowed to collapse and die by the wayside. Africa was cruel and bloodstained, the Dark Continent not because so little was known about the interior, but because so many of its practices could not bear the light of day. It was an image that was to persist well into the twentieth century, perpetuated by snake- and crocodile-filled movies in which courageous white heroes and heroines faced frenzied mobs of blacks.

This was the image of a continent that it would be well to stay out of, except from the fringes where European traders maintained contact with the African middlemen who had previously sold them slaves and now provided them with palm oil in return for Birmingham and Manchester goods. Africa beyond the coasts attracted attention, however, and explorers and missionaries, who sometimes acted like explorers, provided the reasons for increasing involvement with the continent. They revealed that the ravages of the slave trade had crisscrossed the continent and that no indigenous people were either willing or powerful enough to stop it; this was something for the humanitarians to slowly mull over. Meanwhile, the explorations satisfied other urges—to be the first, for example, to stand at the source of the Nile River, or to provide information about areas of the world as yet little known to Europe. Information stimulated the imagination, the spaces of Africa suggested resources, and the odd clue, a piece of fertile land, a copper bangle, a lump of raw gold, rapidly converted dreams into certainty: Africa contained vast resources that needed to be exploited in the European fashion, with proper European-run farms and plantations growing cash crops, and mines to which railways must extend in order to bring in the machinery necessary to extract the ore efficiently, and on which the ore could be funneled to ports modernized by European capital and European technology. Since British explorers did a great deal of the opening up of the continent, it seemed only logical that the British should grab the lion's share of the benefits of these resources. In return, they would stop the slave trade that was killing Africa and the Africans, and modern development would be their weapon.

Medical knowledge in the nineteenth century only near its end came to an understanding of the causes of the major killing diseases, which made the penetration of Africa by Europeans for any reason a courageous act, more courageous than the exploits of European imperialists in most other parts of the globe. Silent death, or agony and disability, waited to claim its victims, and the courage of the battlefield alone was not sufficient to meet such a menace. The books written by the participants in numerous tropical dramas always sorrowed at the loss of colleagues to disease more than if they were killed in action in the line of duty; there was the background feeling of the waste and the lack of dignity of such an ending. By taking such risks, the British often felt that they had proven their courage and worthiness. It was a frame of mind that could be very conducive to imperial theorizing.

The roots of British interest in Egypt were much more mundane and pragmatic. Egypt, like many of the Near Eastern countries, was a source of exotic Asian luxury goods, but by the nineteenth century, it was more important as a state that lay across one of the routes to their Indian empire and to the growing trading interests in China. The strategic protection of power and profit need always be of concern to a British government, and consequently prudence dictated that French interest in the area be kept under control; Napoleon had already found that out at the end of the eighteenth century, when a British fleet helped deny him the opportunity to emulate the exploits of Alexander the Great. When modernizing Egyptian rulers began to demand the luxuries of an industrialized state, Egypt emerged as an opportunity to the modern entrepreneur, to deal not in the importation of perfumes and flummeries but in the supplying of the technological hardware and services that a bourgeois state required. Why then should not the leading industrial and business state in the world be interested in these developments?   When later Egyptian rulers added extravagance to their modernizing proclivities, then money lent and the payment of interest became of concern, especially when the newly constructed Suez Canal added urgency to the strategic question. Compelled to choose between a perceived chaos and a desired stability that would preserve all sorts of mute British interests, the choice became clear, and the British became an Egyptian government, condemned to attempt to create efficiency in a people for whom, perhaps, efficiency had not been a priority. The seeking of solutions to age-old problems turned the British to theorizing and moralizing the very practical, mundane, financial interests that they had developed in Egypt.[31] The common image of Egypt, the Egypt of the tourists, was of sand and pyramids, Nile boats and beggars in the street; very quaint, but hopelessly out of date, and in need of a heavy dose of westernization. Even the desert could be made to bloom with the proper techniques, and British civil servants were there to ensure that this happened.

British interests in the Sudan were much more distant and exotic. There were no direct financial interests in the area, at least, none that would seriously concern the British government. Earliest interest was in the exploration of the Nile Basin and in the activities of the two Britons, Samuel Baker and Charles Gordon, who, as agents of Khedive Isma'il of Egypt, attempted to extend Egyptian control far to the south and to eliminate the powerful slave traders who operated there. Apart from the humanitarian involvement of the antislave-trade movement, there was little to interest the British, except, of course, the Nile. The Nile was enhanced as a long-term interest of the British when they became effectively the governing presence in Egypt. The religious fanaticism of the Mahdi and his followers, who by 1885 had virtually eliminated Egyptian rule over the area, would have been of little concern to Britain, save for the death of General Gordon and other British officers in the service of the Egyptian government, if it were not for the fact that the dervish state lay across the Nile River, the lifeline of Egypt. Again, this might have remained of little concern to British officials if Europe had not at this point entered its imperial expansionist period. The Mahdist forces, for all their fanatical courage, obviously would not be able to stand up to a disciplined force armed with modern weapons, and consequently the Sudan could fall victim to any of Britain's rivals, such as a France dedicated to making the British position in Egypt more uncomfortable. Building dams on the Upper Nile might appear to be a chimerical project, but in an age when all kinds of imperial projects were taken seriously, no British foreign secretary could afford to take chances with what appeared to be vital British interests. The reconquest of the Sudan by General Kitchener[32] brought out a number of war correspondents, who reacquainted the British public with burning sands and ragged dervishes charging fiercely into the devastating fire power of a modern army.[33]

If British interests in the Sudan were not always clear to the unbiased eye, there were few that would have serious doubts that Britain had major interests in India and the regions surrounding India. Many books were written about India, some by travelers, but even more by sojourners, people who had spent most of their working lives in India. They were soldiers, civil servants, missionaries, and wives of men who had made their careers in India. Occasionally, there were books by persons who might be termed extended travelers, like Emily Eden, who accompanied her brother, Lord Aukland, to India for the period of his governor-generalship.[34] Impressions of India coming from such a variety of authors might vary a great deal, and certainly different aspects of the Indian experience were stressed, but most writers were impressed with the solemnity of British achievements and obligations in India. From their books came a very detailed picture of India, the activities of the British in India, and their reactions to their position in the subcontinent.

The constant reader of travel books would have indelible images of the geography of India, beginning with the landing through the surf at Madras, or sailing on the way to imperial Calcutta along the sluggish Hughli, with its human bodies occasionally floating past. Sacred rivers, dusty plains, cool hills, majestic mountains, and scrubby jungles were traversed with often exasperating, and monotonous, description. The cities and villages, temples, palaces and hovels, fortresses and burning ghats, all with their crowds of extremely varied individuals were lovingly portrayed. The sacred cows strayed everywhere, as apparently did the red-faced Englishman. The grandeur of the past and the squalor of the present were examined in exhaustive detail.

To the writers India was like a diamond, the sumptuous symbol of a glorious empire, but many faceted in its needs, and the pressures it placed on the British to maintain its brilliance. There seldom was any question that the possession of India was a matter of gain to the British, from the virtual monopolization of a large market for manufactured goods to the maintenance of a power base from which Britain could protect its other interests in much of the rest of Asia, and even in Africa. There was also obligation. This obligation was not simply the necessity to provide good government for the Indian people. The rulers had frequently proclaimed their duty to train the Indians to govern themselves as well as the British could govern them, though British appetite for this work, or even the belief that it could or should be done, noticeably cooled by the end of the nineteenth century. The problem was that the heirs apparent were people trained by the British in British ways—they were imitation Englishmen—and the British increasingly felt less inclined to hand over power to what they saw as carbon copies of themselves; after all, carbon copies are never as good as the originals. When even learned Indians still retained their beliefs in and practices of Hinduism—and the average British at home had been taught in the books that they had read, written by people they considered to be experts on the subject, that the Hindu religion was ignorant superstition, full of myths that would not convince an English child—then it appeared obvious that the educated Indians had absorbed only the externals of civilization and had not achieved that internal conviction which was necessary to run governments of true liberty.

Another obligation of the imperial crown was to protect the jewel of India from the covetous hands of greedy external powers. The price of possession then was eternal watchfulness, and the willingness to act to prevent the shaking of the foundations of empire. Considerations of European politics and the realization that Britain was not all-powerful was much more apparent to statesmen in London than to writers on Indian affairs or to Indian civil servants.[35] A reputation for power was worth having, but Indian civil servants were always more convinced that there was reality behind the reputation than were their counterparts in London. In the outposts of empire, the proconsuls, almost of necessity, must feel more vividly the responsibility of power, and the necessity of being constantly alert and willing to exercise that power.

Power, along with the proper, judicious acknowledgment of the necessity of trade for the welfare of Britain, was the major reason for keeping a very careful watch on India's neighbors in any direction. The eye of the traveler to the border areas, besides being fixed upon the picturesque, was always on the lookout for the possibilities for a developing trade and observant of strategic considerations. Was there a potential enemy? What were the passes like? What supplies were there on the travel routes for an army? What areas could be quickly fortified and held? How would the local population react to an invading force? Would they welcome and join foreign intriguers against the British, or would they recognize the basic altruism of their British neighbors and cooperate instead with the imperial Raj?

India and its surrounding territories, in the writings of travelers and adventurers, were romantic, but it was a romance laced with a peculiarity that was particularly British; the writers appeared to feel that a goodly portion of discomfort must accompany any romantic adventure worth having. It would never do when on the road to be too comfortable. Even those who traveled with full retinues of tents, silver services, and myriads of servants must emphasize the inconvenience of it all, the sheer torture of having to live in the middle of a human zoo.[36] Dampness or all-pervading dust always qualified comfort even in the midst of palatial surroundings. On the frontiers, the grandeur of mountain passes, cascading streams, and breathtaking panoramas came along with narrow, shale-laden tracks over which only surefooted beasts could move, and a single incautious moment brought death or injury. Glaciers were not only the fantastic playgrounds of the gods, but were crevice-filled, tortuously cold, and agonizingly difficult to cross.[37] The people were either loyal, courageous, and dirty, or suspicious, sly, lazy, and dirty, and the traveler was never really sure which characteristic would predominate, except, of course, the one that controlled the propensity for slovenliness. Travelers in frontier areas often worked themselves near to the point of exhaustion, and had to make frequent calls upon their innermost resources, but the dangerous beauty of the remote was seductive, calling them back as often as possible, at times calling them back to their deaths.

It was difficult for the British to pretend that they were explorers in the Chinese empire, though in remoter provinces such as Manchuria and Yunnan, some did manage to create the illusion. Most British were in China for a particular reason, and when they traveled, they traveled mainly as tourists, through well-settled, well-cultivated areas, seldom seen, perhaps, by Europeans, and therefore bearing the stamp of novelty, but lacking the element of danger and adventure associated with travel in the border regions. Despite this, what they saw made a deep impression.

For the most part, what the travelers saw was a fertile, well-worked land, full of an industrious population whose devotion to labor they admired, no matter what reservation they might have about their personal habits. The white man's burden, except to the missionary, who was obsessed by the number of souls daily slipping away to damnation without the benefit of the Christian message, did not apply here with the same intensity as in other parts of the world. The Chinese were even relatively well-governed by an educated bureaucracy. Also, the Chinese empire did not in itself constitute a strategic danger, except insofar as Britain began to develop interests in such areas as Burma and Tibet, which in the past had a Chinese association. In these circumstances, British interest in China could be more frankly, if not more realistically, commercial and economic. Huge potential markets appeared to be readily reachable, either because major centers of population were near the sea, or because river and canal systems gave access deep into the interior. All that appeared to stand in the way of the achievement of the potentialities of this market was a suspicious government, and an obscurantist, backward bureaucracy that stubbornly refused free access to the Chinese people.

Though large areas of flat paddy land could become as monotonous as similar reaches of Canadian prairies, in general, the British were impressed by the well-ordered, regimented countryside, which sought to make use of all possible pieces of economic land. And there was enough that was exotic, with picturesque bluffs, river gorges, and distant temples, to lend a patina of fascination to the landscape. River life, especially, was full of flavor, with quaint sampans, stately floating houses, and the myriads of barges and high-castled, cranky looking junks. Much could be made to look mysterious about essentially a simple way of life because it was different from anything to be found in Europe. England's own waning canal system did not achieve such exuberance and variety. Once freedom of movement was conceded, after three wars, the travelers became more aware of the vastness of the land, and the deserts, forests, and thinly populated mountain regions, the resources of which could only be speculated on. China was the best illustration of the timelessness of the Orient, with links everywhere to Marco Polo and the dreaded Mongol and Tartar hordes that had occasionally erupted into the peripheries of European history.

The Chinese could be interpreted in many ways. Peacefully working, they were a productive people dear to the heart of any proper English, especially those English eager to provide them with the means to work more efficiently. In a mass they became threatening; angered, they were a dangerous mob ready to tear a foreign devil to pieces. Their elegantly dressed officials were supercilious, with their faces hiding their arrogance and natural cruelty; in private, they could be polite and learned, as were many of the better merchants. The priests of the various religions could appear venerable and pious, but just as often gross, greedy, venial, and stupid, their faces revealing brutal lusts and degraded superstition. Lower-class Chinese were either stolid and patient, or stubbornly conservative, set in the ways of their ancestors, obsequious to their priests and officials, and impolite to foreigners. Women, depending on their class, were either fragile, painted, and decked out in finery proclaiming their basic uselessness, or were sturdy peasants, sharp-tongued, and as coarse as their menfolk. And, of course, prolific in child production. From the people in general could be drawn many qualities to be admired, including deference to authority, especially within the family, and much that was to be derided, such as the lack of the independence of judgment that was taken to be a hallmark of the European. They were not, obviously, a people that needed to be ruled by an imperial power; perhaps they needed only to be advised and assisted, by a Robert Hart in Customs, for example,[38] to help make the proper decisions. The British-run colonies of Hong Kong and Singapore appeared to be examples of how British administrative genius unfettered Chinese commercial genius.

Japan, on the other hand, was quaint and doll-like, with interesting ceremonial. It shared Chinese characteristics in having a numerous and industrious population, ready to be translated into eager buyers of European goods by the application of proper marketing techniques. It also had a definite warrior class, with a code that could be understandable if not completely acceptable to a ruling imperial caste that had some interest in the revival of chivalric ideals.[39] On the surface, the Japanese had the same good and bad points as the Chinese, but by the late nineteenth century it was obvious that they were making much more effective use of their contacts with the West, and were building a superior civilization on the ruins of an ancient Japan shot to pieces by the bombardments of the British and American fleets in midcentury. They were now a people to be admired, perhaps feared a little, whose alliance might be of some value.[40]

Southeast Asia, though in some instances showing the qualities of the Far East, was much more the frontier world. It was sparsely settled and heavily forested, promising and producing hints of great resources in mineral wealth and timber. It was rough country, requiring considerable stamina to travel across, even though the distances involved were not often very great. Disease, wild animals, and wild men, the ever present bandits, made travel hazardous, as did the incessant rainfall and hilly terrain. The people were less civilized, possessing excellent qualities in many cases, but were basically not to be trusted because they were too subject to their own personal whims and the arbitrary orders of their rulers. "Oriental despots" exercised life-and-death powers over their subjects without any apparent checks, or even a rational framework within which the government operated. This made a small Malay chieftain sometimes as difficult to deal with as the emperor of China, whose arbitrary will was much more tied down by the advice of an educated bureaucracy. Life in this area appeared to be uncertain, and therefore in need of the steadying hand of a British advisor, the type of advisor that helped turn the Malay States into the model of prosperous colonies by the outbreak of World War I.[41]

In the Far East and in Southeast Asia, the British travelers came face to face with peoples of long imperial traditions, with the habit of rule and authority. They did not always like what they saw. In the presence of imperial authority that they chose to term despotism, and which they felt was in no way related to their own exercise of imperial power, they tended to become stiffly democratic, expressing libertarian sentiments that might have amazed their Indian subjects if they had bothered to take them seriously. The difference, to the British, was clearly a matter of intention. To their mind, the only thing that motivated the arbitrary power of an oriental despot was the sheer love of power itself. If it should be used by a ruler for the benefit of his people, this was strictly a matter of whim; no concept of a higher duty seemed to inform such an action. The British, on the other hand, did have a duty to govern in a specific manner, and though individuals did abuse this duty, this abuse was not officially countenanced. A great deal was made of the altruistic, long-term benefits of a properly motivated arbitrary government.

To shift from reading the accounts of travels in the Orient to tales of the South Pacific is almost like going from adult literature to stories meant for children. Civilization, with its elaborate structures and ceremonies, appears to give way to naked simplicity, complicated only by primitive ritual. Highly cultivated rice paddies give way to yam gardens tucked away under swaying palms, a sturdy peasantry bent-backed over its labors to a pleasure loving people gamboling in the sea. In the South Seas there were no cities, few idols or temples, and almost nothing to remind men that they owed some thought to matters beyond the immediate moment. The South Sea islands appeared to be like gardens tended by children who were half-wild, often beautiful, and devoted to their games. Flower scents and gentle breezes and sparkling seas made the islands a dreamland, but like all dream landscapes, these too had their nightmares. Tropic storms wrought havoc on shore and sea; the childlike minds of the people harbored dangerous perversities. The most idyllic beach could be rendered hideous by the cannibalism to which the travelers were certain the population were addicted. Mild-mannered savages in an instant could be turned into ferocious killers when thwarted, or when an innocent ran afoul of one of the many taboos that to the European were the surest sign of the infantile minds of the islanders. Beauty of natural form and line could be distorted and made frightful by beastly ornamentation or unglamorous tattooing. Pleasant idleness for the sophisticated European spending a long time there could turn into a sense of mind-numbing isolation among a people that appeared to lack any evidence of higher philosophical speculation, and appeared to feel no need to remedy its absence. The South Seas, then, could be made to appear to be almost a play world, a sideshow to the real world; and in the scale of importance by which European governments liked to apportion their concentration and effort, it definitely was a side issue.

Nonetheless, the islands did attract a number of fervent devotees who idealized their experiences there. They became the very image of paradise, the Garden of Eden, from which the serpent needed to be kept at bay; the identity of the serpent varied with the writer. To a world wearied of its sophistication, the simplicity of the islands beckoned. Unfortunately, too often the greatest simplicities occurred in the writings of the observers, who caught neither the complexities of the islands, nor the irreparable changes that the real world was making in this child's garden of coconuts and yams.[42]

Given the land area and the number of people involved, the Pacific islands perhaps have had a disproportionate amount of attention from travelers and fiction writers. The voyages of Captain Cook[43] helped pin an earthly paradise label on them, the effect of which was enhanced by the Enlightenment discussion of the noble savage, his customs and his environment.[44] The story of Captain Bligh and Mister Christian in its own way helped to maintain a romantic glow over this area, with seamen so smitten by the beautiful island women that they are brought to the point of mutiny, the most heinous of maritime crimes.[45] The tales of castaways and cannibals helped to retain the image of an exotic locale in which definitely exotic events could take place. In the romantic conscience rose a composite picture of the geography of the islands; they were emerald jewels in blue, sometimes stormed-tossed seas, and to the weary sailor they appeared with unexpected welcome out of the horizon. Coral islands with their reefs, placid lagoons, and sandy, palm-fringed beaches were mingled and then mixed up with the images of volcanic islands, whose forest-covered mountain peaks offered magnificent views of the Pacific. There was always something hedonistic and even guilty about the geographical pleasures of the islands; tropical storms were nature's way of balance.

The people were divided into two kinds, basically revolving around the image of Tahiti and the image of Fiji. The Polynesian islanders were presented as examples of almost perfect and sensuous beauty, with magnificent eyes, languorous forms, and carefree personalities with whom the sound of laughter predominated. The Melanesians and the Micronesians were wilder, less beautiful, though there were fine specimens, and often ferocious; they were the serpent element in the garden of paradise, who profaned paradise with the image and actions of the beast.

For the missionaries, who began their penetration of the islands late in the eighteenth century,[46] the latter image, the image of the satanic beast, was the dominant one and one that applied to all of the islands. Not for them carefree islanders engaged in the pleasures of living; the islanders in a state of nature were engaged in sin, and too many of their pleasures were symptoms of the depravity from which they had to be rescued. So, coming from the opposite direction, the missionaries reinforced the image of the islands as some kind of sexual Gomorrah, where an outsider could easily fall victim, unless he were very firm of purpose. The implication of the descriptions of the islands was that not many of the outsiders in the South Pacific were that firm of purpose, and even the occasional missionary yielded to the lure.[47] The missionaries also, incidentally and certainly not intentionally, strengthened another image of the islands when some highly publicized individuals such as John Williams, Bishop Patteson, and James Chalmers got themselves killed, and apparently eaten.[48] This provided a shiver of delight for those who needed a streak of danger and adventure in their paradise, and the challenge of martyrdom for the serious-minded individuals who were determined to reduce the world to their own brand of moral behavior.

The West Indies were another form of tropical paradise, but not nearly so romantic as the South Sea islands. The West Indies were nearer to home and much more frequented and described over a long period, and they were, from too early a period, the home of plantation slavery, which, given the ferocious laws in place to maintain order, was hard to gloss over with a romantic glow. At the beginning of the Victorian period, the West Indies had just undergone a drastic revolution which appeared to match if not supersede one that had been going on for the past half-century. To the slow decline of the islands as the centerpiece of the old imperial system—as sugar dominance eroded with the fertility of the soil, and as the competition from other sources of supply increased and the mercantile system that had propped up the plantations waned—was added the emancipation of the slaves, which converted the large majority of the population from an unfree to a free labor force. Much of the Victorian period was taken up with the working out of the consequences of these revolutions, and with the very obvious evidence that moral rectitude had not brought with it the economic revival that could have made such a change tolerable to the indigenous white population.

The West Indies became, unlike in the previous century, the poor relations of the British Empire, and to the visitor, everywhere there were evidences of its decline.[49] Other parts of the empire were being built up under the paternalistic direction of the British, but it appeared that in the islands the British had abandoned their native genius for progress, and the situation had gone into permanent reverse. Beautiful the islands might still be, though with the sultry, not to be trusted, sensuous beauty of the South, but the people almost everywhere were unlovely, sunk in apathy, and content with Thomas Carlyle's "pumpkins" raised with a minimum of labor,[50] rather than with the hard continuous labor that might have restored this corner of empire. The sullenness and suspicions that grew prodigiously in this tropic climate finally exploded in 1865 in the Jamaica Rebellion, and Governor Eyre's savage repressions had long repercussions in England itself.[51]

The ambivalence of feeling toward the West Indies, children of great sin and great humanity, emerged in the bitter debates in Britain that followed Eyre's actions. The North American colonies might represent failure, in that a mistaken policy had led to the collapse of the first British Empire in 1783, but after all, the United States had then gone on to be an enormous success, and certainly an imperialist could proudly attribute this success to the British heritage of the new state, fed by the contribution of a continuing stream of Anglo-Saxon immigrants. The West Indies, which had not rebelled, had gradually turned into a failure despite its loyalty, and this was a failure that was galling to imperialists who wanted to make claims for the value of empire to its participants, voluntary or involuntary. Scapegoats were clearly in order, and both sides sought their scapegoats, but obviously in different people.[52] If many of the attackers of Governor Eyre tended to be anti-imperialist in sentiment, they still had to explain how a system that was governed so closely on the British model, and in which the vaunted British principles of justice should have held, had managed to go so wrong. Britain with or without the empire might have deep basic flaws, and this was disturbing; it was better to push the blame on evil administrators. To the imperialists as well, such flaws could be fatal; it was best to place the blame on wrongheaded philanthropists.

All that was needed was to get on the right track again, and all would be well with empire.

The empire had a great diversity of geographical features and physical resources. The peoples of the empire differed equally widely in appearance and culture. Some appeared to be at the height of a vigorous civilization, others on the downgrade of what had been sophisticated, but were now decadent, societies; still others were in the midst of static and barbarous social systems, and some had little apparent system at all to their societies. Some of the travelers and adventurers of Britain saw only a part of this "Greater Britain," and others traveled extensively, touching in their lifetimes on many continents and islands, and sailing on many seas. Almost all had the conviction that their home civilization was superior in virtually every way and that the new societies that they saw, where they were not already conscious imitators of the British model, would benefit from a greater infusion of spirit and direction from the British Isles. To them, it seemed that the Briton abroad, whether a traveler, a trader, an administrator, or a colonist, was an agent of the British spirit, a proselytizing advance guard of the British race, and that in some way there was a divine purpose behind their actions and the impact of their activities around the world.

To the Briton, the diversity of his world did not really matter. Like a jigsaw puzzle, all the pieces, no matter how strange and singular they looked when they were examined individually, fit together to form the larger picture and the grander concept. The strength of the sense of the reality of the picture varied from writer to writer. Some did not even feel the need to speculate on it. To them, the picture was there, and they were merely describing one particular corner of it. For others, there was a desperate necessity to convince the readers that the picture did exist, and that all the various parts fit in and, perhaps, that the picture was expandable. The picture needed to exist because what it portrayed was either so desirable that it would be a crime against humanity if the artist was in some way blocked from his creation, or because the very purpose of the British people—and a people must have a purpose—must be expressed through it. In a world society where other peoples were beginning to flex the muscles of their purposes, and were murmuring their own versions of divine plans, the larger picture was necessary to ensure that the people who had been vouchsafed the finest revelation of the Duty and the Law by which mankind must be governed would be safe in carrying out nature's plan in the world.

NOTES

1. For convenience, I have included in this group people who filled for a time administrative posts in different parts of the world, as well as soldiers and sailors.

2. Thomas Cook (1808–1892). Began making travel arrangements for the British public in 1841.

3. Edmund Swinglehurst, *The Romantic Journey*, 66–75. See also Edmund Swinglehurst, *Cook's Tours: The Story of Popular Travel* (Poole, Dorset: Blandford Press, 1982), Chapter 3, and Piers Brendon, *Thomas Cook: 150 Years of Popular Tourism* (London: Secker & Warburg, 1992), 87–91.

4. Kenneth Rose, *Superior Person: A Portrait of Curzon and His Circle in late Victorian England* (New York: Weybright & Talley, 1969), 217.

5. See Frank McLynn, *Hearts of Darkness: The European Exploration of Africa* (London: Pimlico, 1993), for a general discussion of African explorers that indicates from time to time the source of their funding.

6. Geoffrey Dutton, *The Hero as Murderer: The Life of Edward John Eyre, Australian Explorer and Governor of Jamaica, 1815–1901* (Sydney: Collins, 1967), 80. Eyre also relied on being able to sell the livestock he brought with him on his journeys, in new markets, at good prices.

7. Arthur Connally (1807–1842), officer in East India Company army, and political agent, and Charles Stoddart (1806–1842), British army officer and diplomat. Stoddart and Connally were killed by the emir of Bokhara in 1842. A. R. Margary (1846–1875), member of the British Consular service, killed on the frontiers of Burma and China. William Henry Shakespear (1874–1915), British army officer and political agent, killed in an Arab conflict in Arabia.

8. Charles Darwin, *The Voyage of the Beagle* (New York: Bantam Books, 1958 [1839]).

9. See James A. Froude, *Oceana, or England and Her Colonies* (London: Longmans, Green & Co., 1886).

10. Mary Kingsley, *Travels in West Africa, Congo Francaise, Corisco and Cameroons* (London: Frank Cass & Co., 1965 [1897]), Chapter 1.

11. See, for example, Charles Dickens, *American Notes* [1842], from *The Works of Charles Dickens* (London: Chapman & Hall, 1907), Vol. 12.

12. See Herbert Grange, *An English Farmer in Canada and a Visit to the States. Being Notes and Observations by a Practical Man and Commercial Man on Canada as a Field for British Capital and Labour* (London: Blackie & Son, 1904), Catherine Parr Traill, *The Backwoods of Canada, being Letters from the Wife of an Emigrant Officer, Illustrative of the Domestic Economy of British America* (Toronto: McClelland & Stewart, 1929 [1836]), and Samuel Strickland, *Twenty-Seven Years in Canada West, or The Experiences of an Early Settler* (Edmonton: M. G. Hurtig, 1972 [1853]).

13. Robert M. Ballantyne, *Hudson's Bay, or Every-Day Life in the Wilds of North America During Six Years Residence in the Territories of the Honourable Hudson's Bay Company* (Rutland, Vt: C. E. Tuttle Co., 1972 [1848]). Captain John Palliser led a British expedition to Western Canada and wrote a report of its findings for the British government, published in a Blue Book. The report is summarized in Irene M. Spry, *The Palliser Expedition: An Account of John Palliser's British North American Exploring Expedition, 1857–1860* (Toronto: Macmillan Co. of Canada, 1963).

14. Major W. Ross King, *The Sportsman and Naturalist in Canada* (Toronto: Facsimile edition by Coles Publishing Co., 1974 [1866]), and Frederick C. Selous, *Recent Hunting Trips in British North America* (London: Witherby & Co., 1907).

15. G. M. Craig, ed., *Lord Durham's Report* (Toronto: McClelland & Stewart, 1963), 17–18.

16. The Earl of Southesk, *Saskatchewan and the Rocky Mountains: A Diary and Narrative of Travel, Sport, and Adventure, During a Journey Through the Hudson's Bay Company's Territories in 1859 and 1860* (Edmonton: M. G. Hurtig, 1969 [1875]).

17. See the descriptions of the West in William F. Butler, *The Great Lone Land: A narrative of the Red River Expedition and other travels and adventures in Western Canada* (Edmonton: M. G. Hurtig, 1968 [1872]), and *The Wild North Land: The story of a winter journey, with dogs across Northern North America* (Edmonton: M. G. Hurtig, 1968 [1873]).

18. See, for example, Ronald A. Wells, ed., *Letters from a Young Emigrant in Manitoba* (University of Manitoba Press, 1981), for the adventures of a young Englishman, Edward ffolkes, on a Manitoba farm in the 1880s.

19. Susan Jackel, ed., *A Flannel Shirt and Liberty*, "What Women Say of the Canadian North-West," 33–65.

20. Patrick A. Dunae, *Gentlemen Emigrants: From the British Public Schools to the Canadian Frontier* (Vancouver and Toronto: Douglas & McIntyre, 1981), Chapter 8, on the Cannington Manor settlement.

21. See Edward John Eyre, *Autobiographical Narrative of Residence and Exploration in Australia, 1832–1839* (London: Caliban Books, 1984), for descriptions of numerous such adventures.

22. John R. Godley, ed., *Letters from Early New Zealand by Charlotte Godley* (Christchurch: Whitcombe & Tombs, 1951), 62.

23. Their journeys are described in Charles Dilke, *Greater Britain* (London: Macmillan & Co., 1869), Anthony Trollope, *Australia and New Zealand* (Leipzig: Tauchnitz, 1873), and James A. Froude, *Oceana.*

24. See Noël Mostert, *Frontiers: The Epic of South Africa's Creation and the Tragedy of the Xhosa People* (New York: Alfred A. Knopf, 1992).

25. E.E.K. Lowndes, *Everyday Life in South Africa* (London: S. W. Partridge & Co., 1900). Lowndes came to South Africa as a settler but writes with the eye of a traveler. Strangely, Robert M. Ballantyne's *Six Months at the Cape, or Letters to Periwinkle from South Africa* (London: James Nisbet & Co., 1880), written by an author normally very observant, concentrates mainly on the English settlers.

26. Roger C. Thompson, *Australian Imperialism in the Pacific: The Expansionist Era, 1820–1920* (Melbourne University Press, 1980), Chapter 5.

27. Eric Walker, *The Great Trek* (London: Adam & Charles Black, 1965), Chapter 2.

28. Frederick C. Selous, *A Hunter's Wandering in Africa* (London: Macmillan & Co., 1907 [1881]).

29. Joseph Thomson, *Through Masai Land* (London: Frank Cass & Co., 1968 [1885]), 144.

30. Philip Curtin, *The Image of Africa: British Ideas and Action, 1780–1850* (London: Macmillan & Co., 1965), 23–24.

31. See The Earl of Cromer's two volumes, *Modern Egypt* (London: Macmillan & Co., 1908), and Viscount Milner, *England in Egypt* (London: Edwin Arnold, 1920 [1892]).

32. General Sir Herbert Kitchener (1850–1916), soldier and administrator, created Earl of Khartoum as a result of his victory at Omdurman in 1898.

33. See Winston Churchill, *The River War: An Account of the Reconquest of the Sudan* (New York: Award Books,1965 [1899]), Chapter 15.

34. Emily Eden, *Up the Country: Letters Written to her Sister from the Upper Provinces of India* (London: Oxford University Press, 1937 [1866]).

35. Edward Ingram, *Beginning of the Great Game in India, 1828–1834* (Oxford: Clarendon Press, 1979), Chapter 11.

36. Jennifer Labach, "Responding to Adversity: British Women in India, 1813–1914," (master's thesis, University of Saskatchewan, 1991), Chapter 2.

37. Francis E. Younghusband, *The Heart of a Continent: A Narrative of Travels in Manchuria, Across the Gobi Desert, Through the Himalayas, The Pamirs and Chitral, 1884–1894* (London: John Murray, 1896). George Seaver, *Francis Younghusband*, prints extensive extracts describing his journey through the high Himalayan passes in Chapter 8.

38. Robert Hart (1835–1911), British consular official who spent the years 1863–1911 as Inspector General in the Maritime Customs Bureau in China.

39. Mark Girouard, *The Return to Camelot: Chivalry and the English Gentleman* (New Haven: Yale University Press, 1981) deals with the revival in the nineteenth century of chivalric ideals. Gordon Stables, *Captain Japp* (London: S.P.C.K., 1891) is a fictionalized account of the attractions that the ideals of the Japanese warrior class had for young

Britishers.

40. J.A.S. Grenville, *Lord Salisbury and Foreign Policy: The Close of the Nineteenth Century* (London: Athlone Press, 1964), Chapter 17.

41. See Sir Frank Swettenham, *British Malaya: An Account of the Origin and Progress of British Influence in Malaya* (London: George Allen & Unwin, 1955 [1906]).

42. Craig Charabin, "Voyages to the Gates of Dawn: Official Exploring Expeditions to the South Pacific, 1767–1857," (master's thesis, University of Saskatchewan, 1999) examines this topic.

43. Captain James Cook (1728–79), made three voyages to the Pacific, 1768–71, 1772–75, 1776–79.

44. Alan Moorehead, *The Fatal Impact: The Invasion of the South Pacific, 1767–1840* (New York: Harper & Row, 1987 [1966]), Chapter 3.

45. See Richard Hough, *Captain Bligh and Mr. Christian: The Men and the Mutiny* (New York: E. P. Dutton & Co., 1973).

46. The London Missionary Society sent thirty missionaries to the South Pacific in 1796, to work mainly in Tahiti. See David Howarth, *Tahiti: A Paradise Lost* (London: Harvill Press, 1983), Part 3.

47. Ibid., 177.

48. John Williams (1796–1839), John Coleridge Patteson (1827–1871), and James Chalmers (1841–1901).

49. See Anthony Trollope, *The West Indies and the Spanish Main* (London: Dawson's of Pall Mall, 1968 [1859]).

50. Thomas Carlyle, "Occasional Discourse on the Nigger Question," first printed in *Fraser's Magazine* in 1849. From Philip Curtin, ed., *Imperialism* (New York: Walker & Co., 1971), 135–165.

51. See Bernard Semmel, *The Governor Eyre Controversy* (London: Macgibbon & Kee, 1962).

52. Geoffrey Dutton, *The Hero as Murderer: The Life of Edward John Eyre*, Chapter 20.

3

World Pictures: The Fiction Writers

During the Victorian period and after, a number of fiction writers spoke favorably of empire in their works, or were viewed as being pro-imperialist. Their commitment to empire existed with varying degrees of intensity. In some cases, colonial and imperial settings were convenient locations for works of adventure, and the pro-imperialism appeared vague. In others, the imperial message was more overt, with some attempt being made to present the positive benefits of the empire and the qualities inherent in the people who built the empire. Some writers presented the imperialist message with great skill, at times in a subtle and seductive manner. In others, the methods were crude and obvious, with plot and style often giving way to the authors' other intentions, or lack of literary talent. Writers of both types achieved a considerable market for their wares and played a significant role in the popular culture of their time, if little or none in the later works of those whose business it is to analyze the "literature" of the period.[1]

For most writers, speaking for empire was not the primary intention behind writing their books and seeking to get them published. Most of the writers involved, especially the ones who developed a considerable following and reputation, at some point in their lives became "professional" writers and relied upon their books to provide them with all or a substantial part of their living. Consequently, a preoccupation with money at times colored the view of empire presented in their works. There was a lot of emphasis on the acquisition of riches on the microcosmic level, the riches gained by the individual rather than the riches that created general economic benefit to the British community. Even here, the emphasis usually was not on the prosperity available to a hardworking farmer or busy merchant or salaried imperial civil servant, but on the windfall gain that could create sudden wealth for the individual through the finding of treasure or loot or through some other fortunate occurrence. The object appeared to be to make the fictional hero totally economically secure, a life destination that the authors themselves must have surely envied.

Most of the better-known writers came from moderately well-off middle-class families; most were therefore educated up to the level of their abilities, or desires, and their interest in education usually showed in their works—academic achievements were not despised. Again, most of the writers followed their academic training with substantial experience outside of the British Isles, and sometimes in one or more of the British colonies. Therefore, they could add considerably to the authenticity of their works, and quite often their most effective books were the ones that closely reflected their personal experience. The experience itself was quite varied. Captain Frederick Marryat entered the navy at the age of fourteen and eventually reached the rank of post captain. He fought in a number of wars, including the War of 1812 and the first Burmese War. In addition, he did some traveling in continental Europe and in North America. Mayne Reid had considerable experience as a civilian and a military man in the United States, and fought in the Mexican War. W.H.G. Kingston belonged to a merchant family with strong interests in Portugal, to which he traveled by ship frequently and learned to love the sea; he also spent his honeymoon traveling in the United States and Canada. Robert Ballantyne spent his early years employed in the fur trade in British North America, and later often traveled to the locations in which he set his novels, in order to get a better feeling for the setting. G. A. Henty in the army served in the Crimean War, and as a war correspondent covered campaigns in Europe and Africa. He visited India and the United States. Gordon Stables was a Royal Navy surgeon who traveled extensively before settling down to a writing career. Rider Haggard was a civil servant in South Africa, as was John Buchan. Rudyard Kipling was born in India and was a journalist there for a number of years; he also traveled around the world and spent considerable time in the United States and South Africa. Many of the lesser writers, and occasional fiction writers, also had some experience with the imperial world.[2]

Firsthand experience was undoubtedly an asset in adding a note of authenticity to the works of the writers, and, in fact, this was a selling point that the publishers were not reluctant to exploit. Still, not many writers could afford to supplement their experiences with further travels once they had reached the writing stage of their careers. Writers were, consequently, heavy users of libraries, especially relying on works of history, travel, and geography. Some, like Rider Haggard, wove their information skillfully into their narrative and brought it to life as an integral part of their stories. Others, like Henty and Mayne Reid, allowed huge chunks of borrowed material to float intact like icebergs through the thin seas of their story lines. Because there was often a reliance on secondary sources, the accuracy level of the information in the stories could not be trusted to the extent of the stories informed by personal experience, though firsthand experience did not always ensure accuracy. Frederick Marryat, who had visited and had been impressed by Niagara Falls prior to writing *Settlers in Canada*, allowed his heroes to travel from Lake Erie to Lake Ontario without encountering that majestic phenomenon. Not all the writers seemed to make full use of their experiences. Henty had published two books based on his reports as war correspondent in Abyssinia and in West Africa, and though he did send one of his young heroes to travel with Wolseley to Kumasi, none of his young men marched with Napier to Magdala.[3]

By the end of the nineteenth century, the genre of imperial adventure stories especially aimed at the juvenile market was so well established that personal experience was no longer a major qualification for access to the periodicals and to book publication. "Herbert Strang," who began operations shortly after the Boer War, was an amalgam of two members of a publishing firm.[4] The formula and imperial message was so firmly set that all it needed was a moderate amount of literacy to reach an increasing market. Conan Doyle's historical tales, of which the best was *The White Company*, an imperial tale of the fourteenth century, drew their material from the study, and were successful because the stories were entertaining as well as informative.[5]

The romances of Sir Walter Scott, successful as they were, and great moneymakers, provided an incentive and inspiration to the imperial writers of the Imperial Century.[6] To a certain extent, most of these writers attempted to produce romances, or at least, tales of romantic adventure, that incorporated a code of behavior from a romantic past, bringing in a concept of chivalry that was quickly engrafted to the code of behavior of the imperialist. The most skilled practitioner of the art of imperial romances was H. Rider Haggard, and if his works have not until recently achieved the same attention from literary critics as those of Scott, he did extremely well from a long series of popular books beginning with *King Solomon's Mines, Allan Quatermain*, and *She*.[7] Most of the books of other authors were primarily adventure stories, with elements of romance thrown in to a greater or lesser extent, depending upon the skill of the practitioner.

Both these elements were important in the promotion of the imperial ideal. Imperialism, through constant repetition, especially in the reading material of the young, became identified as the ideology of action, and the Victorians, who were proud of the British achievement of creating the world's first great industrial state, valued a life of action over a life of contemplation. British industry and the British Empire were created by doers, and action and virtue gained a degree of synonymity. It did no good to sit and lament over misfortune; misfortune could be overcome by the resolute determination to "do something," and by never giving way to despair. The imperial writers taught the lesson that in doing something, the hero created. He created his own salvation in the face of danger; he also created an image that made an impression on friends and foe alike. His vigorous reaction to events was exactly what fit him for his role of imperial mentor to subject people. The subject people might believe in action as well, but it was seldom to the same purpose and consequently was not as effective as the action of the Briton. This was where the element of romance entered in; like the missionaries who believed that right action without proper motivation was of little value, the imperialist believed that he behaved according to a certain code, which immediately placed his actions at a different and higher level than those of his opponents. Imperial writers were propagators of these important codes.

What the actual code was differed from writer to writer. The fitting of the precepts of chivalry to the ideal of the gentleman was an ongoing process in the nineteenth century, and the appropriation of the gentleman by the imperialists developed most especially in the 1880s. Before that, the codes followed were those of a devout Christian, perhaps as would be defined by Thomas Arnold, and were popularized by Thomas Hughes in *Tom Brown's Schooldays*, or of the politically conservative landed gentry, as advanced by Captain Marryat, especially in *Midshipman Easy*,[8] and carried influentially to the end of the century in the books of G. A. Henty. The difference between the code of the conservative gentry and the chivalric ideal might not be apparent at first, but can best be seen within the imperialist field by contrasting the works of Henty with those of his otherwise imitator, Captain Brereton.[9] Henty's heroes, based as they were on himself, slightly idealized, were much more realistic and down-to-earth than those of Brereton. A Henty hero could see an ambush as a legitimate military ploy, and use it repeatedly without the qualms of conscience that forbade a Brereton hero from taking advantage of a strategic position to strike a mortal blow at an enemy. In Brereton chivalry is taken to such an extreme as to provide some of the most unintentionally humorous pieces to be found in imperialist literature. By the end of the period under study, the romantic chivalric adventurer was so common—witness John Buchan's otherwise charming creations who were always among the "at, or near, the top of the form,"[10]—that he was as easily caricatured as admired, and this proved to be an important development in the decline of popular imperialist sentiment. The man of action with his romantic and exclusively masculine codes overstayed his welcome in imperial epics and was to find refuge in the detective fiction, and particularly the thrillers, so popular in the twentieth century. James Bond has a strong resemblance to the imperialist hero, though some of his traits would be thoroughly shocking to the moral purists of the previous century.[11]

In a sense, the picaresque novel of adventure was totally appropriate as a representation of the imperialist ideal. The twentieth century developed all sorts of moral qualms about the rightness of imperialism, and the agonizing of Leonard Woolf and George Orwell about their functions as imperial officials, as well as their eventual abandonment of their imperial careers,[12] was generally accepted as the epitome of how right-thinking individuals should approach the subject of empire. There is no evidence that the people engaged in gaining or in administering the colonies had severe doubts about what they were doing, or that most of the people who directed their activities from London had qualms about the morality of the enterprise. Therefore, the novels that were a string of action stories designed to show how the empire was acquired, and the character of those involved in the acquisition and retention, were probably an accurate portrayal of just how colonialists regarded their activities. They accepted their positions within the empire and did what they felt they had to do. Whatever private doubts the British might have about their religion,[13] the advantages of colonies seemed to be less questionable. Even when an imperial policy did come into question, the most searching doubts concerned its practicality and its cost in men and money. A Gladstone might have his doubts about the propriety of one nation ruling another,[14] but this, like his salvation work among prostitutes, was more an indication of eccentricity than a generally accepted trend of thought.

British liberalism did exist, and early in the nineteenth century it reached out to encompass other nations' colonies and subject peoples. It took another century before the belief that liberalism should extend to all parts of the British political structure gained much credence. Up until the First World War, at least, the books of imperial adventure, with what would be for modern taste an excessive amount of violence and bloodshed to be suitable as children's fiction, were regularly given as prizes in schools and Sunday schools. The world that they described, with its principles intact, was simply accepted as the world as it really was, and the books were a change of pace from George MacDonald's fairies[15] and James Barrie's Peter Pan.[16] And perhaps the stories were realistic. Though the nineteenth century was not a century of world wars on the scale of the previous century, even exclusive of events within the British Empire and involving the British Empire there were a great many wars throughout the world. Life was violent, death a commonplace, and with the prospects of heaven still generally accepted, there was less positive insistence that life on this planet should be made more acceptable, or even that each individual had a positive right to survival. Indeed, with the growing strength of Darwin's theories in the second half of the century, all the scientific evidence seemed to point in the opposite direction. If the books handed out to youngsters were teaching anything, they were surely teaching that imperialism was as certain as a scientific law of nature.

Teaching was a major intention of a great many of the writers of imperial fiction. The teaching function was intended to extend to both adult and youthful readers, though this was most obvious in the children's literature. The reading public expected to be edified as well as entertained, and certainly those who bought books for the young expected that they would get their money's worth only if the books carried in them a considerable freight of instruction, usually in more than one area.

First of all, the books were expected to teach a great deal of religion and morality, and this they did do throughout the century, though in lessening quantity and less obviously. When the imperial books engaged in reports of religious conversations, they were following a well-established pattern of literature for the young, and indeed for everyone, following the influential evangelical revival.[17] In the earlier imperial adventure stories there were often set piece sermons, as well as a good deal of general religious matter included. Captain Marryat's book *Masterman Ready*[18] would be a slim book if the religious element were left out. The earlier novels of W.H.G. Kingston often were held together by their religious framework. R. M. Ballantyne included a lot of religious material, though usually in a more lively fashion than found in some of his contemporaries.

G. A. Henty, perhaps the best known of the imperial writers of boys' stories, and conventionally religious,[19] actually had very little religion in his books. Christianity, if mentioned at all, was merely the accepted background from which his characters worked. Consequently, the moral teaching in these works was not so much religious as an illustration of what qualities were possessed by a virtuous and manly individual. Even these were usually presented, unlike his set piece battle scenes which are long digressions from the plot, as morality in action—the proving by example of how a right-thinking young man should act in the face of challenge and temptation, though there was very little temptation. The character of a Henty hero was set in the opening pages of the book, and it remained steadfast right through to the end. The lesson was there for young boys. Act correctly now, and you will act so for the rest of your life.

Many of the writers also saw themselves as schoolmasters, with a mission to impart information. The boys' and girls' magazines of the period were full of items of information in articles on how to do things, or incorporated into works of fiction. Sports, careers, the army, the navy, animals, plants, and industries were all discussed and illustrated. The novels followed the same pattern. G. A. Henty claimed that "My object has always been to write good history,"[20] and since large chunks of a number of his novels were simply extracted from his sources, it is possible that his books came up to the state of historical knowledge of his time. W.H.G. Kingston, Mayne Reid, and others were interested in giving detailed descriptions of plants and animals in their habitat, as well as detailed descriptions of exotic geographical locations and various natural phenomena. Many writers also took a traveler's delight in describing foreigners and their customs, with a special emphasis on how these customs differed from those of the British. Such novels did perform a function in broadening the education of the young people, and presented instruction in a palatable form, easily devoured.

Among the lessons taught were lessons in right living, in proper behavior under a variety of circumstances. There were lessons on manners, politeness, and cleanliness, on avoiding strong drink, especially in excess, and, occasionally, on avoiding tobacco. If the books were condescending toward the social inferiors of the heroes of the stories, they at least prescribed courtesy to all, and definitely proscribed the "blow and kick" school of treating servants. The authors maintained that having an education was a good thing and that work was better than idleness, even for the rich. They advocated that people take an interest in their surroundings and never submit to boredom or despondency. Many authors were insistent upon the variety of activities that a young man should be able to undertake—running, rowing, wrestling, cliff- and tree-climbing, swimming, sailing, boxing, and even manual labor. The writers were convinced that the empire was not built in the study and therefore could not be maintained from the study, and the young must be suitably prepared.

Right living was also decreed to be simple living; luxury should be avoided, and even comfort should not be avidly sought. Those who would conquer and hold an empire must be inured to discomfort, to cold and wet if necessary, or hot and parched, with hard beds and little food to eat. Hardiness was useful not only in maintaining the health of young imperialists under the most trying of conditions, but in serving as a valuable example to those beneath them, showing them that the leaders were prepared to make the same effort and sacrifices that they would ask of their men. The qualities of right living, of course, quickly assumed moral properties. Those who habitually lived right, and the young middle- and upper-class English were frequently presented as best exemplifying this trait, were thereby revealing their moral superiority. Even lower-class English lived too much for the present, and could not forbear from satisfying their desires to the limit whenever they could, though they were seen as being capable of purifying endurance when necessary, and when properly led. Peoples of other nations, especially those lower on the cultural scale, were too often incapable of right living and degenerated into licentiousness when unrestrained, and consequently fell all the more easily under the control of the abstemious and morally upright Europeans. And rightly so. Bad living certainly could not be shown as claiming rewards—the example would be too seductive.

The major lessons that the fiction writers hoped to teach concerned imperialism, though not jingoism, and the importance of maintaining, defending, and developing the empire in such a way that the British could benefit from it to the maximum extent, and yet the subject peoples could do likewise within the orbit of a superior civilization. Their books were often little sermons on power, how the power of Britain gained an empire, and how, in turn, the empire interacted and ensured that Britain would remain powerful and in a position to compete with the other great nations of the world. The scope of the books were worldwide, and together they present a comprehensive picture of how each part of the world contributed to the imperial position.

A very important part of the empire, and, in fact, often viewed as an extension of England, was the sea. The sea figured in whole or in part in a great many of the imperial stories, and few of the writers were impervious to its lure. The sea was the home of great adventure and the source of immense danger, but it was also the pathway to prosperity. It was the home of scoundrelly pirates, of black-hearted slave traders, both usually of foreign extraction, and of the bold and stout men who hunted them. Pirate treasure abounded, to be sought with enormous hardship and won with deeds of great courage, suitable reward for enterprise. The sea was also important as the field for the odysseys through which the young men wandered, developing their knowledge of people and things, and revealing to themselves and others their strength of character and their worthiness.

The sea was also magnificent, stirring even in prosaic writers some element of romance. The awesome and destructive storm at sea, described with breathtaking detail, was a common element in many stories, so common in the works of Harry Collingwood, for example, that in his writings at least one shipwreck was inevitable, with heavy loss of life. This was only fitting. Empire, including dominion over the sea, could be won only at great risk. That many died enhanced the value of the survivors and placed a greater premium on their achievements.

Best of all, the sea was the pathway to the colonies. On the fictional seas were to be found colonists, administrators, soldiers, and sailors, all of whom in the lengthy voyages had time to make friends, learn new languages, and perform deeds of valor; they could prepare themselves mentally for their imperial roles. Through their books flowed a love of the sea, the assumption that the sea formed an essential part of the British national character, and the conviction that on the sea lay the defensive outworks of a great imperial state. The sea was hypnotic, and in the best writers,[21] it became a character integral to the story, shaping as it did the nature of the British people, and the mythology of the empire. The sea was the element which through its presence appeared to give the imperial dream more validity, more reality—the sea was forever, and like the sea, the empire would endure.

Apart from the sea, and Great Britain itself, the most compelling part of the empire consisted of the settlement colonies. Consequently, it was a matter of regret that the wealthiest, most populous region, the region with the greatest potential, had already broken away from the empire long before the imperialist writers began to write. The American Revolution and the demise of the American colonies as part of the imperial system was always an embarrassment to the writers. After all, most colonial Americans had been British, and in the Seven Years' War they had acted like true Britons; it was hard to dismiss them as mere traitors on account of the Revolution. Most writers tended to accept the American interpretation of what had happened. A terrible wrong had been done to the colonists, and despite the impropriety of their action in breaking up the British Empire, it appeared so obvious that they had justification for what they did that it was difficult not to treat them sympathetically. It is interesting, too, that the writers tended to accept James Fenimore Cooper's view of the Indians and their relationship with the rebellious colonists. The "good Indians" were the friends of the American frontiersmen, who, themselves, were the embodiment of virtue, and the "bad Indians" were those who, though British allies, ambushed the American pioneers, attacked their settlements and farms, and killed, scalped, and carried off captives to slavery and torture.

As a result of this residual feeling of guilt, the United States was often treated as an extension, if sometimes a quaint one, of the British state. Americans might be presented in a humorous way, as brash, too democratic, boastful, and somewhat lacking in manners,[22] but generally they appeared in a favorable light as still sharing the qualities of the parent peoples. They were a courageous, intelligent, persevering, loyal, hardworking, and morally upright people, a people who could be relied upon. If they were more openly interested in money and the acquisition of great wealth than the British writers wished to acknowledge that they and their heroes were, they were also basically kindhearted and ready to help their neighbors and even strangers who found themselves in distress. When the Americans fought each other, as they did in their Civil War, it became difficult for the British writers to come down decisively on one side or the other. Popular sentiment might be on the side of the South, where the plantation gentry appeared, at least from a distance, to live in the manner of the chivalric gentry whose ideals the imperialists were busy appropriating, and gallant Confederate officers were holding off faceless hordes from the factories of the industrial North, but popular sentiment was also influenced by decades of battle on the Atlantic against the slave trade, and was against slavery; it was felt instinctively that the moral case, as distinct from the sentimental one, was on the side of the Northern states. This was not a matter of foreigners fighting wars of their own concern; to the writers this was a family fight, with unfortunate cousins engaged in a struggle that the British had already settled peacefully.

In general there was much more sentiment in favor of Cousin Jonathan than there was for brother Pierre, who had found himself unceremoniously bundled into the British Empire when France was no longer able to protect its North American possessions. The habitants, though living in a British colony, were clearly still unassimilated aliens. They spoke a different language, their religion was superstition, and they were led, usually astray, by their priests and their seigneurs. They were slow-witted, boisterous, often comic, but possessed admirable prowess in woods and in canoes. Usually, the writers ignored these uncomfortable denizens of the remnants of the French empire, except in historical accounts of the Seven Years' War[23] or when they were portrayed as voyageurs in the West.[24]

That part of New France that became the colony of Upper Canada, and later the province of Ontario, was more suitable territory for imperial exposition. Unfortunately for the writers, it appeared to lack the high drama of other colonial areas; the War of 1812 and the Upper Canadian Rebellion failed to catch the imagination as a setting for heroic deeds, and the Indians of this area never had the same high profile as the Iroquois or some of the western tribes. Instead, this was an area of relatively peaceful farmers and fishermen, and apart from a few novels in which such a life was emphasized, there was not enough glamour in it to arouse interest. Marryat and Kingston might present the advantage of such a life to families whose alternative in Britain was poverty,[25] but for the most part writers chose not to concentrate on this area. When they thought of Canada as a setting for their epics, they usually arrived at the far north, the prairies, or the Rockies, where the backdrop appeared grander and the inhabitants more untamed and challenging.

Most of the stories of the Canadian West had to do with the period before the great migration to the plains by those who traveled on the new railways to the free and cheap land available in such huge quantities. Firsthand accounts of the exploits of the Northwest Mounted Police did not start appearing until later in the period under study. British attention instead was caught up with figures of American myth; G. A. Henty wrote a novel placing one of his young heroes among the cowboys of the American West,[26] but he did not send one adventuring in the Canadian West in 1885, when the Métis and Louis Riel were stirring up considerable excitement.[27] When the authors did move into a more modern period, it was usually to take their heroes goldhunting in the Caribou or the Klondike, or, perhaps, cattle ranching in the foothills of the Rockies.

No matter what the period of the stories, the underlying themes remained the same and, indeed, can be said to be a basic theme of Canadian literature to the present.[28] Nature in all its moods was clearly dominant, and survival in the west involved monumental struggles with the elements. Always there was an emphasis on space, the great distances and the lengthy journeys involved in getting anywhere, and the certainty of mishap along the way. Depending upon the season, there was always a storm to enliven proceedings. Indians wandered in and out of the stories like the forces of nature, some of them purely malevolent and adding the complications of raid and massacre to the other dreadful hardships of survival. Others intervened at critical times to ensure the survival of the heroes. Gold claims attracted claim jumpers as regularly as the summer travelers attracted mosquitoes, and they were equally pernicious and in need of being slapped down before justice triumphed.

Life in this west was free and exhilarating. Nature provided an environment full of adventure, and in following the paths of nature a young man became strong, resourceful, and independent. Hunting, fishing, trapping, and camping out beneath the stars was glorious compared with hunching over on an office stool doing accounts.[29] It was clear that the heroes of the stories were pioneers, opening up the west. After them would come the settlers, and the books scattered abundant hints about the potentialities of territories currently under the sway of fur trader and

Indian. The land was fertile, and once transportation difficulties were solved, the west would be the homeland of a prosperous people who would still retain the characteristics of the frontiersmen, living as they did on the doorstep of a nature that was constantly beckoning them to health-giving adventure.

While British North America attracted a fair amount of attention from writers of imperial stories, Australia and New Zealand were not so favored. Writers as well as emigrants preferred to cross the Atlantic rather than sail to the antipodes. There are a number of reasons why this was so. No long-term economic product like furs existed to establish a valuable connection with the southern territories, so that there was no tradition of interest in the area. There was no viable threat of a rival power to dispute possession of a continent and lead to sometimes bitter wars. Though coexistence with the aborigines of Australia was not always peaceful, and the spearing of stock herders was too often followed by massacres of almost helpless natives,[30] and though the Maori of New Zealand certainly proved they were warlike and valorous, there was not the tradition of epic confrontations with native peoples that the expansion of settlement in North America provided. There was little that was romantic in man's conflict with man in Australasia. The Australian continent had the size, but it quickly was perceived as a vast, inhospitable desert, except on the fringes, mysterious because unknown, but carrying with it the danger of one of the least glamorous of deaths—death by thirst. The continent appeared hard, bright, harsh, and unyielding, with little in the way of big-game hunting that made other wild areas attractive. New Zealand, on the other hand, while it had green landscapes and fertility, and almost the languorous softness of Britain itself, was small. To move from one small group of islands to another did not overly stimulate the imagination, and cannibalistic Maori could not quite provide the counterbalance.

What Australia and New Zealand did provide, apart from gold, was the concept of a new beginning, a second chance. This is a legacy of the convict heritage in Australia,[31] spread to encompass New Zealand since many of the early settlers came from Australia. People with troubled backgrounds sensed almost instinctively a refuge in an area meant to redesign people, especially those of even more troubled backgrounds. In this case the pastoral life, lived on horseback, raising cattle or sheep, created a healthy and prosperous future for the enterprising immigrant. Here, as in the Canadian West, when the immigrant became identified with the land, working with his hands to create prosperity from the soil, or at least from animals who fed on the grasslands, he was more likely to stay, raise his children, and become a permanent Briton abroad. Those who found their wealth in the mining camps were more likely to retire with their spoils to enjoy the comfortable existence of the gentry of rural England. South Africa was a special case for writers of imperial fiction. The "native" threat was always a staple of adventure stories set in the colonies, and British writers had followed the American writers in romanticizing the wars of the Indians and white settlers. But the truth was that in British-held territories there was little of that type of warfare on the American scale still in existence in the nineteenth century, and the writers had to borrow and transpose a good deal from the American scene in order to create the climate of danger into which they wished to immerse their heroes. In South Africa, on the other hand, at all times there was a native population that was volatile and many times larger than the white population, creating the potential for conflict. A writer could, if he wished, conjure up a black Napoleon to lead his people in concerted warfare against the white settlers, as John Buchan's black preacher did in *Prester John*.[32] There were enough contemporary disturbances in South Africa, such as the Zulu War of 1879, to lend credence to the most imaginative of writers.

Beloved of many writers were the hunting stories, and certainly the North American stories had their buffalo hunts and grizzlies and wolves. But again, South Africa seemed to be so much more dramatic. The epitome of the hunt stories concerned the elephant. The sheer size of the beast impressed, as did the difficulty of bringing it down. It was a dangerous pursuit as shown by many true stories of hunting in Africa, because an enraged elephant, even a wounded one, could so easily kill or maim. The elephant could also be made to yield a handsome profit in ivory, and for a real or fictional hunter, this was often a serious consideration. The lion, next to the man-eating tiger of India, was another favorite beast to stir shivers in readers and test the mettle and steady nerves of the adventurous. Vast migrating herds of antelope and zebra and other exotic animals could thrill the reader with expectations of luxurious profusion. The bad-tempered rhinoceros, the canoe-tipping hippopotamus, the graceful giraffe, and the fleet-footed ostrich added their excitement and promise to young nimrods hunting by proxy in the pages of their favorite authors. To add to the sense of adventure, there was also the chilling lure of poisonous snakes in abundance, and rampaging ants marking their destructive paths with the bones of anyone foolish enough to stay and attempt to fight.

South Africa as well, more than the other settlement colonies, was regarded as an area where one could get very rich very quickly. This was especially true after the discovery of diamonds in the 1860s and the gold strikes of the 1880s. Rider Haggard touched a special chord with *King Solomon's Mines*, a tale of a mysterious kingdom reached overland from South Africa, and an enormous fortune there for the taking by anyone lucky enough to find it. In his books, South Africa emerged as a land of great romance, where behind desert and mountains could exist pockets of ancient civilizations, guarding equally ancient treasure troves. Haggard was also adept in picking out and making credible the mythology of such people as the Zulu, with an emphasis on magic, communication by some fashion superior to the telegraph, and fortune-telling developed to a fine art.

Much of what has been said about South Africa can be said of the view fiction writers had about the rest of Africa south of the Sahara. If anything, the African tribes farther to the north were portrayed as being more savage and even more deadly to the very small white population that came among them. They were more superstitious, and were dominated by their fetishes and strange and bloodthirsty gods who demanded human sacrifices, and by secret societies that engaged in dangerous conspiracies. In the more northern regions there was also an emphasis on hunting, with the gorilla presented as a supposedly dangerous opponent to thrill the European readers. Because a great deal of this area was unexplored by Europeans before the twentieth century, it too provided excellent settings for adventure, with the kingdoms east and north of Lake Victoria good models for hidden kingdoms that could only be reached by heroic treks through jungles, rain forests, waterless wastes, and mountains with fascinating names such as The Mountains of the Moon.

On the other hand, there was also more depiction of disease, which affected both man and beast of burden. Carriage was reduced to long lines of porters or travel by river. Malaria and other forms of deadly fever could strike at any time, laying low the unlucky adventurers. There was little suggestion that most of this territory was ever "white man's country" just waiting for the enterprise of the European entrepreneur to settle and develop it on a large scale. It was accepted that the white population would always be small here and that imperial responsibilities would be carried out by handfuls of dedicated administrators and army officers risking their lives in a deadly environment. Their presence would be supplemented by the European traders who had centuries-old connections with parts of the west coast, and by the missionaries who had penetrated the interior, often before the merchants, and sometimes just behind the explorers when they themselves were not the explorers. Factual accounts and fictional ones made it clear that imperial service in this region demanded sacrifices.

The issue that most set off sub-Saharan Africa in the minds of the writers was slavery and the slave trade. To the writers the fight against the slave trade justified intervention in African politics in order to secure the destruction of that noxious business. Though the novels were seldom outright jingoistic, demanding that the problem be solved by the "simplest" method, annexation and outright control of the interior sources of slaves, fictional heroes felt that they could with impunity invade the creeks and rivers of the coast, raid slave-holding stockades and villages in what was undoubtedly the independent territory of African rulers, fight battles, release slaves, and pressure chiefs into dropping their support of the trade.[33]

West Africa and, to a certain extent, East Africa were the areas of the most stereotyped view of tropical Africa. They were the Africa of jungles and heavy rains, stinging insects and virulent disease, oppressive heat and mildew and rot, and nature rioting in mangrove swamps and creeper-festooned rain forest. A thin veneer of civilization, partly European in West Africa, Islamic in the East, covered savage brutality and heathenish religious practices. It was also the Africa that gave some pause to the whole theory of the superiority of the white men, because here the whites died and the blacks survived; only the repeating rifle and the Maxim partially restored the balance. It was the Africa of potentially dangerous confrontation with other European colonizing states, but surprisingly, the fictional potentialities of this were usually ignored. Perhaps the possibilities of war between "civilized" states was too dreadful to consider when writing imperial propaganda for the young.[34] The restraint, of course, did not extend to the Africans; you could not have omelettes without breaking eggs,[35] and in the heated atmosphere of the 1880s and just after, omelettes were suddenly very desirable.

If West Africa was a territory that became fraught with international tension, so too did the Valley of the Nile, and the imperial novelists became very interested in the area. Oddly enough, unlike most other areas, a reading of the fiction located here would give very little inkling of Britain's real interests in the region. The bondholders who were in danger of losing their money in Egypt did not strike a note of sympathy among the writers, and the Suez Canal was accepted as an established fact that in no way had to be explained, economically or strategically. The security of the Red Sea was taken for granted to be a British responsibility, and Aden was a natural part of the British Empire. There were, apparently, self-evident interests that Britain had in Egypt, and these interests were sufficient to justify the bombardment of Alexandria in 1882 and the sending of military forces to Tel-el-Kebir. The resistance of "ignorant fanatics" to British activities here was all the more reprehensible because the Egyptians were "almost" civilized and needed only some further English help in reconstituting their finances and economy to become almost as the European states.

Ignorant fanaticism was for the novelist the major story of the Sudan. The Mahdi represented the fury and irrationality of a demagogue driving his people to destruction, and the task was being completed by his successor, the Khalifa. Fantastic courage that compelled admiration[36] was the only positive aspect of the whole Mahdist phenomenon. Abandoning the Sudan to these slave-raiding, arrogant, warlike fanatics who were turning the basin of the Nile into an area of plague and famine looked like derogation of duty to the imperialist; the Sudanese as a people surely were worthy of saving. Overshadowing the whole picture of the Sudan was General Charles Gordon and his "martyrdom" at Khartoum. The fact that Gordon was left to die "alone," supported too late by his government, was regarded as a monumental betrayal, and even a Scottish patriot like Robert Louis Stevenson could express his sense of shame about such perfidy.[37] Consequently, the bulk of the Sudanese fiction circulates around this central event of Gordon's death, and we have the attempt to rescue Gordon, the effects of not rescuing Gordon, the impact of having a hostile people on the borders of British-held territory, and the final reversal of the ignominious policy. Again, one of the curiosities of imperialist literature, is that the international ramifications of the aftermath of the reconquest were virtually ignored by the writers; no one marched with Kitchener to confront Captain Marchand at Fashoda. Perhaps the patriotic press, operating at white heat,[38] had already said all that needed to be said about this issue and had wrung the emotional content out of it. After all, the real "glory" of these events belonged to graying gentlemen poring over maps in London and Paris, and there was not much imperial glamour in this kind of process.

If there was a connection between power and empire, this connection was most clear in the minds of the imperial image-makers when it came to India. More than any other part of the empire, India and power seemed synonymous. Almost all the stories about India at some point or another concentrated on the military, with stirring pictures of marching regiments, or regiments at rest but ready to march at a moment's notice. British regiments were celebrated, with all their long traditions of heroic action, but so also were Indian units, with their gallant handful of British officers who kept their men to the paths of duty or who died in the attempt, as so often happened in the tales of the Indian Mutiny. The Indian Mutiny was power shaken through treachery; the campaign against the sepoys and their allies was power regained through a reassertion of the British virtues that had gained the Indian Empire in the first place. The reestablishment of power was presented not only as a flexing of military muscle that overwhelmed the deluded rebels, but as a proclamation of moral superiority; the British won because they knew they were right, and the sepoys, deep down in their fury, knew that the British were right and feared the consequences of all their moral power flaring forth to punish transgressions. Power was to be exerted on the frontiers as well, and to this end the diplomacy of India was concentrated. The "great game" as a phrase might have been popularized by Rudyard Kipling,[39] but the maintenance of the British position on the frontiers by secret means or open was a major theme in Indian stories, attracting writers to the north of India much more than to the south.

The rightness of the British position in India was something that came out very clearly. There was very little discussion of the benefits of the connection between Britain and India for the British, and almost no discussion of the economic value of India apart from windfall gains; tea planters and opium merchants did not figure extensively in the literature of the period, but there was a considerable elaboration of the benefits of British rule for the Indians. Above all, British government provided security against the "incessant" warfare that had been motivated by the rivalries of countless Indian princelings. In the stability of the British administration, Indian peasants could go on farming, knowing that their little disputes would be solved by a wise district officer.

What the British did in India was done under conditions of considerable hardship. A difficult climate, sometimes very dry, sometimes very damp, often very hot, laid a heavy hand on the gallant band of civilian and military officials who were at the core of Britain's control in India. Disease appeared to be endemic, with a variety of fevers claiming their victims, as well as the dreaded cholera. The company of like-minded individuals, except in the largest stations, was limited, and any company at all could prove monotonous, which in turn could breed trouble. Life, on the other hand, was usually lived in a crowd, with servants ubiquitous, and the general population crowding in on the personal space held sacred by the Europeans and assailing their senses with noises, smells, and unnatural sights.

India in many ways was disturbing to the minds of the average Englishmen who appeared in the stories.[40] Indian religions were strange, and could be set down as ignorant and gross superstition, but on the other hand, Hinduism was much more ancient than Christianity. The brooding remnants of religion, the ruined temples, snake-infested, with suddenly thrusting statues of grotesque deities, were disquieting; they fit in so well with the languorous sensuousness of the land, much more than the brash and unimaginative Christian. They reeked of mystery, suggesting strange and perhaps perverted rites, even human sacrifices, and the atmosphere made the British uneasy, all the more because they could not understand how such religions could gain and maintain a hold on the minds of men. There was a magic in it, and even the most skeptical mind could yield to the force of it, especially when face to face with a genuinely skilled magician. Rope tricks, conjuring, and illusions of all types were part of an atmosphere where they could be so much more easily credited than on the pavements of London.

India had several other advantages for a romantic storyteller. It was the land of enormous riches in gold and jewels, which put real meaning into the native word from which "loot" sprang[41] and suggested the prospect of turning adventure into profit. And India was the land of adventures. It had its share of martial peoples who glorified deeds of valor and who struck a responsive chord in the breasts of the British imperialists who held similar values. Best of all, with India the writer did not have to rely on invention to create his adventures; he simply had to turn to the records of British military and civilian achievement in India for his examples and the settings into which to plunge his heroes. The Indian Mutiny was especially prolific in creating settings for particularly desperate adventures, with heroes plummeting to the depths of defeat and soaring to the giddy heights of victory.

When the writers moved on to Southeast Asia, China, and Japan, they had to admit, reluctantly or not, that the British had economic interests in those regions, and the economic interests were why the heroes were to be found there. The background of the main characters was often commercial, but for the purposes of an adventure story, the concentration was on their exploits in killing their enemies and not on their successes in making a killing in the market. Most though, ended up doing very well in that regard before the end of the adventure. As in India, there were palaces to plunder, cities to loot, and rich princes to be suitably grateful to enterprising young Britons.

Writers' attitudes to China were really very mixed. Villains to be found there were among the blackest in the fiction of the period, thoroughly depraved and vicious, without conscience or sense of humanity, with a cunning all the more dangerous because it was informed by an ancient civilization that placed a good deal of emphasis on education. On the other hand, Chinese characters could appear to be very sophisticated, polite, and trustworthy. Scholars were highly intelligent, pirates vicious, merchants good-tempered, officials supercilious, peasants ignorant, and servants faithful. Certainly, China was a very slippery area to deal with, and in contrast, Japan appeared to be straightforward. The Japanese could be either tradition minded and cast in the heroic feudal mode, which could be very attractive to the British, or they could be very progressive, with a specially keen interest in the modern navy, an interest that also made them attractive.[42] To British writers not yet concerned with the "yellow peril," the Japanese appeared to be the most admirable of the Oriental peoples, almost the Englishmen of the North Pacific.

The Orient quickly established itself as a place of mystery, a reputation it was to retain in popular fiction and movies well into the twentieth century. It was an area of obvious attractions; the fact that such vast numbers of people created enormous potential markets did penetrate to writers who normally were not concerned with such matters, and market potential made this an area of international concern and intrigue. It was obvious that great power politics would operate here, and a watchful eye had to be maintained by all devoted imperialists to ensure that British interests were here properly looked after.

If the Orient was a land of mystery, the South Pacific was paradise, though for writers of a particularly evangelical bent, it was a paradise with some very large flaws. The scenery might be beautiful, even spectacular, but the habits of the population were unfortunate. The natives were given to cannibalism, head-hunting, and licentious behavior. On top of that, they were not the least bit inflicted with the desire for hard and continuous work. All but a fortunate few were, regrettably, pagans. The attractions of a licentious life of subsistence idleness were not apparent to the group of writers under study here. Most of them had not been in the South

Seas and relied for their information mainly on the publications of the missionaries, who did tend to approach the question of the lifestyle of the islanders from a definitely subjective point of view. Travelers to the Pacific islands who were not missionaries generally tended to be more sympathetic to a culture that was rapidly disappearing under pressure from the missionary societies, and exposure to modern civilization.

With the best of wills, it was not possible to present the South Sea islands as an area of great actual or potential wealth. A few pearls might be found, some sandalwood logs, and gold might be sought in New Guinea and some of the larger islands. Otherwise, the achievement of prosperity was a slow business, based on trading with the islanders for natural products, and sometimes recruiting them for work elsewhere. The fictional islands, therefore, were most useful as settings for idyllic adventure stories and as fields for the reclamation of souls. Because there were temptations in this natural paradise, the effects of succumbing to temptation could be portrayed, and redemption could be earned.

Wealth, piracy, and temptation, on the other hand, seemed to be naturally allied in the West Indies, which were a field for international conflicts; all this provided plentiful and tempting possibilities for imperial adventuring. Although planters were to be found, the major emphasis was on the seas and the possibilities for heroic exploits in the naval arena. A lot of stress was placed on greed and savagery, and in this case not all the savages were natives, and on a lifestyle that was as violent as the hurricanes that frequently visited the area.

The islands were also an entry point to the mainland colonies of the Spanish Empire and the independent states that replaced them in the nineteenth century. These also provided settings for many imperial adventure stories because, throughout, there was an undercurrent of the sense of opportunity missed, the feeling that South America was a natural field for British enterprise. The fact was that there was a solid basis for this feeling; British economic enterprise did penetrate substantially into these states,[43] but this is not what concerned the fiction writers. As A. P. Thornton has pointed out, no one celebrated *A Venture in Argentine Rails*.[44] The fiction writers were more concerned with two things, regret that these regions were not actually under the British flag, which would have enabled them to make their way in the world so much better, and the windfall gain that the adventurer could discover in Inca treasure or, perhaps, lost gold mines.

Taken as a whole, the empire and those other parts of the world that were a field of activity for enterprising Britons were places of adventure and potential sources of great wealth. But for most writers, the heart of the empire was still Britain itself, and on Britain the most affection was concentrated. It was a special Britain; only incidentally was it the Britain of the nineteenth-century industrial revolution, which aroused boasting but little love.[45] For the imperial writers, the Britain that was the starting point for most of their adventurers was the Britain of rural estates and small towns and villages, often located on the seacoast. It seemed as if the imperial adventurer always carried a patch of British green within his soul, refreshing him in the arid and dangerous portions of the world, inspiring him to fight and win, as he so often had done on the village green, and acting as a magnet to bring him back after the empire's work had been done.

The world pictures created by the imperial writers were a series of often vivid illustrations presented in a gallery to tempt the palates of their readers. They did not constitute a whole and continuous tapestry, and did not aspire to reveal a seamless image of the empire as it was or as it might be. These pictures were disparate pieces of the imperial story, and they did not portray anything approaching a "plan" for empire. Nor was this their intention. One writer, however, early in his career as a successful purveyor of romances of adventure, did try his hand at providing something approaching a plan and a philosophy for the rose-colored imagery of empire that the fiction writers were creating. This was John Buchan, who, upon his return from South Africa, published in 1906 *A Lodge in the Wilderness*.

NOTES

1. Rudyard Kipling is virtually the only "imperialist" writer to make it into the serious works of literary criticism. Rider Haggard occasionally appears.

2. For example, Harry Collingwood (real name, W.J.C. Lancaster) served in the Royal Navy and then became a civil engineer, specializing in sea and harbor work and hydrography, and traveled extensively in both careers; Verney Lovett Cameron was a Commander in the Royal Navy and led explorations in Africa; Charles Gilson served in the army in many parts of the empire; Frederick Sadleir Brereton was an officer in the British Army; and David Ker was a war correspondent and served in the Russian Army in Central Asia.

3. Henty's war-correspondent books were *The March to Magdala* (London: Tinsley Brothers, 1868) and *The March to Coomassie* (London: Tinsley Brothers, 1874).

4. George Herbert Ely and James L'Estrange worked for Oxford University Press. Ely did the writing and L'Estrange the research. W. O. G. Lofts and D. J. Adley, *The Men Behind Boy's Fiction* (London: Howard Baker, 1970), 323.

5. Arthur Conan Doyle, *The White Company* (Toronto: Musson Book Co., 1945 [1891]).

6. See Martin Green, *Dreams of Adventure, Deeds of Empire* (London and Henley: Routledge & Kegan Paul, 1980), Chapter 4.

7. *King Solomon's Mines* in 1885, *Allan Quatermain* in 1887, and *She*, also in 1887. He had other published fiction in this period, *Dawn* in 1884, *The Witch's Head* in 1884, and *Jess* in 1887, which did not sell very well.

8. *Mr. Midshipman Easy* (London and Birmingham: Rylee, n.d. [1836]).

9. Captain (later Lt.-Colonel) Frederick S. Brereton was a cousin of G. A. Henty and wrote books like *One of the Fighting Scouts: A Tale of Guerrilla Warfare in South Africa* (London: Blackie & Son, n.d.).

10. Richard Usborne, *Clubland Heroes* (London: Constable, 1953), 95.

11. Hugh David, *Heroes, Mavericks and Bounders: The English Gentleman from Lord Curzon to James Bond* (London: Michael Joseph, 1991), 237–42, maintains that Bond is a species of post-World War II English gentleman. One of my former students, Anthony Appleblatt, frequently remarked on the resemblance of James Bond to a Henty hero, a contention that Henty fans might not appreciate.

12. Leonard Woolf (1880–1969) left the British Colonial Service to become a publisher, and George Orwell (Eric Blair, 1903–1950) left the Indian Civil Service to become a novelist and essayist.

13. Herbert Tingsten, *Victoria and the Victorians* (London: George Allen & Unwin, 1972), 32–43.

14. C. C. Eldridge, *England's Mission: The Imperial Idea in the Age of Gladstone and Disraeli, 1868–1880* (London: Macmillan, 1973), 227–29.

15. George MacDonald, *Dealings With the Fairies* (London: Strahan, 1867).

16. James M. Barrie, *Peter and Wendy* (London: Hodder & Stoughton, 1911).

17. Ford K. Brown, *Fathers of the Victorians: The Age of Wilberforce* (Cambridge: At the University Press, 1961), 444–73, 507–20. See also Gillian Avery, *Childhood's Pattern* (London: Hodder & Stoughton, 1975), Chapter 5.

18. *Masterman Ready, or the Wreck of the "Pacific"* (London: T. Nelson & Sons, n.d. [1841–42]).

19. Guy Arnold, *Held Fast for England: G. A. Henty, Imperialist Boys' Writer* (London: Hamish Hamilton, 1980), 49.

20. Quoted in Guy Arnold, *Held Fast for England*, 92.

21. In Joseph Conrad's novels and stories, for example.

22. See, for example, Charles Dickens, *Martin Chuzzlewit*, Margaret Cardwell, ed. (Oxford: Clarendon Press, 1982 [1843–44]).

23. Such as Gilbert Parker, *The Seats of the Mighty* (Toronto: Copp Clark Co., 1902 [1896]).

24. As in Robert M. Ballantyne, *The Young Fur Traders, or Snowflakes and Sunbeams: A Tale of the Far North* (London: Blackie & Son, n.d. [1856]), which is Ballantyne's first novel, based on his years as an employee of the Hudson's Bay Company.

25. Captain Frederick Marryat, *The Settlers in Canada* (London: The Boy's Own Paper, n.d. [1844]), and W.H.G. Kingston, *The Log House by the Lake: A Tale of Canada* (London: S.P.C.K., n.d.).

26. *Redskins and Cowboys* (London: Blackie & Son, n.d. [1892]).

27. John George Donkin, *Trooper in the Far North-West: Reflections of Life in the North-West Mounted Police, Canada, 1884–1888* (Saskatoon, Sk.: Western Producer Books, 1987), 152, says that "Mr. Henty, of the Standard, was visible among the staff," the staff being that of General Middleton during the Riel Rebellion, but if this was indeed G. A. Henty, he does not seem to have written a boy into the Rebellion's adventures.

28. Margaret Atwood, *Survival: A Thematic Guide to Canadian Literature* (Toronto: Anansi, 1972), Chapter 2.

29. R. M. Ballantyne, *The Young Fur Traders*, 52, in which one of the young heroes, Charley Kennedy, complains to his sister "If I don't run away, I must live, like poor Harry Somerville, on a long-legged stool; and if I do that, I'll–I'll–."

30. Geoffrey Blainey, *A Land Half-Won* (Melbourne: Macmillan Co., of Australia, 1980), Chapters 5 and 6.

31. Russel Ward, *The Australian Legend* (Melbourne: Oxford University Press, 1977), 32.

32. *Prester John* (London: T. Nelson & Sons, 1963 [1910]).

33. As in W.H G. Kingston, *The Three Midshipmen* (London: J. M. Dent & Sons, 1920 [1862]). The morality of doing this is not even discussed in Kingston.

34. Gordon Stables, *Cruise of the "Vengeful,"* is one of the few books written by a "boys'" author on this theme.

35. In the words of Colonial Secretary Joseph Chamberlain. J. C. Anene, *Southern Nigeria in Transition, 1885–1906* (Cambridge: At the University Press, 1966), 217.

36. See Rudyard Kipling, "Fuzzy Wuzzy," and G. M. Fenn, *In the Mahdi's Grasp* (London: S.W. Partridge & Co., n.d.), 183–84.

37. Derek Ferguson, "Robert Louis Stevenson and Samoa: A Reinterpretation" (master's thesis, University of Saskatchewan, 1980), 78.

38. J.A.S. Grenville, *Lord Salisbury and Foreign Policy*, 227.

39. From *Kim* (New York: Doubleday, Page & Co., 1914 [1901]), 279.

40. See Flora Annie Steel, *On the Face of the Waters* (London: William Heinemann, 1897), which was not written for children, and has adult themes of adultery and betrayal, but portrays well the English lack of understanding of the native population of India.

41. The real profits in the early days of the establishment of British power in India came from "presents." See Michael Edwardes, *The Nabobs at Home* (London: Constable, 1991), 25–33. Loot was usually for soldiers, who were very much interested in it; G. A. Henty, *In Times of Peril: A Tale of India* (Chicago: M. A. Donohue & Co., n.d. [1881]), 320.

42. Gordon Stables, *Captain Japp*, 223–24.

43. P. J. Cain and A. G. Hopkins, *British Imperialism: Innovation and Expansion, 1688–1914* (London: Longman, 1993), Chapter 9.

44. A. P. Thornton, *For the File on Empire* (London: Macmillan, 1968), 19.

45. Martin J. Weiner, *English Culture and the Decline of the Industrial Spirit* (Cambridge: Cambridge University Press, 1982), 81–88.

4

John Buchan and the Imperial Colloquium

Elections, in societies where elections do make a difference, are traumatic events. During the course of the campaigns, extravagant hope and emotion build strong expectations of policies vindicated, of visions shared. Election day itself brings jubilation and despair. Winners hurry on to create or extend their New Jerusalems; losers survey the wreckage of their dreams, and freely predict disaster to their nation, or to a particular cause that would suffer in the profane hands of the victors. The most creative among the losing side soon cast about for means of minimizing the effects of loss by finding ways to rescue cherished ideas in danger of perishing. This John Buchan set out to do in 1906, in defense of his vision of the British Empire, a vision that appeared to be in some jeopardy as a result of the events of that year.

In January of 1906 the voters of Britain gave an overwhelming majority in the House of Commons to the Liberal Party.[1] Though there were imperialists in the cabinet of Prime Minister Sir Henry Campbell-Bannerman, notably Herbert Asquith as chancellor of the exchequer, Sir Edward Grey at the Foreign Office, and R. B. Haldane as secretary for war, the results of the election were not encouraging to imperialists of any party.[2] Directly or indirectly, imperial issues had played a role in the election campaign, and had undoubtedly influenced the outcome. The length and costliness of the Boer War, the inglorious defeats at the beginning of the war, and the apparent ineffectiveness of large numbers of British soldiers against a handful of Boer guerrillas in the later stages of the conflict rebounded against a Unionist government that had not scrupled to use the issue of patriotism and empire in the election of 1900, fought in the midst of the war. The morality of farm burning and the use of concentration camps, with their heavy mortality rates, during the war, had been relentlessly debated, as was the issue of Chinese "slavery" in the gold mines in the period of reconstruction. The conflict that had already racked the Unionists over Joseph Chamberlain's tariff policies had been extended to the nation and had highlighted some of the economic issues of imperialism, with debates on imperial preference, imperial unity, "free food," and prosperity for the workers of Britain. The election among the hordes of Liberals of a great many nonconformists and radicals who appeared to owe their inspiration to Gladstone, as well as the appearance of a substantial contingent of Labourites and the by-now usual solid block of Irish Nationalists, certainly held out little hope that the new administration would be a strong supporter or promoter of the British Empire. Priorities would obviously be different, and a confirmed imperialist could well wonder whether indifference or outright hostility would prove most damaging to his cause.

To imply that John Buchan was defeated in the election of 1906 is somewhat misleading. He was not a candidate, and he was not even a member of a political party. Though in 1911 he was to run unsuccessfully in Scotland as a Unionist and many years later was to sit in the House of Commons as a Conservative, he had what can be called a "cross-bench" mind—he was not committed to the full program of any party.[3] But he was committed to imperialism. In 1900 he had published a novel, *The Half-Hearted,*[4] with a strong conclusion concerning the hero's duty to empire. From 1901 to 1903, Buchan was in South Africa on Lord Milner's staff, aiding in the reconstruction of the Boer colonies. Calling upon this experience, he had published *The African Colony*, his analysis of what was needed in South Africa.[5] In London in 1906, during the election campaign, Buchan was juggling the possibilities of a legal and a newspaper career with the prospects of an appointment in the Egyptian administration. He was contributing regularly to *The Spectator* items on imperial and foreign affairs. Among his wide spectrum of friends and acquaintances he numbered prominent imperialists such as Joseph Chamberlain, Lord Lugard, and R. B. Haldane.

Distressed as he was about the general anti-imperialist tenor of many of the candidates during the campaign, Buchan was most distressed at what he considered to be unjust attacks on Lord Milner. He had been strongly impressed by Milner during his two years in Africa, and for a time many of his imperial ideas ran closely parallel to those of his old boss who had given him so much scope and freedom in the Transvaal.[6] When Milner was attacked in the election campaign, even by people that Buchan felt should have known better, Buchan decided to write a book, *A Lodge in the Wilderness.*[7]

A Lodge in the Wilderness is the closest that English novelists in the Age of Imperialism came to presenting a blueprint of imperialism. It is not a jingoistic novel, and it does not present a plan for the acquisition of more empire; in this it foreshadowed Lord Milner's own dictum "It is not a question of more acres on the map painted red. Quite enough have been painted red already."[8] Instead, the book creates a vision of what could and should be done with the empire that already existed, accumulated by Britons in the heroic age.

Though it includes a lion hunt and a light romance, *A Lodge* is not a novel in the conventional sense. It is a symposium, a series of long discussions on a congenial topic, such as Buchan had enjoyed as an undergraduate at Oxford, as one of Milner's "young men" in South Africa, and as a guest in the houses of the rich and influential to which he had entry upon his return from South Africa.   The fictionalized form of these discussions allowed Buchan flexibility to present a variety of points of view, which could be delivered in a light but more compelling fashion than a political treatise on the subject. In this form it is a "pep rally" to encourage the faithful after the disheartening experiences of the election. It is also a spiritual retreat that would enable the readers who were apprehensive imperialists to engage in quiet contemplation of their ideals, and emerge with new resolve to face the problems of empire.

The plot of the book is simple. To his home in East Africa millionaire Francis Carey invites eight men and nine women to share a vacation under idyllic conditions, and to engage in serious conversations on the state of the empire and its future. During the day the guests were to enjoy the luxuries of Musuru, the grand bungalow set atop the Great Rift Valley, and after dinner they were to explore the various ramifications of the subject of their common interest. There is also an excursion to a mission station and a detailed description of that staple of books with African settings, a lion hunt. Almost as light relief are the faint suggestions of a budding romance between two of the guests, who, in fact, represent Buchan himself and the lady who was soon to become his wife, Susan Grovenor.[9]

Buchan included at the beginning of the book a list of "The Characters." The characters are clearly drawn from his own experience, with most, despite the disclaimer in the preface to the 1916 edition that "None of the characters are designed as portraits of actual men or women," being modeled on individuals or combinations of individuals from Buchan's milieu. They are intended to represent a wide variety of pro-empire sentiment, though none of them are "jingoist." There are also no anti-imperialists present to give their points of view. All the guests are aristocratic or members of the upper middle class.

At the head of the list is Mr. Francis Carey, the host, "An intelligent millionaire," who had left home as a young man for the sake of his health and had by sheer ability made himself extremely wealthy. His enterprises spread around the world, but in Africa "half a continent waited upon his will."[10] Carey is clearly based on Cecil Rhodes, but a Rhodes with the warts taken off—Buchan had not been impressed by his first encounter with Rhodes.[11] A businessman and a philanthropist, Carey is also a man for whom imperialism "was a creed beyond parties, a consuming and passionate interest in the destiny of his people."[12] Carey is a "'man of destiny'"[13] whose imposing figure impresses all, and whose speeches—a mixture of common sense and romantic poetry, "'blank verse'" as one of the guests complained,[14] even though delivered in a thin, high-pitched voice—complete the impression of an overwhelming presence. Carey's views on empire probably owed a great deal more to the program of R. B. Haldane for the Liberal Imperialists[15] than to the sentimental romanticism mixed with unscrupulous opportunism that marked Rhodes's contributions to imperial thought.[16]

Lord Appin is "A Conservative; sometime Prime Minister of England," and, given his interests in philosophy, has obvious similarities to both Lord Rosebery and Arthur Balfour. Appin is inclined to be a theorist, a student of politics more than of men, though at the end of the book he is planning to visit the dominions in order to add fact and experience to theory. Lord Launceston, "an Ex-Viceroy; attached to no political party," represents many of Lord Milner's views, and certainly stands for the voice of experience in the administration of empire. Reserved and weary, Launceston often sums up important discussions on imperialism with a well-chosen blend of vision and reality, his views being somewhat less rigid than those of Lord Milner. Both Appin and Launceston present a picture of idealized aristocracy, the graceful natural leaders of an imperial state.

Mr. Ebenezer Wakefield, "A Canadian Statesman," and the only colonial present as a guest, comes dangerously close to providing comic relief for the book. An ex-premier and "'a wise old philistine,'"[17] he is always demanding solid, fact-laden discussion and is uneasy with poetic and philosophic talk. He is a stereotypic rustic colonial from the wild frontier, though one able to spout snippets of "dead languages," and is included in the book to be the voice of budding colonial nationalism, a crude Sir Wilfrid Laurier, whose arguments vividly illustrate the problems in the way of the achievement of such dreams as imperial federation, or even imperial cooperation in defense and foreign policy. Mr. Eric Lowenstein, "A Jewish Financier" and business associate of Francis Carey, is timid, and not in the best of health at the beginning of the book. He shares Carey's passion for certain aspects of empire. Lowenstein represents the new Edwardian aristocracy of wealth, and is meant to be a counterbalance to the unfavorable image of the Rand Lords who were blamed by many for the tremendous sacrifices imposed upon the British people by the Boer War. Jewish millionaires also, as another guest remarked, "'have the infallible good taste of the East.'"[18] In this case, Lowenstein has the good taste to be a British imperialist, contrary to the image of the internationalism of the European Jewish financial community.[19]

The younger male members of the distinguished gathering are Sir Edward Considine, "An Explorer and famous Big-game Hunter," who is much more at home in the wilds of the world than in the drawing rooms of London where his wife prefers him to be; Colonel Alastair Graham, "A Soldier and Traveller; now of the Intelligence Department," a prime example of the solid, omnicompetent Britons who so cooly administered the empire; Mr. Lewis Astbury, "A Journalist," mountain climber and world traveler, whose major purpose in the book appears to be to testify to the lure of the tropics; and Mr. Hugh Somerville, a young man who has travelled and now under the tutelage of Carey is seeking to make his fortune. Somerville represents the dreams and excitement of Buchan himself in the imperial world. Three of them, Considine, Astbury, and Somerville, were defeated candidates in the recent election, but this does not appear to bother them. They are, or soon become, bronzed and rugged-looking, thoroughly at home amid the discomforts of the wilds, adventuresome, capable, fine shots, particularly under desperate conditions, and able to cap their conversations with classical quotations acquired during their public school days. They are, as Considine, who is deeply gone in wanderlust, points out, "'the advance-guard, always pushing a little further on and making the road easier for those who come after us, the serious solid fellows who make laws and create industries, and generally reap where we have sown.'"[20] The dullest appearing among this type of young Briton has the inner spark which will surface when needed, as the pride of the white man, and will help him establish superiority over less civilized peoples.[21]

The Duchess of Maxton, "Wife of George, 14th Duke of Maxton and Champfleury, at one time a Liberal Secretary of State; sister of Lord Appin," at the request of Francis Carey chose the female members of the symposium. The most human of Buchan's creations in this book, she appears to be at times confused,[22] but her instincts are as determinedly liberal as her politics are Liberal. In her, almost blindly at times, shines the whole Whig tradition of English history. Her foil is Lady Amysfort, "A Tory; wife of a well-known member of the Jockey Club." She is the elegant defender of Toryism as distinct from the Conservative Party,[23] a Toryism that pays attention to the natural temperament of the English people. Mrs. Wilbraham, "Wife of Colonel Wilbraham, C.B., on service in South Africa," though an imperialist, is very much embarrassed by the fact that so many imperialists have no sense of proportion and no sense of humor, and harm a good cause by their excesses. Lady Warcliff, "Wife of Sir Arthur Warcliff, K.C.B., K.C.S.I., General Officer commanding in India," is a social Darwinist of a particularly ferocious type, who believes that the undeserving poor should be strictly controlled by the state, and that the empire should be used to settle the deserving poor in the colonies where they would do the most good for themselves and their country. Lady Warcliff is most concerned with white migration, but Lady Lucy Gardner, "Wife of Sir Hamilton Gardner, G.C.M.G., High Commissioner of East Africa," presents Buchan's defense of Milner and the Chinese coolies question.[24] She makes a strong case, based on the freedom of choice, for the use of temporary contract labor, which could be shipped back home.

The remaining ladies are more decorative than political. Mrs. Yorke, "An American; Wife of the Rt. Hon. Henry Yorke, a Liberal Secretary of State," seems to be in the book primarily to relate a strange Kiplingesque story about one of her husband's relatives, a staid politician and lawyer, who, in his diary, lived a swashbuckling life as a conquering Byzantine general and emperor.[25] Its relationship to the imperial theme is dim except insofar as it holds that we all have the stuff of conquerors, and therefore imperialists, buried within us. Mrs. Deloraine, "Of Deloraine Manor, Shropshire," is beautiful, sings beautifully, and delivers a discourse on art and the empire. Lady Flora Brune, "Niece of the Duchess of Maxton," is the somewhat naive socialite who is searching for a purpose in life and asks many questions on all aspects of the empire. Miss Marjorie Haystoun, seriously intellectual, writes poetry on imperial themes.

The guests are obviously not a cross section of British society, and there is no evidence that Buchan felt this to be a shortcoming. As he shows in his later books, primarily thrillers, Buchan was interested in people who got things done. His heroes are at the top, sometimes by breeding, most often by ability. The guests at the Lodge belong to the influential upper classes, and it is their duty to spread the good word about imperialism to the members of their own castes. With the influential people won over, government policy would all the more easily be influenced in favor of the definition of and the organized development of the empire that was so desperately needed. The guests are to be an informal lobby group whose efforts would rescue the cause of empire from the despair caused by the election. For such a purpose members of the lower middle and working classes, from Buchan's point of view, would not be effective. They are instead the people that are to receive their marching orders from the top and are to effectively carry out the instructions of their superiors. Francis Carey shows his awareness of this political equation when he calls together the white residents of his district of East Africa and *tells* them how to behave to the black population.[26]

Though not mentioned in the cast of characters, the house, Musuru, is important to the discussions. At one level, it is John Buchan's dream house,[27] modeled on the Cape farmhouse and full of the luxuries and comforts of civilization. On another level it can be seen as a metaphor for empire, or at least empire as it should be, with all of Joseph Chamberlain's estates fully cultivated.[28] The house is set in the middle of a Garden of Eden, where different climatic zones in descent from the high ridge on which it was built are appropriately and beautifully developed. Musuru is an island placed in a savage setting to show what a dedicated Briton could establish with the rawest of materials. The house and grounds are maintained by an army of servants, mainly African, but with a Scottish butler. Fierce and dreaded Masai warriors here are tamed into noiseless and efficient servants, operating at what Carey would maintain was their best level of usefulness. Musuru is a "a place to work, to talk, to think, but not to idle in—a strenuous and stimulating habitation,"[29] just like the empire itself, which calls forth dedicated and inspired effort from the British. It is also an illustration of a "vantage point" from which the white man can dominate the tropics, and to which he can retreat from time to time to restore his health, his spirit, his morale, his will to rule.[30]

An elegant setting is also an elegant incentive for elevating discussions on imperialism. Whether in the drawing rooms of London or the drawing rooms of Musuru, civilized people hold civilized discourse; the real advantage of Musuru for these discussions is its isolation, its freedom from the distractions of London, of family, and of society and from the obligations that are part of the daily routines of most of these people. The ideas that the guests express are not new or startling, but they are well expressed; everyone talks in paragraphs, as one guest half complains.[31] What results is not full-fledged debate, but series of set-piece recapitulations of pro-imperialist viewpoints, with the viewpoints of opponents of imperialism being brought in usually by way of newspapers or newspaper clippings. Carey from the beginning repudiates the intention of establishing hard-and-fast blueprints for empire. The discussion is to be a refresher course designed to reach some common grounds among a variety of opinions and to clarify some of the central ideas of imperialism. Differences of opinion are never carried to extreme, and the bases of reconciliation become readily apparent, perhaps too readily.

The discussions on imperialism begin and end with definitions. With his liberal arts and humanistic tendencies, Buchan does not feel the need for hard-and-fast formulas, pinning down imperialism onto a drawing board and labeling its exact components. A series of working definitions are for this sometimes political man sufficient—indeed necessary—to get a variety of people into the proper frame of mind to cooperate voluntarily in working for a common cause.

A considerable portion of the guests at Musuru are romantics, and their attempts to define their views on imperialism tend to have a poetic, sometimes insubstantial, quality. "'It is a spirit, an attitude of mind, an unconquerable hope. . . . It is a sense of the destiny of England. It is the wider patriotism that conceives our people as a race and not as a chance community,'" begins Carey, who for a hardheaded businessman reveals a distressing tendency toward airy flights of fancy.[32] Mrs. Deloraine, understandably looking "a little confused," adds "'I call it an enlarged sense of the beauty and mystery of the world.'"[33] This is encouragement for more rhapsody, and imperialism becomes successively "'a spirit moving upon the waters, a dumb faith in the hearts of many simple men up and down the world,'" "'the impulse to deeds rather than talk, the ardour of a race which is renewing its youth,'" and "'the spirit which giveth life as against the letter which killeth. It means a renunciation of old forms and conventions, and the clear-eyed facing of a new world in the knowledge that when the half-gods go the true gods must come.'"[34] The initial offering of the philosophical Lord Appin is not much clearer; for him imperialism is "'the realization of the need of a quantitative basis for all qualitative development.'"[35]

The exercise of such flights of fancy might have been quite satisfactory in the social and academic society of Edwardian society, but Buchan does realize that if an ultimate propaganda effort were to be put forward, a more substantial diet would be required to convince the general public. Lady Amysfort, ever political, must have definitions that are strictly political; imperialism is simply synonymous with Toryism, but this is a definition that is self-limiting in its appeal. More appropriately, Mr. Wakefield, the practical man, gives a practical definition, one that for most purposes could be accepted as describing the British Empire until after World War II: "'I define imperialism as the closer organic connection under one Crown of a number of autonomous nations of the same blood, who can spare something of their vitality for the administration of vast tracts inhabited by lower race—a racial aristocracy considered in their relation to the subject peoples, a democracy in their relation to each other.'"[36]

Near the end of the book, after a great deal of discussion of various facets of empire, Lord Launceston attempts to sum up the various viewpoints and to produce a definition satisfactory to all. Imperialism is a "'living faith.'"[37] As in any other faith, there must be variations within it to encompass a large number of people, but the believers must be imbued with the fanaticism that will not rest until the purposes of the imperial faith had been carried out.[38] For the future it would not be necessary to create a new political party to embody this faith, because all existing parties should be convinced that imperialism must form the essential element in all their policies. When all the parties finally get down to dealing with the practical details of imperialism, then the dream of empire, with all its spiritual greatness, can be realized:

> I can forsee an empire where each part shall live to the full its own life and develop an autochthonous culture. But behind it all there will be the great catholic tradition in thought and feeling, in art and conduct, of which no one part, but the empire itself, is the appointed guardian. In that confraternity of peoples the new lands will redress the balance of the old, and will gain in return an inheritance of transmitted wisdom. Men will not starve in crowded islands when there are virgin spaces waiting for them, and young nations will not be adventures in far lands, but children in a great household carrying the fire from the ancestral hearth. Our art will be quickened by a breath from a simpler cleaner world, and the fibre of our sons will be strung to vigour by the glimpse of more spacious horizons. And our English will vindicate to mankind that doctrine which is the noblest of its traditions—that liberty is possible only under the dominion of order and law, and that unity is not incompatible with the amplest freedom.[39]

To Carey this is perfectly in keeping with his conviction that religion and politics are really one, fanatical in spirit,'"as fierce and stubborn and consuming as life itself.'"[40]

The "living faith" is the very essence of a rose-colored vision—beautiful in form, ultimately unrealistic in construction. The concept has two major points of interest. First of all, it is some sort of indication that a compelling force has been at work in the nineteenth century, which has led these late Victorians to convert what after all should have been a pragmatic interest in the course of empire into the tenuous emotionalism of religious faith, for while *A Lodge in the Wilderness* is a work of fiction, Buchan is speaking for a conviction strongly held by a substantial number of his contemporaries. It is hard to envision Lord Palmerston, for all his "Civis Romanum Sum," speaking in such terms; to him the relationship of power and empire was not a romantic theology but a simple fact of life.[41] Disraeli did bring a romantic element to his concept of empire, with its strain of oriental grandeur, but he would have found Lord Milner both amusing and dangerous.[42] Gladstone would have found the concept simply blasphemous, and it would have confirmed his view that imperialists were dangerous fanatics.[43]

The second factor of interest in this equation of religion and imperialism is its implications for the future of imperialism in Britain. What Buchan seems to be saying is that the successful defense of the British Empire depended on the conversion of a majority of the British public to the same view of empire as was arrived at by the Musuru group—first by converting the upper classes, then by filtration to the rest of the political-economic nation. This required the effort to successfully wean the British public from whatever view it had of the empire and propel it into a theological vision held strongly enough to prompt the required actions, and this appeared to be beyond the technical capacity of British society at this time. The immediate necessity for the conversion would not have been readily apparent, and a medium such as television, which perhaps could have been used by a chauvinistic leader to arouse in large numbers of individuals the type of anxiety great enough to lead to the spiritualization of their attitudes to empire, did not exist. Consequently, if the success of the Buchan plan from *A Lodge in the Wilderness* did depend to a significant extent on further emotionalizing the idea of imperialism, then the British Empire was in deeper trouble than Buchan seemed to realize. Though he includes a "practical" character, Mr. Wakefield, in his party, Mr. Wakefield seems unable to jolt the bulk of the rest of the group out of their blank versifying, and by the end of the book he seems more inclined to put on the rose-colored spectacles himself than to fight to remove the scales from the eyes of the rest and to convince them to concentrate fully on the difficulties of achieving what they had set out to do.

One of the curiosities of the imperial literature of the Victorian period is that most of it is not highly descriptive. There are few long word-pictures of imperial places or the wild reaches in which the deeds of empire could transpire. Brief phrases about sandy wastes, dark jungles, and windswept prairies could quickly and firmly set the readers in a mental territory perhaps previously furnished by the works of popularly read travel writers, and make them receptive to the nonstop action that was the usual staple of imperial stories. Action itself, described in detail, became synonymous with the empire and cast a glow over the activities of

Britons overseas. This is why some action, a hunting episode, for example, and references to others, as well as excursions to various locations in eastern Africa, had to be present in *A Lodge in the Wilderness*. The exotic locale and the promise of action were all part of the rose-colored vision.

Sir John Seeley, in his popular lectures, *The Expansion of England*, had highlighted the problems that England could and would face in a world composed of superstates and pointed out that the empire, properly utilized, could keep the British Empire on a par with the United States and Russia.[44] Any vision of the future of empire had to take into account the creation of a unity from the diverse components of the existing empire, and Buchan undertakes a discussion of the topic. The problems that were in the way of greater unity were much easier to state than a plan of successful amalgamation devised. Mr. Wakefield stood as the sole representative of the forces of paradox existing within the empire.

The existence of the autonomous, self-governing colonies, later to be known as the "dominions," was both the pride of British achievement and the hindrance to further development of the empire along closer lines. The existing imperial government by Crown, cabinet, and British Parliament was inappropriate for a more closely coordinated empire. The white colonists, proud of their achievements, were not about to allow a British Parliament, concerned chiefly with local affairs, and in which colonials were not represented, to make important decisions for all parts of the empire. The British public would not be enamored of a situation in which a pack of colonials sat in judgment over its local affairs. There appeared to be too many barriers, both physical and mental, in the way of creating an alternative government that would rule an imperial federation.

In the end, the best suggestion that Buchan's debaters can make is one that relied heavily on intangibles; the counterforce to colonial pride and incipient nationalism would be "'a sentimental attachment to the parent race, an eager desire to acquire those other elements of civilization which their new land can give them.'"[45] On this basis compromise can be reached, involving the trade of the manly virility of the colonists for the sophisticated culture of the parent peoples. This compromise can be reached slowly, by evolving solutions for individual problems, such as those of imperial defense and trade, and by allowing these limited solutions to grow into a desire for the greater creation. A transitional Imperial Council, with colonial representatives, meeting every two or three years to discuss issues of common interest can, if worked successfully, be the forerunner of an imperial legislature, once distrust has abated and obstacles to closer union removed. Home Briton and colonial stalwart would then unite to rule the lesser peoples of the dependent empire.[46]

Ruling the dependent empire was one of Buchan's concerns, and this was consequently a concern of the Musuru colloquium. It was a problem that had occupied Buchan previously, when he wrote the novel *The Half-Hearted;* the novel centers on defining the characteristics of the British that peculiarly suited them for their imperial role. In *The Half-Hearted* the hero, Lewis Haystoun, is a wealthy young Scot, well thought of by his friends and acquaintances, and an adventurous traveler. He had published a book about his travels on the dangerous frontiers of British India. He is "half-hearted" because he cannot take domestic politics seriously enough, and loses an election to a less glamorous, duller man; he also loses the girl he loves because he hesitates when she falls into a river, and she is saved by another man. He is consequently too full of self-doubts to declare his love until it is too late. Despite these drawbacks, when he is put to the test of his courage, he does not fail, but saves the British Empire in India from Russian hordes and border ruffians; he sends out warning messages to the British garrisons and ensures the vital delay necessary for preparation by a desperate stand in a narrow pass, which led to his own death but stopped the invasion.

In *A Lodge in the Wilderness*, Buchan once more takes up a similar theme, through a story told by the two restless adventurers, Considine and Graham. It concerns Lacey, "'an ordinary stupid fellow'" who had been to Eton with them and had died near Chitral on the Indian frontier, holding "'a border fort with a dozen men for five days against several hundred ruffians.'"[47] His stand made such an impression on his opponents that they offered to spare his life with honor, an offer that he refused. His diary revealed his reasoning—"'it was a case for the white man's pride.'" He chose to die "'because he fancied it was his duty. And of course he was happy.'"[48] His death had the impact that he expected it would; his courage was so impressive that that portion of the frontier was to remain quiet in the future.

Considine maintains that Lacey is typical of adventurous young Englishmen, the idea of duty burning as strongly within them as the restlessness that sends them exploring all over the globe. Considine himself, bored by too much civilization, must always be on some frontier, and he feels that he has performed a very useful function in the process:

> We are the advance-guard, always pushing a little further on and making the road easier for those who come after us, the serious solid fellows who make laws and create industries, and generally reap where we have sown. You cannot measure the work of a pioneer by the scale of a bagman. We keep the fire burning, though we go out ourselves. Our failure is our success. We don't found colonies and build cities, but unless we had gone before no one would come after.[49]

The people that Considine/Buchan are talking about are the "gentlemen" adventurers, the restless gentry of sufficient income to feed their inclinations, and they present a very romantic picture indeed. It is therefore unfortunate that there is no strong evidence that Considine's type of wanderer ever contributed a great deal to British imperial development. A much more likely pioneer is an Edward Eyre, whose explorations were designed to open up sheep runs in Australia for economic gain,[50] and whose public school education was more conspicuous by its absence, or a Henry Morton Stanley, whose motives were as thoroughly mixed as his methods were often reprehensible, but which included personal economic and social advancement.[51]

The Musuru party generally agreed that the tropics are important, and that those parts that had fortunately fallen to Britain's share should be firmly and judiciously ruled and developed. The tropic colonies needed capable and dedicated Englishmen as administrators, willing to put up with the debilitating effects of the climate. They could only do this effectively if each colony had a "'vantage ground,'"[52] a high place to which the administrators could come periodically to restore their health and recover vitality and mental vigor. In these highlands the great problems of the colony could be worked out in an atmosphere more conducive to a '"workshop of government."'[53] Britain was especially fortunate to have gained the most hospitable parts of Africa, with its '"great undeveloped speculative dependencies,"'[54] some of which were destined to be white men's colonies, and others the administrative centers of the less climatically desirable portions of the globe. If Carey had his way, tropic administration would be specifically studied and young men trained in the various aspects of efficient governing in such areas, before they went out to the colonies.[55] The vantage points would then perform their function by keeping colonial officials fresh and dedicated to their colonial service.

Without a doubt the function of the tropic administrators was to rule the native population, and to rule them according to a fairly strict set of guidelines. Francis Carey, were his mind not set on so many enterprises, would have been perfect for the job. The members of the Musuru group are carried off to a mission station, where Carey first addresses an assembly of chiefs and warriors—all armed— '"I will not have these people meet me except as free men, and in this country it is the badge of the free man to carry spear and shield."'[56] Free they might be, but even the chiefs stood at Carey's approach and gave him the royal salute—'"He once told me he thought he had over thirty native names, and they are all flattering."'[57] Carey speaks to them in their own tongue, and speaks with '"a superb air of authority,"'[58] friendly talk of crops and diseases changes to a tone of "sharp command" when his word is questioned.

Carey then goes on to speak to an assembly of the local white population about their mission and duty to the native population. They have a responsibility for the welfare of the country, and though mainly farmers, they, simply by virtue of being white men, have some of the duties of colonial administrators '"to fight against ignorance, stupidity and barbarism."'[59] It was important that they keep clear of the extremes—'"The first is the danger of underrating the status of the black man, and the second is the still greater danger of overrating it."'[60] They must ensure that the native population be granted, in justice, the full protection of the British legal system, and they must not take on the onus of inflicting punishment themselves, except under unusual circumstances when breaking this rule might be justified. The native must not be treated as a child, no matter how great the temptation.

On the other hand, it would not do to overestimate the abilities of the black. No matter how apt he appears at assimilating the gifts of civilization, it must be remembered that the native is only beginning his journey down that path, and his achievements are not really what they might seem to be because '"Between his mind at its highest and ours at its lowest there is a great gulf fixed, which is not to be crossed by taking thought. It is less a difference in powers—for he has powers as remarkable often as our own—as in mental atmosphere, the conditions under which his mind works, and consequently the axioms of his thought."'[61] Educational policy must take into account this difference. '"Teach the children to read and write, but do not aim at higher education, for that means black parsons and black schoolmasters, and for that class the market is overstocked, and they are outcastes from the society they would claim as intellectual equals."'[62] The unreality of the last contention Buchan himself was to acknowledge in his book *Prester John*, in which the black pastor, John Laputa, is an eminently respected leader of his people. Instead of the frills of education, the natives should be given solid, practical training in the trades and manual skills that would give them the background for a "decent life." Despite the shortcomings in his view of the Africans, he does maintain that all natives in the dependent empire had recognizable rights. These rights might even extend to the right, as Lady Lucy Gardner stoutly maintains, to make a contract of labor indenture to work in other colonies, and to enjoy the prosperity that this could bring them.[63]

It was not enough simply to rule a dependent empire. In some way this empire must be made to appear to be of value to the people of Britain as well as to the subject population. Settlement, said Mr. Lowenstein, quoting John Ruskin, is the answer. Britain today was suffering from the evils of the industrial society, with a large portion of the population, even of the skilled workers, caught in the insecurities of the industrial system. The empire will provide the land for these people, and the need for their industry and enterprise. The empty lands of the empire and the unfortunate masses of an urbanized industrial society must be brought together, in the view of Lady Warcliff, by determined government action. Though people are free to emigrate they often cannot afford to do so. State-supported migration would "'send the right man to the right place in the right way,'"[64] and create benefits for the migrant, the home country, and the colonies.

Though the empire could bring many good things, Lord Appin points out that there are dangers inherent in dedication to a large imperial state. Size is not a problem of itself:

> I believe most firmly that in the deepest sense Providence is on the side of the bigger battalions. I cannot see why size should not have its ideal as well as littleness. All the world inclines to reserve its affection for small things—a small country, a small people—because I assume there is a stronger sense of proprietorship attaching to what is limited in bulk. Yet I can conceive of as deep a patriotism in an empire as in a city, and a love of great mountains and plains as real as any affection for a garden.[65]

Obsession with size can lead however to the evils of "'jingoism,'" of "'braggart glorification,'" which is a shallow view of empire, not true imperialism. The true imperialist is more concerned with his duty to solve the problems of every part of the empire, and is not interested in an empty England-centered trumpeting about the glories of mere possession. Because he is interested in the colony as a "'trust,'" he is "'the best guardian of the peace.'"[66] War has its place in society—"'the purpose of God is best attained by the strife of race with race and ideal with ideal'"—but war must not come about as a result of a mere "'lust of possession.'" There is enough real work in the peaceful development of the existing empire to take up all the energy of England's sons—this is true empire building and "'above all things it is the labour of peace.'"[67]

Imperialism expressed in such ideal terms will naturally appeal to the upper classes; it is part of their duty and training, part of the process of governing at which they are so adept. But Britain is also a "'rising democracy,'" and the lower classes, which have been brought into the political process and are often still struggling to gain the basic necessities of life, must be convinced that support for the imperial mission is in their interests, but not simply in the material sense.[68]

The natural appeal of imperialism is the appeal to "'a wider patriotism'" that stirs the "'civic conscience.'" It appeals to the basic nature of the British race, which will not confine itself to tiny European islands, but sees that its "'task has been to absorb the unfamiliar and to lay bare the unknown, admitting no *terra incognita* into its scheme of things. There is always the home country, the centre of memories, but the working loyalties of life go to the lands it has created. As every man loves the work of his own hands, so any race must love what comes from its own toil and adventure.'"[69] It is this sense of accomplishment in the imperial sphere, this response to an innate racial sense of duty, that justifies the Musuru project, and demands a stalwart work of propaganda to convince the general British public that the vision is truly one worthy of pursuit.

If the poetic vision of *A Lodge in the Wilderness* is in itself an inspiration to the cause of imperialism, in practical terms this blueprint for the future has some odd omissions. There is remarkably little interest shown in India and the problems of India within the empire. Buchan's imperial experience had been in Africa, and it was on Africa, "the tropics," that he concentrated when he wrote about the dependent empire. As a transplanted Scot, Buchan did have a greater awareness than many of his contemporaries of the difficulties posed in the dominions by the existence of large Boer and French Canadian populations,[70] but *A Lodge in the Wilderness* appears to show little sensitivity about how they contributed to the growth of dominion nationalisms, and how they would complicate the growth of a closer commonwealth.

Foreign nations are also virtually ignored. Nothing in the book suggests an awareness that there was an international competition for empire, a competition that was often tense and bitter and sometimes threatened to explode, as it did over Morocco in 1906, into dangerous confrontation. The problems considered by the Musuru guests are all internal, to the extent that it appears at times that Buchan considered imperialism to be a game played by the gallant sons of the gentry, and there was no indication that he was aware that the gallant sons of other nations did not necessarily play by English rules. Most of all, there is no suggestion in this book that the members of Buchan's ruling class were aware that other nations might no longer be willing to allow the British the room to play out elegant imperial experiments, and that Edwardian England might not be in a position to insist on having its own way. Buchan's debaters could discuss potential limitations on British power if the empire were not consolidated in the fashion that they advocated; they do not take into account the possibility that many of the limits of power had already been arrived at and that Britain's freedom of action was now considerably circumscribed.

Even though the book makes a great show of discussing the economic problems of Britain and the empire, it does not really confront many of the hard problems of the economic situation. The overall economic structure of Britain, the question of whether the Britain of 1906 could afford to be the center of such an empire as was discussed, was not considered, and, indeed, neither Buchan himself nor any of his characters were really qualified to discuss this crucial aspect. Carey and Lowenstein, though presented as economic geniuses, were, like their models Cecil Rhodes and Sir Alfred Beit, inspired banditti, creating their fortunes out of the peculiar circumstances found at the fringe of empire, where chance and instinct often played a greater role in success than understanding of economic forces. Nothing in their experience would fit them to comprehend the problems of an industrial state in relative decline, whose vast resources were rapidly being concentrated in the financial, *rentier* sphere.[71]

But if Buchan and his characters were in the dark about these realities, they were not alone. There were, of course, voices of doom that decried Britain's weakness and offered new remedies, from conscription to pacificism. The popular writers of imperial fiction, the successors of G. A. Henty, such as Herbert Strang and Percy Westerman, still wrote, as their predecessors had for more than half a century, of an imperial universe more in tune with Buchan's picture. Critics such as H. G. Wells, George Bernard Shaw, and Joseph Conrad appealed to a more limited public than the people who were to provide an audience and a market for Buchan's thrillers. In time Buchan's vision of empire would become a commonplace dream, inspiring the young while they were still young, and the dream was good at least until the Second World War. But Buchan's young men grew up, and while the rose-colored vision was a cherished part of their boyhood memories, the colder realities of a world in which Britain was increasingly not one of the superpowers, began to freeze and fade the vision.

NOTES

1. The election resulted in the return of 400 Liberals, 157 Unionists, 83 Nationalists, and 30 Labourites. A. K. Russell, *Liberal Landslide: The General Election of 1906* (Newton Abbott: David & Charles, 1973), 160.

2. A great many radicals were elected.

3. Janet Adam Smith, *John Buchan: A Biography* (London: Rupert Hart Davis, 1965), 180–83.

4. *The Half-Hearted* (London: Hodder & Stoughton, 1935 [1900]).

5. *The African Colony: Studies in the Reconstruction* (Edinburgh and London: William Blackwood & Sons, 1903).

6. J. A. Smith, *John Buchan*, 133, 183.

7. I have used the 1916 edition, published by T. Nelson & Sons.

8. Lord Milner, *The Nation and the Empire* (London: Constable & Co., 1913), xxxii.

9. J. A. Smith, *John Buchan*, 136, 160. Buchan was married in 1907.

10. *A Lodge*, 12.

11. J. A. Smith, *John Buchan*, 139.

12. *A Lodge*, 13.

13. Ibid., 142–43.

14. Ibid., 32.

15. See H. G. C. Matthew, *The Liberal Imperialists* (Oxford University Press, 1973), 288.

16. R. I. Rotberg, *The Founder: Cecil Rhodes and the Pursuit of Power* (New York and Oxford: Oxford University Press, 1988), 679–92. Chapter 25 presents Rotberg's assessment of Rhodes's career.

17. *A Lodge*, 215.

18. Ibid., 23.

19. J. A. Hobson, *Imperialism: A Study* (Ann Arbor: University of Michigan Press, 1967 [1902]), 56–57, refers to "men of a single and peculiar race" as being involved in the "central ganglia of international capitalism."

20. *A Lodge*, 103.

21. Ibid., 100.

22. Many Liberal Imperialists appeared to be confused, caught between Gladstonian principles and their own strong interest in imperial matters. H.G.C. Matthew, *The Liberal Imperialists*, 287.

23. Buchan himself was more of an old-fashioned Tory, rather than a Conservative or Unionist. Guy Vanderhaeghe, "John Buchan: Conservatism, Imperialism, and Social Reconstruction" (master's thesis, University of Saskatchewan, 1975), 10.

24. *A Lodge*, 160.

25. Ibid., 183–190.

26. Ibid., 137–42.

27. J. A. Smith, *John Buchan*, 136.

28. J. L. Garvin, *The Life of Joseph Chamberlain*, Vol. 3 (London: Macmillan & Co., 1932), 19–20.

29. *A Lodge*, 19.

30. Ibid., 119.

31. Ibid., 114.

32. Ibid., 28.

33. Ibid.

34. Ibid., 28–29.

35. Ibid., 28.

36. Ibid.

37. Compare Lord Milner, "Imperialism . . . has all the depth and comprehensiveness of a religious faith." *The Nation and the Empire*, xxxii.

38. For this reason Alan Sandison entitles his chapter on Buchan, "John Buchan: The Church of Empire." *The Wheel of Empire* (New York: St. Martin's Press, 1967), Chapter 6. Sandison tends to overplay this idea, for Buchan's ideas are not necessarily those of Milner. Buchan was interested more in imperialism as part of an organic state.

39. *A Lodge*, 244.

40. Ibid., 245.

41. The "Civis Romanum Sum" speech is extensively discussed in Donald Southgate, *The Most English Minister: The Politics of Lord Palmerston* (New York: St. Martin's Press, 1966), 263–78.

42. Disraeli was primarily a political man, which Milner was not.

43. A "fanatic" like General Gordon in Khartoum in 1884 could get "reasonable" politicians into a lot of trouble, as Gladstone found out.

44. Sir John Seeley, *The Expansion of England*, 18.

45. *A Lodge*, 79.

46. Ibid., 83–84.

47. Ibid., 99–100.

48. Ibid., 100.

49. Ibid., 103.

50. Geoffrey Dutton, *The Hero As Murderer*, Chapters 3–8.

51. See Frank McLynn, *Stanley: The Making of an African Explorer* (London: Constable, 1989) and *Stanley: Sorcerer's Apprentice* (London: Constable, 1991) for an attempt to explain psychologically Stanley as man and explorer.

52. Ibid., 117.

53. Ibid., 119.

54. Ibid., 117.

55. Ibid., 115–16.

56. Ibid., 134.

57. Ibid., 135.

58. Ibid.

59. Ibid., 137.

60. Ibid.
61. Ibid., 139.
62. Ibid., 140.
63. Ibid., 160.
64. Ibid., 158.
65. Ibid., 227.
66. Ibid., 228.
67. Ibid.
68. Ibid., 239.
69. Ibid., 241.
70. J. A. Smith, *John Buchan*, 183. Unlike Milner, when Buchan returned from Africa he became skeptical about the possibilities of Imperial Federation.
71. P. J. Cain and A. G. Hopkins, *British Imperialism,* discuss this process in Part Two.

5

Settling the Ends of the Earth

To Sir John Seeley it seemed obvious, a "normal extension of the English race," that the English people should occupy the "thinly peopled" areas of the world; natural and fortunate: "For a nation to have an outlet for its superfluous population is one of the greatest blessings."[1] From the beginning of Victoria's reign to 1914, more than 21,000,000 people from the United Kingdom emigrated. Of these, almost 7,000,000 went to the areas that became the dominions, British North America, Australia, New Zealand, and South Africa.[2] Most of the rest went to the United States, a country that Cecil Rhodes believed to be at heart reclaimable as part of the British Empire, having been driven away in the past by the wrongheaded stupidity of mere politicians.[3] It is difficult to say why such vast numbers chose to venture their fortunes in new lands; whether it was the "push" of circumstances at home, overcrowding, unemployment, destitution or hunger, or the "pull" of the destinations, the free or cheap land, the job opportunities, the lure of essentially British societies—even in the United States the new migrants did not have to face the culture shock of having to adapt to a new language and to radically different concepts of social behavior. Only the tiniest fraction of this exodus was directed by the British government itself; if later imperialists saw the advantage of an active pursuance of a policy of establishing New Britains all over the world, which could in due course enhance the power of the old, few if any British statesmen at any point seemed personally motivated to push such a vision. So among the "push" factors the state was conspicuous by its absence. More lively were individuals and colonization societies designed to help specific portions of the population, perhaps those generally in need of assistance to get on their way. More lively still were some of the "pull" factors, the emigration agents who sought out and persuaded thousands of prospective migrants that a secure future lay in the lands that they represented. Among their tools of persuasion, propaganda played a significant role, written works of enticement being paramount.[4] Curiously, the writers of imperial fiction were backward in performing this function, which would seem to be a natural one considering their preoccupations.

They were backward but not totally absent in the presentation of the delights of migration, though their books as immigration literature leave a great deal to be desired. Just why this is so will appear from an examination of the works of a number of writers, spread roughly equally throughout the Victorian period. These are Frederick Marryat, W.H.G. Kingston, R. M. Ballantyne, G. A. Henty, and G. M. Fenn.

The theory behind settlement, especially as enunciated by Edward Gibbon Wakefield, was unexceptionable. If the country could benefit from the departure of a portion of its population, then it became almost a sacred duty for those people to go, and for the rest to assist them. Depression, poverty, overproduction could all be resolved by having fewer people to share in the decreased pie of the nation's economy. Indeed, the spirits of the people at home would pick up once they no longer had to struggle against oppressing odds, and the economy could surge forward. But those who left also had a duty not to go just anywhere, selfishly bettering themselves, perhaps in the United States, without a thought for the mother country. They should be bound for the colonies, stirring them into fruitfulness, creating cultural new Albions, and playing complementary roles in the worldwide economy of the British people.

Not everyone saw colonization in glowing terms. The United States was a standing example that a colonization policy could go sadly amiss. And emigration basically was an admission of failure—the failure of a society to accommodate to all the wishes and needs of its people. The novelists approached the question of actual emigration, as distinct from adventuring or serving abroad for a limited number of years, extremely gingerly, and not at all with the confidence of Buchan's planners.

Most of the fiction written in the Victorian period that can be characterized as imperialist writings cannot be said to be emigration tracts. For the prolific imperialist writers, as opposed to writers like Marryat who were chiefly naval writers and only occasionally wandered into the imperialist field, settlement was almost incidental, a byproduct in what was meant to be a novel of adventure typical of the genre. Emigration in such novels becomes a device to get the hero or heroes into the area of action as quickly as possible, so that he or they could participate in this or that invigorating and enlightening conflict. For the object more often was to teach something about a far-off place than to persuade people that they should pack their bags and move there.

Although the motives for the migration of their heroes could vary from author to author, usually the move was initiated by some sort of disaster that made it difficult if not impossible for the heroes to remain in Britain. Frequently the motives are tied to class—the higher the social standing the more difficult it was to avoid migration, because the consequences of staying could prove embarrassing to those used to a better sort of life. Most often the crises revolved around money, or its absence, and the impact that the absence could have. These were crises that professional writers knew a great deal about and could elucidate most convincingly.

Captain Frederick Marryat published *The Settlers in Canada* in 1844 as one of several books that he wrote specifically for the juvenile market.[5] He had visited the

United States and Canada in 1838, and so had some firsthand experience with the locale. The adventures related in the book begin in 1794 and concern the Campbell family from Scotland and its exploits in that part of British North America known as Upper Canada.

Mr. Campbell is a prosperous doctor who had inherited a considerable estate from a distant cousin. His eldest son is at Oxford, his second son, a midshipman in the navy who has recently passed his lieutenant's examination. Two younger sons and two nieces are being educated at home. The crisis for this family is precipitated by the appearance, after ten years, of a person with a better claim to the estate. When legal fees and other debts are finally settled, the family is left with seventeen hundred pounds and a very uncertain future, since Mr. Campbell feels that he could no longer take up his long-interrupted and previously successful medical career. To the rescue comes the naval son, Alfred; "'The few hundred pounds,' he points out to his father, 'which you have left are of no use in this country, except to keep you from starving for a year or two; but in another country they may be worth as many thousands. In this country, a large family becomes a heavy charge and expense; in another country, the more children you have, the richer man you are. If, therefore, you would consent to transport your family and your present means into another country, instead of being a poor, you might be a rich man.'"[6] With the money that he has, his father in Canada could buy very cheaply an estate large enough not only to provide for himself a comfortable living, but to leave his children in a far better situation than if they had remained in Britain.

Since no one has any better suggestion the decision is made to migrate, and Alfred leaves the navy, reluctantly, but knowing that his duty lies with his parents, helping them to carve an estate out of the Canadian wilderness. And this is just what the Campbell family proceed to do. With the capital available to them, and some excellent letters of reference that gain them the favor and support of the governor at Quebec and the commandant at the nearby fort in Upper Canada, a substantial and increasing enterprise is set up on the shores of Lake Ontario. It soon becomes the center of a satellite community of semi-independent migrants recruited from the lower classes.

George Alfred Henty has long been regarded as the most popular writer of boys' stories in the late Victorian period. A great many of his novels have imperial themes and imperial settings. The earliest of these and the first of his boys' novels was *Out on the Pampas, or The Young Settlers*. It is a story written by Henty specifically for his children; the children of the Hardy family, Charles, Hubert, Maud, and Ethel, bear the names of his own children.[7]

Mr. Frank Hardy is an architect in a provincial English town, whose increasing expenses as a family man are threatening to overwhelm his income from his profession. To stop the decline in his fortunes he decides to give up his professional career and to migrate with his family to Argentina, an area to which a considerable number of British settlers traveled in the nineteenth century. The attraction of the new world was the availability of cheap land, where his limited resources would have greater impact than in England. The Hardy family is able to establish itself on a huge estancia, bring in increasing numbers of cattle, sheep, and horses, experiment with a variety of crops that aided in the self-sufficiency of the establishment, and build a large and comfortable home. Soon the family is surrounded by a great number of other estancias, many of which are occupied by British settlers.

Very few of Henty's prolific writings dealt with actual emigrants. A family caught in financial difficulties is featured in *Maori and Settler,*[8] though as the subtitle, *A Story of the New Zealand War*, indicates, the major purpose of the book is not to detail the act of settlement. In this book, the Renshaw family, father, mother, son, and daughter, are pushed into migration by the loss of most of their money due to the collapse of a bank in which Mr. Renshaw had shares. Mr. Renshaw is an ineffectual scholarly type, paralyzed with indecision in the face of this disaster; the necessary impetus for action must come from his wife and son. In the midst of the lengthy campaign against the Maori, a successful farm is established, as well as a business in providing rare plants for the English market, a matter in which Mr. Renshaw gets himself involved in preference to his scholarly activity and in the process casts off his air of futility and indecision.

In *With Roberts to Pretoria,*[9] a young public school boy, Yorke Haberton, sets off to South Africa to find his fortune, his journey precipitated by the financial failure of his family. He achieves his goal not on the farm where he originally settles, but through his exploits in the Boer War. Only to a limited extent can this be called a settler story, but the motivation for migration does involve loss and the attempt to regain status.

A variation on the theme of migration through necessity is provided by Henty in *A Final Reckoning.*[10] In this case the hero, Reuben Whitney, is not a member of the upper classes; his father had been a miller who had apparently committed suicide when his business venture failed. Reuben is educated to a level above his social origin by a kindly schoolmaster, and this enhances his natural nobility of spirit, which constantly shines through. Reuben's crisis arrives when he is falsely accused of burglary and is acquitted in a trial whose proceedings left most people convinced of his guilt, or at least uncertain of his innocence. In such a situation, as Reuben points out, "'These things stick to a man all through his life,'"[11] and it was better to seek a fresh start in the colonies, in this case Australia, where he could find work at his trade of wheelwright, or some other honest occupation. He works his way to Australia as a carpenter on a convict ship, and through the influence of, first of all, the fiancé of a young lady whose life he has saved, he becomes a bold and successful policeman, and then with the aid of her father, a successful Sydney businessman.

Necessity for the upper classes could take a variety of shapes. The two young heroes of G. M. Fenn's *Diamond Dyke,*[12] the half brothers Joseph and Vandyke Emson, migrate to South Africa and start an ostrich farm to show their father that they can be successful at an enterprise all their own. Success does come in the end, but not through farming; diamonds prove more rewarding than ostriches. In *First in the Field,*[13] the father of the young hero, Dominic Braydon, is forced to migrate to Australia because of ill-health. A successful doctor in London, his health had broken down, and his remedy was to prescribe himself an entirely different type of life, with fresh air and plenty of exercise as a squatter in New South Wales.

Of all the writers concerned with this subject in any way, W.H.G. Kingston was the most involved in the promotion of emigration. In a pamphlet published in 1848 he advocated substantial government commitment, including financial, in promoting emigration.[14] He became secretary of a colonization society whose purpose was to actively promote emigration. Speeches and publications such as *How to Emigrate*[15] tried to ensure not only that prospective emigrants had some financial assistance but also that they had proper moral and religious preparation. Advice, small comforts, provision for educational opportunities for the children of migrants, and provisions for their spiritual welfare, therefore, all formed part of Kingston's activities on behalf of his pet project. When he turned to writing fiction on a full-time basis, a number of his novels were concerned with settlement.

Snow-Shoes and Canoes[16] is a lengthy tale of the adventures of young traders on the prairies of British North America. Curiously, the book ends with several pages designed to promote settlement in the "fertile belt" of what were to become the Canadian prairies.[17] It was an area that was "amply" watered, with a thick layer of rich soil. The climate was "healthy and perfectly suited to British constitutions," as well as being suited to the grains and fruits that could be grown in that area. There was plenty of pasture land for sheep and other animals. The region was now part of Canada, had settlements, and was being surveyed for a railway. The prairie land was

> still wild enough to satisfy the most romantic; but it now contains many of the elements of civilization, and affords every opportunity of success to hardy, industrious men desirous of forming a home for themselves and their families. Numerous English travellers have visited it; and only lately the Governor-General of Canada traversed the whole region from the shore of Lake Superior to Vancouver's Island in the far west without encountering the slightest difficulty, having concluded on his way satisfactory treaties with the Indians, who are never again likely to molest their pale-face fellow-subjects. Intending settlers can now reach the region from Canada with ease. A railway has been designed to extend to the Pacific shore of British Columbia; and until it is opened a succession of post-stations will enable the traveller to pass without impediment from east to west through the whole of the Canadian Dominion.[18]

In this case adventure is the hook to catch the interest—the interest presumably of boys as yet not interested in migrating to a new country no matter how exciting. The message at the end is for any older family members who might be enticed to read along with the children. On a longer view, it was something that might remain with the younger readers when in later days they would be considering their course in life. As was the case of the young Gilpins of *The Gilpins and Their Fortunes*.[19]

Arthur and James Gilpin were the sons of a "squire" with a small property and a large family. While the father could raise and educate his family adequately from his resources, it was obvious he could not provide for their future. The two young men decided to migrate to Australia to see what hard work and resolve might bring them. What hard work earned them was careers as successful and contented stockmen, well able to provide for younger siblings when they in turn came to Australia.

What is significant about the Gilpins is that they are ordinary young men, as defined by mid-Victorian moral and religious standards, who can make the choice for migration unpressured by crisis or disaster. Life in a new country could be the rational choice of those who viewed quietly their prospects at home, and decided that on balance they would be better off in a fresh setting. Kingston was not entirely free of the melodramatic motive. In *Very Far West Indeed*,[20] Peter Burr migrates to the United States because he cannot make a profit on his English farmland, and is evicted. Once settled on a farm in the United States, he is pressured into moving farther west by a series of natural disasters, and then persuaded to move to the Red River Colony of British North America in the aftermath of a serious Indian attack on his wagon train. In the same book Fred Rowland went adventuring to the wilds of North America when his father forbids his marriage to Peter's sister-in-law, Jane, a sweet but now poor woman. He keeps on moving until he ends up with Jane, his deceased father's money, and a prosperous farm on the Red River.

The British government had occasionally taken the initiative in promoting, organizing, financing, and carrying out a migration policy that if pursued more consistently and enthusiastically would have gladdened the hearts of all colonial advocates. In 1820 it sent out almost 5,000 settlers from Britain to settle in the Eastern Cape Province in South Africa, to provide some counterbalance to the Boer population of the Cape, but more specifically to closely settle an area as a barrier in the path of future "kaffir" raids into the colony.[21] Incidentally, this migration was doing something to ease the problems of poverty in Britain, and what was perceived, in the depression that followed the Napoleonic War, as overpopulation. The settlers were chosen from some 90,000 applicants from all areas and most corners of British society.[22]

R. M. Ballantyne, after traveling in South Africa in the 1870s, a visit that he chronicled in *Six Months at the Cape*,[23] had earlier incorporated his knowledge of the South African scene into the adventure tale *The Settler and the Savage*.[24] The settlers in this case were the 1820s settlers sent out to the frontier by the British government, and the book, with a fair amount of humor and some digs at officialdom, deals with the often severe trials of succeeding in what was often a hostile environment. It has no specific heroes, but is composed of a series of vignettes about the adventures of a number of individuals and groups of individuals, spread out over two decades, the 1820s and 1830s.

What the book does not deal with is the motives for the migration. The motives of the British government are briefly indicated when the Scottish parties are settled in a mountainous region where they could act as a barrier to native incursions. The motives of the small number of upper-class settlers are suggested in the somewhat unlikely explanation—they "had resolved to forsake their native land and introduce refinement into the South African wilds."[25] But individual motives for the vast majority are simply assumed, not discussed. The settlers came for the land, and for the opportunity to make a better living than at home. Some were drawn by the adventure, and their lack of any previous involvement with the soil and their consequent lack of farming knowledge soon sent them adventuring into other areas, such as hunting and trading, to make their way. None of the people that Ballantyne deals with are troubled aristocrats, or individuals fighting to regain their positions in society.

The Britons who populate the pages of Gilbert Parker's *Pierre and His People* and *An Adventurer of the North*[26] are most likely to be star-crossed in some way. Duke Lawless is on the prowl through the colonies because of a misunderstanding with the woman he loves.[27] Shon McGann has to leave home and love because of a tangle with the law.[28] Dick Adderley headed into the North country partially out of boredom with London life but mainly because of the story of John York, sent into exile because of the faithlessness of his love, and a quarrel with the Prince Regent.[29] These are all people who have not so much settled in British North America as merely inhabited portions of it, attracted not by the economic potentialities of where they were, but by the mysteries of the wilderness. They are, like Pretty Pierre, the half-breed who is the hero of most of these collections of stories, gamblers, but not gamblers for money. They are gamblers with life itself. They bear a resemblance to Buchan's adventurers, but they have no such pretentious or exalted views of their roles in the scheme of the British Empire. They are living their own dreams, not those of someone else.

To emigrate to a new and distant land obviously involved a major commitment, designed to be permanent. To several of the fiction writers dealing with this topic, the permanency of the arrangement does not appear to be desirable; it is only permanent if there is no alternative. All the detailed delights of the New World, when placed in the balance, could not really measure up to the pleasures of "home." Though the Campbell family in Marryat's *The Settlers in Canada* have definitely created success with the establishment of a prosperous farming settlement, most of them are always conscious of the sacrifices they have made, and of what they are missing by being there. When Mr. Campbell reinherits the Scottish estate, "duty" calls the major part of the family to return to the Old World. Of the prosperous community on the St. Lawrence that they had established, only the youngest son, captured by the life of a hunter and not given to "book learning," remains, along with the Canadians and the emigrants from lower social classes who will likely never have the option of returning to Britain. It might have been "hard to say whether much real joy was felt by any of the party at the prospect of returning to England,"[30] but return they did.

To a large extent the winning through of the hero/heroes to fortune and estates in England is a feature of the novels of Captain Marryat.[31] The same is definitely true of the bulk of the stories of G. A. Henty, whether they be historical novels or his adventures in the empire. It is his version of the happy ending, justice triumphant, the capping of a distinguished career of boldness and virtue. In most cases this is a fitting conclusion to the romance of adventure, but in the case of his settler stories this conclusion is not merely inappropriate, but in fact it is frequently strained and artificial.

The Hardy family from *Out on the Pampas* is not portrayed as a family responding to a drastic crisis and faced with the necessity for migration. The father has spent years, as a young man, in America, and already knows something of the frontier life. The sons have months before they leave to learn and practice useful arts such as gardening, carpentering, shooting, and riding. The daughters practice the domestic arts. The whole family, since it is bound for Argentina, takes tuition in Spanish and attempts to gain some fluency in the language. Once established in Argentina, they are, after a time, no longer on the frontier, but are in the midst of a considerable and prosperous settlement, much of which is composed of Britons of their own class, and with whom they have established extensive and pleasurable social contacts. The eldest daughter becomes romantically involved with a quite suitable neighbor. At this point a lively novel of adventure and settlement has been completed, but it does not suit Henty's purpose. The last few pages are devoted to a rather cold and mercenary calculation by the father who engages in the splitting of the assets of the enterprise. Part of the assets he takes home to England, along with his wife and daughters, in order to develop and farm an estate in that country. The sons are to alternate living and traveling in Europe with managing the Argentine estate until such time as the equity in the land has built to the point that it makes them all wealthy. Then the land is sold, and both sons, now married, settle in England. The daughters also marry, the eldest to her Argentine sweetheart, but only after he has inherited his father's English lands and wealth and has settled back in England. The whole adventure stands revealed as a long-term stock market manipulation.

Financial disaster had precipitated the departure for New Zealand of the Renshaw family in *Maori and Settler*. Here they found suitable land, with friendly neighbors, including two young men that they had brought out themselves, whose father had worked for them in England. Many of their neighbors were perceived to be of their social class. The farm was successfully cultivated, and a profitable sideline in rare plants was established. Best of all, Mr. Renshaw, who had been a vague head-in-the-clouds scholar knowing more about the ancient Britons than about his own children, had now become an active participant in family affairs and a suitable head for the family. Still, when his daughter consents to marry the wealthy Mr. Atherton, Mr. and Mrs. Renshaw are persuaded to return to keep their daughter company in the old land. True, the son remains to maintain the family businesses, which are increasingly prosperous, but in the end he, too, retires to England with his wife and daughters, though he does leave his sons back in New Zealand to continue to manage business.

Both the above books dealt with families that had lived acceptable and comfortable middle-class existences in England before they had made their decisions to migrate. Reuben Whitney, of *A Final Reckoning*, had lived a life of relative poverty and considerable vexation, with the greatest vexation being his trial for the burglary of the house of the squire in whose village he had grown up. In Australia, he became first a brave and respected police captain, then a partner in a prosperous engineering firm in Sydney. He married the daughter of the English squire, a girl who had always believed in him, and he persuaded his mother, his only relative, to come to Australia to live with him. And in the last paragraph he "twenty years afterwards sold his business and returned to England and bought an estate not far from Lewes, where he is still living with his wife and family."[32] For Henty the stamp of real success was still that estate in England, and the leisurely life of the country gentry.

G. M. Fenn was a contemporary of and a biographer of Henty, and prolific in his adventure writings. In many ways he was less given to formula writing than his friend, and probably for that reason he was not as successful; his excursions into whimsy must have been disconcerting to boys expecting straight uncomplicated adventure tales. In his two settler books looked at here, he split his answer to the question of the permanency of settlement. In *Diamond Dyke*, his two young heroes, having won success through the collection of diamonds on their farm rather than from the raising of ostriches, and disgusted by the moneygrubbing propensities of their neighbors on the diamond fields, took their money and their pet lions and went home to England. In a sense this was to be expected; they had intended to return once they had shown that they could be successful. On the other hand, Dr. Braydon of *First in the Field*, having gone to Australia both to improve his health and to change his lifestyle, had no intention of returning to England, with or without his family. He had been successful in London and successful in Australia, and on the whole he preferred Australia.

W.H.G. Kingston had worked in the field of the promotion of emigration, and probably had more contact with people who would choose to migrate. They were people, once the decision had been made to leave, for whom England held nothing, perhaps not even a sense of nostalgia for the life that they were leaving behind. Kingston had a very strong sense of religious purpose, which constantly shone forth in his writings, and the impact of this religious faith appears to have been to make the author fatalistic. If God had directed his heroes to Australia in *The Gilpins and Their Fortunes* or to North America in *Very Far West Indeed*, then he had obviously meant them to be there. The focus of the books consequently was on how the main characters proceeded to make the best of the life that had been ordained for them, but which they had to merit by meeting all the challenges that were thrown in their paths. In a sense, to send them back to England would suggest that in some way God was second-guessing Himself.

The religious element in the works of R. M. Ballantyne was also very strong, but there was much less sense of predestination about *The Settler and the Savage*. The settlers that Ballantyne focuses on all accept South Africa as their home, and Ballantyne does not portray them as in any way, even in the midst of horrendous difficulty, pining for a return to Great Britain. They are, for the most part, ordinary people who have burned their bridges in the old country and have come prepared to make the best of their new life. Both Ballantyne and Kingston, therefore, present conclusions to their works much more in keeping with the vision of developing the empire through the settlement of British people in the vacant areas of the world.

The stories of Gilbert Parker are much more whimsical. It is to be noted that Parker himself, after spending a considerable number of years in Canada, returned to England, was knighted, and became a member of Parliament.[33] His Britons are like flotsam and jetsam tossed upon the tundras and prairies of the Canadian north and west. They are caught by intangible forces, almost by moonbeams, which keep them where they are, or, like Lawless, constantly returning. What does seem to be clear is that in many ways England is soul-wearying, having been numbed by tradition and authority—laws not justice—and it is in Pretty Pierre's country that Englishmen could really come alive, or could earn their deaths in a special and meaningful manner. The underlying message in many of Parker's stories is about commitment, and it is a fitting message for emigrants, for the New World always demanded commitment.

No one reading the novels of the imperial writers would be under the illusion that life in the colonies would be easy. Quite apart from the fact that the writers were writing adventure stories, and obstacles are an essential ingredient of adventure, there is a real sense in the books that, in comparison to England, life in the far reaches of empire could be hazardous to one's sense of comfort and well-being. There were hardships to be faced, and real dangers, all "drawbacks" to the settler experience.

The British climate has its shortcomings, but generally speaking it is not harsh. It is not often possible to freeze to death there, or to die of thirst crawling across a heat-blasted landscape. Most of the rest of the world, on the other hand, has unpredictable and challenging climates that the novels liked to dwell on in loving detail, whether they be settler stories or novels of rampaging adventure. British North America automatically brought forth shivering dissertations on winter; Kingston, for example, sends off four companions on horseback across the prairies in cool but fine autumn weather, when, instantly, they became enveloped in a "fearful snowstorm."[34] Later Kingston informs his readers that "from the middle of October till late in May, during the whole period, the ground is covered with snow, the rivers frozen over, the trees are leafless, every drop of water exposed to the air congeals."[35] Winter came to the Campbells in Ontario in an exceedingly brusque manner: "During that night the gale increased to almost a hurricane; the trees of the forest crashed and crackled, groaned and sawed their long arms against each other, creating an unusual and almost appalling noise; the wind howled around the palisades and fluttered the strips of bark on the roof, and as they all lay in bed, they could not sleep for the noise outside and the increased feeling of cold."[36] Sergeant Fones, staunchly doing his duty of night patrol, and chilled rather than warmed by love, a love that was not returned, lost his way just a few miles away from his mounted police barracks, and was found on a brilliantly clear and cold Christmas day—"Motionless, stern, erect, he sat there upon his horse, beside a stunted larch tree"[37]—frozen but smiling.

Foreign climates were often exuberantly wet, sometimes with fearsome consequences. In North America, a flash flood forced the Burr family, in the middle of a horrendous nighttime storm, onto the roof of their cabin until they were rescued by canoe.[38] Their house, their crops, and part of their livestock were swept away. In South Africa, the Skyd brothers were washed out of their farm and fled to the farm of the Brooks, arriving just in time to rescue their proposed hosts as the waters battered away the small protection of their raised ground.[39] On the other hand, lack of water left the veldt farms parched and simmering in the heat, and left travelers across the wastes of Australia anxiously looking for the next water hole. The storm at sea was a terror to all prospective migrants, and Marryat, a naval man, did not ignore it. A crippling storm in the Indian Ocean set the Seagrave family and an old sailor on an island where they pursued a Swiss Family Robinson type of involuntary settler life for several months before they were rescued. Henty, though not a naval man, loved the sea and often included long passages of sea adventures in his stories. Reuben Whitney and the Renshaws ran into ship-damaging storms on their way to the antipodes; the Hardy family were more fortunate, encountering merely an invigorating gale. Those who sailed on Harry Collingwood's adventures often had their ships blown to pieces by wind and waves.

The vagaries of temperature, wind, and water most quickly came to the mind and hand of the authors, but other drawbacks existed in the imperial setting. In the settlement colonies neighbors were often far away, communities remote and difficult to reach, and loneliness a constant preoccupation for anyone who had not arrived with a company of fellow adventurers. Even in the midst of a family, homesickness could strike, particularly during festive seasons. Travel often involved the danger of getting lost, with consequent dire results. When diseases struck, as they occasionally did, help was a long way off, and uncertain of procurement. Life on a really new frontier meant literally starting from scratch, scratching the earth to make ready for crops or clawing clearances in heavily wooded areas. A new home, most often a log cabin about which the best that could usually be said was that it was "snug," had to be constructed on lines far different from what middle-class emigrants would have been used to in Britain. Though the land was always fruitful, there were times when food supplies could be short, and hunger if not actual starvation threatened.

The way to and the locale of the colonies were often strewn with hostiles, with pirates, "the enemy," the natives, violent animals, and ubiquitous and voracious insects. A great many Kingston and Henty heroes were attacked at sea by pirates who had to be outfought or outrun in desperate little encounters. The battles served as an initiation to what promised to be a lively series of adventures abroad. If pirates were not at hand, their place could be taken by the "enemy"—the French, for example, who sneaked in through the fog to capture the ship carrying the Campbell family to Quebec.[40] Even stopping at a friendly port could be traumatic, as young New Zealand bound emigrants unwisely get themselves lost on the waterfront of Rio de Janeiro and run into a knife-wielding set of muggers.[41] Outlaws and other desperate men frequent the outback of Australia, the plains of Texas, and the goldfields of California, ready to put life and property at risk. The Gilpins on their first employment on a stock farm have to rid the property of a dishonest manager and a bunch of conniving, drunken, slovenly, criminally-minded stock herders.[42] There is no doubt that man could be exceedingly dangerous to his fellow man. Among the most dangerous to be noted by the adventure authors are the "natives," or indigenous peoples of the areas to which the settlers traveled—the Indians, the aborigines, the Maori and other South Sea islanders, and the Kaffirs and their brethren—all "savages" whose characteristics provide counterpoint for the heroic settlers and cool-nerved adventurers.

The writers were not uniformly hostile to the "hostiles." Little Strawberry, the Indian maiden in *The Settlers in Canada*, is kind, gentle, and intelligent, and fit to marry one of the several white men who seek her hand.[43] Angry Snake, on the other hand, is ill-tempered, covetous, and untrustworthy, and leads his band to the kidnaping of first one, then another of the Campbell children, before he is dealt his comeuppance by an expedition from the settlement.[44] Raiders, such as those that strike the Hardy ranch several times in *Out on the Pampas*, are impersonal evil artifacts that can be shot down with satisfaction. A wounded raider, patched up and sent home, can, however, acquire an identity, and can exhibit gratitude as well as intelligence.[45] As individuals, then, they can have an assortment of characteristics, good or bad—and when they are good, they are very, very good, like Cooper's Mohicans,[46] and when they are bad they are positively evil. As a group, a faceless mass, they become relentless foes, determined to steal or kill, or both, because this is their way; their culture is wayward, cruel, and "savage."

Much the same could be said of the other native peoples who crossed the paths of the unfortunate settlers. The wild aborigines speared stockmen and carried off flocks of sheep into the wilderness, and used their unusually capable bushcraft to evade capture. The appearance of even a small group of aborigines at a water hole could cause consternation to immigrant stockmen.[47] Maoris, fine fellows in their way, especially when they were on your side, were arrogant and had no aversion to striking from ambush, or in the dead of night, and killing settlers and their families. The Kaffirs also struck from ambush, and were arrogant, but were more likely to be depicted as cowardly and ignorant, dangerous primarily when they were present in large numbers, and capable of outrageous treachery.

Wild men were an obvious menace to the well-being of settlers, but wild animals were as well. Panthers and wolves stalked the trails of Upper Canada and the western plains, and when they were hungry, as they always seemed to be, they were not at all shy about attacking prospective victims right up to the doors of their residences. The call of the hungry wolfpack at night was enough to keep even the hardiest settlers, safe within their cabins, awake with apprehension. Bears were often large and angry obstacles to tranquillity, and steady nerve and accurate shooting were required to meet their threat. In Africa, lions and elephants turned hunting trips into exciting adventures, while poisonous snakes could transform everyday life down on the farm into unwanted excitement. Swarms of locusts, unstoppable in their mindless migration, did not directly threaten life, but could within a short time strip a homestead of all greenery and destroy a season's work. The simple armadillo and the prairie dogs digging their homes on the plains endangered free-riding horsemen who were not paying sufficient attention to where they were going. Nature frequently showed its teeth, and the settler had to be fully aware of the possibility of harm, and had to know how to react quickly and effectively to ensure safety.

In their picture of emigrant life, the adventure writers did tend to emphasize heavily the minus factors of such an existence. But they did present the "pull" side as well, the positive factors that were to entice adventurous families to make the decision to migrate. The picture that they presented here was largely a product of the writer's conception of the British public; Britons were seen as freedom-loving, impatient of personal restrictions, and as lovers of the countryside and of pursuits such as hunting—few of the fictional settlers came from an urban industrial complex. They were also undaunted by the prospect of hard work and were invigorated by the promise of adventure, even the scent of danger.

The British might be free people, but they lived and worked in a restricted environment, relatively crowded with people, and full of the rules and conventions of centuries of existence. Opportunity there was, but the chances an individual had to progress to or maintain a certain station in British society were often limited, unless one chose to be adventuresome in the field of industrial development, an area not favored by the imperial writers.   What attracted the writers, therefore, to the colonies was the space available and the apparent freedom from the irksome restrictions of home.   The members of the Hardy family simply exhilarated in being able to race their horses across miles of pampas, and enjoyed the freedom they had to experiment with different types of agricultural production.[48]   Along with space came opportunity. Reuben Whitney and the Gilpin brothers set out for Australia convinced that their physical skills and their willingness to work opened all sorts of options for successful careers.[49]

Nature and its attractions occupy varying amounts of attention in the books of the imperial writers. Henty was much more concerned with recording action than locale—as he was in his two books on his experiences as a war correspondent in Africa.[50] Kingston, always somewhat of a schoolmaster, is more concerned to give detailed descriptions of the countryside. What was common to all the authors was the impression that the characters of the story only really reached their potential when they were outdoors, contending with, cooperating with, enjoying nature. Gilbert Parker tended to become almost lyrical in his descriptions of nature, its vastness, its gravity, its exuberance, its dangerous moods, and its playful as well as its essential mystery to man who often appeared puny in comparison. To Englishmen contemplating migration from the rural districts, but most especially to those city dwellers who regretted the break with the soil that the industrial revolution had engendered, the colonies so described must have appeared extremely attractive.

Equally a "pull" was the suggestion that in the colonies adventure was always around the corner. One need not forever be stuck in a rut, perched on a stool, for example, doing accounts, because the opportunity was always there to step out of the countinghouse, onto horseback or into a canoe, and to go adventuring into an untamed countryside. It was always possible to go hunting, and many of the stories had extended descriptions of hunting expeditions, where the wild animals that were normally featured as a danger to peaceful existence now became fitting adversaries in a game of wit and daring. Ballantyne, especially, appropriated the hunting scene and provided graphic descriptions of the fun, the excitement, and the danger of such enterprises as a lion hunt, or hunting the mysterious gorillas, or even moose hunting in the remote frozen regions of the Canadian north.[51]

One of the best examples of the fictionalization of the "pull" factors for emigration is W.H.G. Kingston's little book written for the Society for Promoting Christian Knowledge, entitled *The Log House by the Lake*. The book is about a well-to-do London family—Philip Ashton, his wife, his three sons (a fourth was in the navy and figured very little in the tale), and his three daughters. It begins with Mr. Ashton bringing home the news that he has just lost a lawsuit to a distant cousin, and along with it most of his money. Almost immediately all the children announce that they should work and make their parents comfortable; indeed they had some training to do this since Mr. Ashton, despite his wealth, had taught his sons carpentering and gardening, and the daughters had learned to perform household chores as well as gardening. To put all this energy and increasing enthusiasm to most profitable use, he asks, "'What do you think of Canada?'" and was answered with enthusiastic approval of moving there. So they do, along with two of their servants.

There are many things to marvel at in the new country, the vastness of Lake Ontario, the steamers, the oceangoing grain-laden ships carrying produce through the Great Lakes-St. Lawrence water system directly to England, the fine city of Toronto: "'Why I thought we were about to enter the backwoods by the time we got this far west, and here we are in the middle of as civilized a city as any we have seen.'"[52] Mr. Ashton, after careful inquiries, buys some land near Lake Huron, "wild land" rather than partially cleared because his boys are especially keen on doing all the clearing by themselves. The oldest son, Philip, goes ahead with the hired man, and with the aid of a neighbor, a young Irish gentleman, and his hired man, builds a plank cottage in which the family can live until the main log cabin can be erected; the log cabin itself is put up and made snug before the winter comes. Meanwhile, the family clears land, sketches, canoes, sails, and generally enjoys the colorful sights of a summer passing into autumn. Winter brings skating and iceboating on the lake in front of their cabin, snowshoeing, visiting, maple sugar making, and logging while continuing to clear land—in all "The winter passed by pleasantly and usefully."[53] In the next year the oldest daughter marries the pleasant Irish neighbor, and all the boys go off to excellent Canadian schools, one to finish his university education and to become a minister in the church near the family farm, the other two eventually to study agriculture so that they could more effectively run the family farm. Throughout, it is made clear that if you are of the right sort—and a baker from England could make a fortune—and are prepared to work hard and take advantage of opportunities, your success is practically guaranteed in a colony such as Canada.

In contrast, the family that won the lawsuit suffers disaster. The father speculates and loses his money, and the family members are forced to disperse to find their living as they may. The best of them, a daughter who had had a previous understanding with Philip that her father would not countenance, now comes to Canada as a governess, and meets and marries her successful and hardworking lover. Two sons end up in Canada and are helped by the Ashton family, which does not bear grudges, to establish themselves on the land. Success seeks out those who in their hearts deserve it, and are willing to work for it.

Altogether the life of a settler is presented in the most favorable light. There are dangers—boats overturn, ice breaks, people lose their way in snowstorms, and bears are a threat—but these dangers are never central to the story of how the Ashton family works its way to success. In the end they do not regret the loss of their English fortune, and Philip is convinced "that his father is happier with his children gathered around him and all actively employed, than he would have been had he retained his wealth and lived on in the world of fashion."[54] There are limits to the kind of favorable attention the settler life gets even here; the pleasures dwelt upon are the exotic ones of hunting and fishing and maple sugar making. All the rest, the work of establishing a farm and actually putting it into operation and keeping it there, are generally lumped together under hard work that makes one sober and is good for the soul because it purges it of the frivolities of an English existence. There are no hymns of praise to crop growing, to the sheer ecstasy of the hands-on experience of milking cows; the vision of the new farmer is not poetic. The economic aspects of migration are straightforward and unglamorous, and are taken for granted after the obvious benefits are pointed out.

Though Kingston's descriptions of the settler life in Canada appear idyllic, he is careful not to make it appear to be too easy; the emphasis throughout is on the qualities necessary for success, based on information that he had gathered on his honeymoon trip to Canada. In his description of this personal adventure, he warns that "Hundreds of gentlemen, especially unmarried, go to the backwoods with the idea that they are about to form an Arcadia; but when the stern realities of such a life as they must lead break upon them, their spirits sink before them—they take too probably to drinking, when of course, matters grow worse; and at length, if not ruined in mind and body as well as in property, they go home and abuse the country as the cause of their misfortunes."[55] Kingston admits that "a strong hard-working, uneducated man, who has never known the pleasures of refined society" has a better chance to survive successfully in the backwoods, but he still maintains that middle-class people with income too limited for comfortable survival at home could, through the exercise of judicious common sense in expenditure, produce all that they needed to eat, keep horses, and generally live much better than they could have in England.[56] It was perhaps a conclusion that would have been disputed by Susanna Moodie, whose *Roughing it in the Bush*[57] outlines the follies of expecting a better life in such a situation, but Kingston, who had read her book, would have reemphasized the need for judicious common sense, which appeared to be singularly lacking in the Moodies.

Later writers backed Kingston's personal observations. J. Ewing Richie, who traveled to Canada in the 1880s with a party of emigrants, observed that "Canada is not the place for members of the British Association who long for the flesh-pots of Egypt or the champagne-cup. In Canada one has to live simply and to work hard. He who does so work, though in England he may die a pauper, there becomes a man. Canada offers to all independence, a fertile soil, a bracing air. At present there is little chance of the majority of its people being enervated by luxury or demoralized by wealth."[58] Mrs. Cecil Hall, who traveled out to Manitoba in the same period to visit her brother, and whose letters home were published as *A Lady's Life on a Farm in Manitoba,*[59] having duly noted the prairie—"Its vastness, dreariness, and loneliness is appalling"—the freezing temperatures, the hard work—"We have fallen into it wonderfully quickly; completely sunk the lady and become sort of maids-of-all-work"—and the mosquitoes, comments: "It is very certain that no gentleman ought to come out to this country, or, when here, can expect to prosper, unless he has some capital, heaps of energy, and brains, or is quite prepared to sink the gentleman and work as a common labourer."[60] The new emigrants also must give up the habits of the old country; only when they begin to conform to the "ways and means"[61] of the colony do they begin to really enjoy the life they have chosen. Ladies would always find it difficult: "Colonial manners, somehow, jar a good deal on one; they take it quite as a matter of course that we ladies should wait on them at table, and attend to their bodily comforts."[62]

To the Buchan theorists on empire, an emigration policy actively pursued by government was an integral part of a strong empire.[63] The British government never did get around to doing much in this regard, but the British public developed its own interest in the subject, and in the period 1900–1914 almost seven and a half million Britons migrated overseas.[64] Of these, more than three million went to the colonies, chiefly to the newly developing dominions. Their inspiration probably owed a great deal more to economic conditions than to the writings of adventure novelists, though a substantial number of young men were attracted by the glamour of going out.[65] Even the novelists, as romantic as their plots and descriptions often were, were aware that most people would not choose to emigrate unless there was some compelling reason, usually economic, to go. Still, the very settings of the stories, as a by-product, helped to create a rosy glow around the subject of migration to the colonies to settle on the land.

NOTES

1. Sir John Seeley, *The Expansion of England*, 233.

2. A. J. Christopher, *The British Empire at Its Zenith* (London: Croom Helm, 1988), 37.

3. Cecil Rhodes, "Confession of Faith," in John Flint, *Cecil Rhodes* (Boston: Little, Brown & Co., 1974), Appendix, 249.

4. See for example, Edward Gibbon Wakefield, *A Letter from Sydney* (London, 1829) and *A View of the Art of Colonization, in Letters Between a Statesman and a Colonist* .

5. The others were *Masterman Ready, The Children of the New Forest,* and *The Mission, or Scenes in Africa.*

6. Captain Frederick Marryat, *The Settlers in Canada*, 18.

7. Guy Arnold, *Held Fast for England*, 8.

8. *Maori and Settler: A Story of the New Zealand War* (London: Blackie & Son, n.d. [1891]).

9. *With Roberts to Pretoria: A Tale of the South African War* (London: Blackie & Son, 1902).

10. *A Final Reckoning: A Tale of Bush Life in Australia* (Chicago: M. A. Donohue & Co., n.d. [1887]).

11. Ibid., 80.

12. *Diamond Dyke, or The Lone Farm on the Veldt. A Story of South African Adventure* (London: W. & R. Chambers, 1895).

13. *First in the Field: A Story of New South Wales* (London: S. W. Partridge, n.d.).

14. Rev. Maurice R. Kingsford, *The Life, Work and Influence of William Henry Giles Kingston* (Toronto: Ryerson Press, 1947), 57–58.

15. Ibid., 67.

16. *Snow-Shoes and Canoes, or The Early Days of a Fur-Trader in the Hudson's Bay Territory* (London: Sampson Low, Marston, Searle, & Rivington, 1877).

17. Ibid, 332–36.

18. Ibid., 336.

19. *The Gilpins and Their Fortunes: An Australian Tale* (London: S.P.C.K., n.d.).

20. *Very Far West Indeed or The Adventures of Peter Burr* (London: Sunday School Union, n.d.).

21. Noël Mostert, *Frontiers*, 520.

22. Ibid., 520–23.

23. *Six Months At the Cape, or Letters to Periwinkle from South Africa*, 1880.

24. *The Settler and the Savage: A Tale of Peace and War in South Africa* (London: James Nisbet & Co., n.d. [1877]).

25. Ibid., 44.

26. *Pierre and His People: A Tale of the Far North* (London: George C. Harrap & Co., 1926 [1892]), and *An Adventurer of the North: Being a Continuation of the Personal Histories of "Pierre and His People" and the Last Existing Records of Pretty Pierre* (London: George C. Harrap & Co., 1926 [1895]).

27. "Shon McGann's Tobaggon Ride," in *Pierre and His People*, 118–47.

28. "A Sanctuary of the Plains," in ibid., 258–84.

29. "At Point o'Bugles," in *An Adventurer of the North*, 178–87.

30. *The Settlers in Canada*, 285.

31. Oliver Warner, *Captain Marryat: A Rediscovery* (London: Constable, 1953), Chapter 11, "The Three Million Voyage."

32. G. A. Henty, *A Final Reckoning*, 301–302.

33. For a brief summary of Parker's career, see Elizabeth Waterston, *Gilbert Parker and His Works* (Toronto: ECW Press, 1989).

34. *Snow-Shoes and Canoes*, 11.

35. Ibid., 100.

36. Captain Frederick Marryat, *The Settlers in Canada*, 100.

37. Gilbert Parker, *Pierre and His People*, 29.

38. W.H.G. Kingston, *Very Far West Indeed,* 72–77.

39. R. M. Ballantyne, *The Settler and the Savage*, 229–36.

40. Captain Frederick Marryat, *The Settlers in Canada*, 30.

41. G. A. Henty, *Maori and Settler*, 64–65.

42. W.H.G. Kingston, *The Gilpins*, 48–97.

43. Captain Frederick Marryat, *The Settlers in Canada*, 170–73.

44. *Ibid.*, 267.

45. G. A. Henty, *Out on the Pampas*, 264–95.

46. James Fenimore Cooper's exemplary Mohicans are found in such novels as *The Deerslayer*, *The Pathfinder*, and *The Last of the Mohicans*.

47. G. M. Fenn, *First in the Field*, 120–30.

48. G. A. Henty, *Out on the Pampas*.

49. G. A. Henty, *A Final Reckoning*, and W.H.G. Kingston, *The Gilpins*.

50. In *The March to Magdala* Henty has more descriptive passages than in *The March to Coomassie*, though even these are not of a lyrical nature, but are simple and matter-of-fact, as are his descriptions of events.

51. The lion hunt is in *The Settler and the Savage*, the gorilla hunt in *The Gorilla Hunters: A Tale of the Wilds of Africa* (London: T. Nelson & Sons, 1897), and the moose hunt in *Ungava: A Tale of Esquimaux Land* (London: Ward, Lock & Co., n.d.).

52. *The Log House by the Lake: A Tale of Canada* (London: S.P.C.K., n.d.), 18.

53. Ibid., 113.

54. Ibid., 127–28.

55. *Western Wanderings, or A Pleasure Tour in the Canadas*, 2 Vols. (London: Chapman & Hall, 1856), Vol. 2, 263.

56. Ibid., 263–64.

57. Moodie writes "If these sketches should prove the means of deterring one family from sinking their property, and shipwrecking all their hopes, by going to reside in the backwoods of Canada, I shall consider myself amply repaid for revealing the secrets of the prisonhouse, and feel that I have not toiled and suffered in the wilderness in vain." *Roughing it in the Bush, or Forest Life in Canada* (Toronto: Coles Publishing Co., 1980 [1852]), 563.

58. *To Canada with Emigrants: A Record of Actual Experiences* (London: T. Fisher Unwin, 1885), 5.

59. *A Lady's Life on a Farm in Manitoba* (London: W. H. Allen & Co., 1884).

60. Ibid., 94.

61. Ibid., 116.

62. Ibid., 52.

63. *A Lodge*, 153–55.

64. A. J. Christopher, *The British Empire at its Zenith*, 37, Table 2.1.

65. Patrick A. Dunae, *Gentlemen Emigrants,* 5–6.

6

All That Glitters: Just Rewards

To be a settler, to go out to woodland and prairie, to turn the wild places of the world to the ordered production of agricultural goods, was a laudable ambition, and a suitable career for men and their families of all classes who felt a need to improve on the life that they would have lived had they remained in England. Laudable as it was, it was also slow; the cutting and clearing of trees and the careful husbanding of cattle and sheep on grasslands were not activities that brought instant satisfaction of the urge to accumulate; only with patience, in reality and in fiction, could a state be reached beyond subsistence. Even when comfortable affluence was achieved, seldom would it be possible, except in the works of determined fiction writers such as G. A. Henty, for the settlers to reverse the process, sell their colonial possessions, and retire to England to live a life of quiet gentility. The fiction writers who were anxious to promote the varieties of adventurous experience and the potentialities the wide world held for acquiring sudden and substantial sums of money therefore needed some alternatives to sober settlement. A truly enticing way to escape the grinding path to prosperity was to find treasure, already gathered, lying hidden perhaps for centuries and waiting for the adventurers to come along to liberate it, and take all or a large part of it back to England.

Though a considerable number of stories in the Victorian and Edwardian periods did deal with spectacular acquisition of hidden treasure, the two books most commonly associated with this concept are Robert Louis Stevenson's *Treasure Island,* first published in 1883,[1] and Henry Rider Haggard's *King Solomon's Mines*, published in 1885.[2] Both were almost instant best-sellers, appealing to young and old alike, and have continued in print ever since. Stevenson was not the strong overt imperialist that Haggard was,[3] and *Treasure Island* does not carry the same heavy load of imperialist preconceptions as *King Solomon's Mines*, yet both authors appealed to the same sense of romantic adventurism that made imperialism an increasingly popular emotional theme over the next two decades. Lotteries had been banned through evangelical pressure since 1826;[4] substantial efforts were made to curb the gambling instincts of the English people, with mixed success, but with the result of driving much of the activity underground. To many young Englishmen the treasure hunt, whether fictional or real, was a substitute for gambling; it was legal and patriotic, and apparently calculated to build up moral character through the strenuous use of characteristics that had made England great.

There were many reasons why the adventurers should go seeking treasure. In *Treasure Island* occurs perhaps the simplest; the treasure is there and the heroes of the story have a map pinpointing its location. The map had been in the possession of the "Captain," a rough old sea dog who terrorized the customers of the "Admiral Benbow," an isolated inn on the road to Bristol; it passes into the possession of young Jim Hawkins the night the captain dies and the inn is raided by a gang of cutthroats guided by Blind Pew, who terrifies Jim much more than the captain ever did. Jim takes the map to Dr. Livesey and Squire Trelawney, and the decision is made to outfit a ship and to go fetch the treasure. No decision appears to be more natural, and the entire book is then structured around the difficulties of the treasure hunt.

In contrast, the treasure hunt in *King Solomon's Mines* comes about more indirectly. Allan Quatermain, the white hunter hero of the book, has had a map, given to him by a descendant of the mapmaker, for many years without feeling tempted to search out the treasure himself. The adventure starts instead with a different kind of search, the search of Sir Henry Curtis for his younger brother, who two years earlier had gone in search of King Solomon's treasure and had disappeared. The book then develops into the grand adventure by which the search party's servant, Umbopa, turns into Ignosi, the rightful heir to the throne of Kukuanaland, the land where the treasure is. Only after the great battle that is the central epic of the novel is won by the forces of light and reason, though not of civilization, since gunpowder plays but a small role in the outcome, does the search for the legendary treasure of Solomon begin.   When the treasure is found, only Quatermain, who styles himself a poor man who must provide for his son studying medicine in England, shows enough interest, in the midst of the tragedy and potential disaster of that event,[5] to take a generous helping of diamonds on the desperate flight to safety.

G. A. Henty, though very much concerned with the prosperity of his heroes, came late to treasure hunting as a plot; *The Treasure of the Incas* was published in 1903, the year after Henty's death.[6]   The origin of the adventure for Harry Prendergast and his younger brother Bert is an affair of the heart; young Harry has fallen in love with Hilda Fortescue, whose father sees little merit in giving up his daughter to a half-pay naval lieutenant with very little money. Having secured Hilda's promise to be true to him for two years while he seeks such a fortune as would capture the interest of Mr. Fortescue, Harry decides that the only way to do this is to find hidden treasure. Fortunately for someone in such desperate circumstances, one of the trustees of his small estate, a Mr. Barnett, had saved the life of an Indian muleteer in Peru many years before, and the man had hinted that he would be able to make his benefactor very wealthy, a hint that could only refer to ancient Inca treasure. Mr. Barnett was not interested and had not taken up the opportunity, but now is willing to give a letter of warm introduction to his young charges, and the search is on. The book is concentrated mainly on the search, with only a few excursions into battles with thugs, Indians, bandits, and ransom seeking military desperadoes.

Love also motivates the treasure hunt in George Manville Fenn's *The Golden Magnet*.[7] Harry Grant leaves home and his father's faltering soap-making business to seek his fortune in South America at the estate of his Uncle Reuben, and promptly falls in love with his cousin Lilla. But all is not well on the estancia, since it is mortgaged heavily to a nasty neighbor who wishes to marry the fair maiden; to save her parent's home she must acquiesce, and certainly must not give her heart to the penniless newcomer. Buoyed by stories of hidden Inca treasures, Harry and his young companion/servant, Tom, begin the search through a nearby cave for the golden treasures that in due course will save the financial situation of his uncle and, later, his father, and win him the girl that he has been increasingly brooding over.

The young Thomas Gaythorpe, in Captain Charles Gilson's *The Lost Island*,[8] is enticed by a devious and murderous Chinese cook to go seeking the Casket of Heaven, a heavily jeweled box containing Guatama's Eye, a gem of fabulous value that had been earned by his great-great-grandfather a hundred years before, but which has been stolen by a treacherous Buddhist priest who has sailed with it to a South Sea island; the location of the island is now unknown, but a chart of its supposed location remains in the monastery. The young boy's motive for going under dubious circumstances on this search is to restore the family fortunes and allow his mother to live a comfortable lifestyle once again.

In two more stories the treasure motif again is secondary. John Buchan's *Prester John*[9] is mainly about the Reverend John Laputa and his fight to stir the southern African tribes into a rebellion that will sweep the white men from their land, and about the young Scottish storekeeper, David Crawfurd, who foils his plans. Only at the end does it become a matter of treasure, with a struggle for the great ruby necklace, referred to as The Snake or the Collar of Prester John, and the diamonds and other treasures that were the war chest of the rebellion. *The Lost Explorers*[10] by Alexander Macdonald starts out like a settler yarn, with two young men, working in a British engineering works, lamenting the slow pace of their advancement: "'Engineering is good enough for the few; but I can plainly see that life is too short for us to make a fortune at the game. The fact is . . . this country is too crowded for us, and too old. Everything is standardized so accurately that we are little more than machines; and we must exist on our paltry pittances, seeing nothing but grime and smoke and fog, until we become old and brain-sodden, with never a hope beyond the morrow.'"[11] So they decide to migrate to Australia, and meet a Scottish-Australian adventurer who takes them first of all on a successful gold-mining venture, and then on a desperate sortie into the Never-Never land of central Australia in search of revenge for the massacre of a previous exploring party, and in search of whatever else might profitably turn up. The finding of treasure in the enemy camp is almost an incidental by-product of their adventures.

Treasure hunting could be a delicate subject to handle in imperial fiction, especially fiction designed to show the positive side of imperial adventuring, and more especially in fiction often designed for the education as well as the amusement of the boys. By its nature, seeking for treasure can arouse the baser human passions, especially greed, envy, and ruthless violence in reaction to any possible opposition or threat. It becomes especially necessary to ensure that the heroes, the role models of the situation, should not be tainted by these all too natural expressions of human weakness; motives had to be pure, and actions restrained.

Jim Hawkins of *Treasure Island* certainly knew what greed is, as he acknowledges when he watches his mother endanger their lives through her determination to get all that is due to her from the newly dead Captain; she painfully searches through his coin bag for coins familiar to her, and enough to make up the exact sum. Jim, on the other hand, is seized with the anticipation of exotic adventure, and throughout the book he often behaves with the exuberant irresponsibility of a high-spirited youth, dashing off to his own adventures, leaving his companions in considerable distress. When being hauled along by the buccaneers to the resting place of the treasure as marked on the map, he is more "haunted by the thought of the tragedy that had once been acted on the plateau"[12] than excited by the find. When at last he sees the piles of gold, seven hundred thousand pounds worth, where they had been placed in a cave by the marooned buccaneer, Ben Gunn, his thoughts are: "That was Flint's treasure that we had come so far to seek, and that had cost already the lives of seventeen men from the *Hispaniola*. How many it had cost in the amassing, what blood and sorrow, what good ships scuttled on the deep, what brave men walking the plank blindfold, what shot of cannon, what shame and lies and cruelty, perhaps no man alive could tell."[13] Safely home with the treasure, Jim's conclusion is that he would never go back for the bar silver still left on the island, and nightmares of the events were to haunt him. It is a very moral conclusion, and one not really borne out by the story of his personal adventures; he has had an exciting time on the island, and even his almost accidental shooting of the buccaneer, Israel Hands, had not greatly dampened his spirits. Stevenson was too obviously trying to establish Jim as not being greedy to care much for consistency at this point. There are other "heroes" in *Treasure Island*, the talkative and pugnacious squire, the sober and resourceful doctor, the straitlaced and honest captain, and even the flighty ex-pirate, Ben Gunn; at no point do any of them show any particular interest in or excitement over the gold, or an overwhelming urge to possess it; to the squire the search for the treasure is the spirited action of a true Englishman; to the doctor and the captain it is a solemn responsibility, and perhaps a business proposition; even Ben Gunn who had found and dug up the treasure on his own does not therefore claim it all—or even a just share—he merely wants to be taken care of handsomely.[14]

The heroes of *King Solomon's Mines* are a mixed bag of characters. Sir Henry Curtis is little more than a big blond warrior, a throwback to the Vikings when his blood becomes aroused in armed combat; Captain John Good on the other hand is largely comic relief. Allan Quatermain, the narrator and central character of the trio, is a curious creation for a hero; he is at times offensively racist and arrogantly high-handed; he is often cloyingly coy about his prowess and courage—and as a writer he is careful to see that his deeds are set forth; it is difficult to see why he was so popular that Rider Haggard chose to reintroduce him time and again into his extravagant romances.[15] It is Quatermain who has any vestige of a motive for a treasure hunt, and it is Quatermain who in the end is most affected by the wealth in the treasure chamber, though at the beginning the shock of seeing all the diamonds affected all three to one extent or another. They were soon laughing beyond control: "There we stood and shrieked with laughter over the gems that were *ours,* which had been found for *us* thousands of years ago by the patient delvers in the great hole yonder, and stored for *us* by Solomon's long-dead overseer. . . ."[16] Such a lapse from Victorian good taste must inevitably be punished; within a short time Gagool the witch who had guided them to the chamber has stabbed Foulata, the beautiful maiden whose life they had saved, and has let down the great stone door to the chamber, which crushes her in her frantic effort to get out before it totally closes; the three adventurers are trapped in the dark chamber that is now likely to become their tomb. It is a sobering experience.

As a result, when the next day hope flares and they find a trapdoor that promises an exit and safety, only Quatermain remains interested in the diamonds, filling his pockets and a basket with handfuls of gems, and calling on the others to do the same. He meets with a dusty response from Sir Harry: "'Oh, come on, Quatermain! and hang the diamonds! . . . I hope I may never see another.'"[17] and from Captain Good, still brooding over the death of Foulata, no answer at all. Quatermain philosophizes that in the circumstances his own response was not strange and that "If, from the habits of a lifetime, it had not become a sort of second nature with me never to leave anything worth having behind if there was the slightest chance of my being able to carry it away, I am sure that I should not have bothered to fill my pockets and that basket."[18] After all, what had looked to be an outbreak of greed has quickly subsided before the great issues of love and life and death, and is replaced in the case of Quatermain with a simple and fortunate, since they do escape and cannot find their way back into the chamber, attack of prudence.

Harry Prendergast seeks *The Treasure of the Incas* with single-minded determination, refusing to let the great variety of obstacles discourage him, but throughout his motivation is pure; when at last he finds the gold he says, "'Thank God, Hilda is as good as won!'"[19] A short time later he is less able to contain himself; "'I am too excited even to think,' Harry broke out. 'It is time for dinner. When we have had that and smoked a pipe I shall be able to talk calmly over it.'"[20] Throughout the search, his brother Bertie is most interested because of his brother's need; otherwise, to him the whole enterprise is a lark. The three natives, Dias, his wife Maria, and his nephew José, who had accompanied him, are only excited on Harry's behalf; they refuse to share in the gold, and are only persuaded to take some pre-Inca silver very reluctantly. Nothing remotely connected with greed clings to the heroes of this story.

The Inca treasure of *The Golden Magnet* does for a time affect the hero, Harry Grant, in an unpleasant manner. As he searches for the gold, and thinks he has found it, he becomes immensely excited, his hands trembling, but also very suspicious of his true companion, Tom: "'Suppose,' I thought, 'Tom should murder me now to possess himself of the treasure, load the mules, and then bury me in the grave we had dug. The water would flow over it again in a few hours, and who would ever suspect the man who went away laden with wealth?'"[21] But before too long he is mourning his friend, whom he thinks dead, as "'worth ten thousand times more than the vile yellow trash,'"[22] and is aware that the love of a good woman is worth even more.

The heroes who go treasure hunting to *The Lost Island*, young David Gaythorpe; the gigantic Irish seaman, Robert O'Shea; Old Dan, the ship's carpenter; and Mr. Wang, the best detective in the East, must surely rank as the most naive of treasure hunters, even more so than Squire Trelawney of *Treasure Island*. Faced with the competition of a master criminal and a Chinese secret society, they seek the Casket of Heaven with an expedition that is most inadequately armed, and suffer severely in consequence. The desire for wealth and the suspicions of what others might do to gain it barely gave them pause. In *The Lost Explorers*, on the other hand, a party of gold hunters travel deep into the Australian wilderness well-armed and ready and willing to deal death and destruction to treacherous savages, especially to the group one of their number blames for the previous massacre of his fellow explorers. The presumed dead explorers are found alive, however; their colleague, an experienced bushman, James Mackay, had mistaken the burned bones of a *camel* for the bones of his friends. The now united expedition takes away quantities of rubies, sapphires, and perhaps even diamonds from the settlement of the clearly maligned aborigines, and sorrows to leave behind the piles of gold because it certainly could not kill enough of the natives to be able to get away safely with such a burden. David Crawfurd looked upon the treasure of *Prester John* as something he has rightfully earned: "My money seemed pleasant to me, for if men won theirs by brains or industry, I had won mine by sterner methods, for I had staked against it my life. I sat alone in the railway carriage and cried with pure thankfulness."[23] Crawfurd does what he can for the preservation of the empire, and that taken care of, he very prudently looks after his own interests.

The question of rightful claims of others to the treasure does occasionally trouble the treasure seekers, but not for long. Jim Hawkins might sorrow over, and perhaps even have nightmares about, the victims of the buccaneers, but there is no suggestion that the rightful owners be reimbursed for their losses, or even partially compensated. Ben Gunn, who had dug up the gold and stacked it in his cave, is not allowed a claim, on the principle of "finders keepers," to a share in the treasure; he ends up living on the charity of the squire. Allan Quatermain is so taken with the treasure of Solomon that he loses sight of the fact that if it belongs to anyone, it belongs to the Kukuana, in whose territories the mines are located; the treasure is not in any sense a "lost" treasure, and the adventurers really do, in justice, need the permission of the new ruler, Ignosi, to take away any of it. The Incas, of course, no longer needed their treasure, even that which they had preserved from the Spaniards, because the Inca kings no longer ruled, but for Henty this did not mean that the Peruvian government has any moral claim to it; and as for a legal claim, it is best that an occasion for debating this not arise. It therefore was prudent to smuggle the gold out, leaving the smaller amount of silver to be used by the native allies of the young heroes to operate charities for the Indians who perhaps do have some moral right to it.

Quantities of gold also are smuggled out of South America in *The Golden Magnet*. Harry Grant does have some qualms about this but decides that because he will make good use of it, this is better than leaving it hidden in the cave.[24] The right of usefulness can be very convincing for anyone proposing to appropriate the wealth of others; Alexander Macdonald's explorers could carry off all the pretty stones that they find in the lost land of the aborigines because the natives do not value all the precious minerals in their midst. Even Prester John's treasure could be forfeit to the civilized David Crawfurd because the Kaffirs to whom it did belong had proposed to use it only for war and the destruction of the colonial rule that could bring them within the grasp of civilization.

Treasure could not be won without hardship and danger; the imperial philosophy of the Victorian writers was not one of sloth and ease. Jim Hawkins and his friends have to face the very stiff competition of the mutinous crew members of their ship, many of them buccaneers who had sailed with the notorious Captain Flint. Long John Silver, a more interesting creation than any of the heroes, and his allies have no aversion to greed as a motivating force, or to murder as a means of expediting their desires. The witch, Gagool, takes a delight in thwarting the seekers of King Solomon's treasures, and keeps her evil intentions sufficiently masked to trap the hunters in the treasure chamber: "'There are the bright stones ye love, white men, as many as you will; take them, run them through your fingers, *eat* of them, *hee! hee! drink* of them, ha! ha!'"[25] and they come close to having to do so. The trek for treasure could lead through stormy oceans and deadly wastelands where water is scarce; it often leads into the way of hostile natives and greedy bandits. Courage and perseverance and a talent for improvisation, as well as a considerable amount of ruthlessness, are qualities necessary to ensure success in a treasure hunt, and even then the element of good luck frequently enters before the treasure can be brought home.

When the treasure is brought home, it is interesting to see what happens to it. The story of *Treasure Island* takes place in the eighteenth century, possibly before the industrial revolution, and certainly its English setting is in a nonindustrial area. Of the survivors of the quest who left the island, Long John Silver steals a bag of gold coins and disappears, not to be seen again; the rest divide the treasure, and "used it wisely or foolishly, according to our natures."[26] Captain Smollett retires, but the seaman Gray rises in the mercantile naval world, becomes an officer, and buys into a merchant ship. Ben Gunn spends his small share quickly, and becomes a lodge-keeper. The after careers of the squire, the doctor, and Jim Hawkins are not mentioned, but suggestions in the book indicate a life much like that of the squire before the treasure hunt.

In *King Solomon's Mines*, the treasure is divided among Allan Quatermain, Captain Good, and Sir Henry Curtis's brother; they all retire to live in Britain the lives of men of leisure. Only the sequel, *Allan Quatermain*, indicates that such an existence could be boring, and Quatermain, Good, and Sir Henry set out again on an African adventure. Both brothers who sought *The Treasure of the Incas* return to England, retire from their naval careers, marry, and settle into the lives of leisured gentlemen. Harry Grant, who also brings home Inca treasure, rescues his parents from bankruptcy, marries, buys an estate, and indulges his wife's charitable activities. David Gaythorpe and his friend Robert O'Shee bring the Casket of Heaven to Britain, and David returns to his mother and an unspecified career, and O'Shee to an Irish estate, his butterfly collection, and literature. The Australian adventurers return to England, but there is some indication that some at least would go adventuring again in Australia. Buchan's David Crawfurd returns to Scotland to finish his education, and thinks about coming once again to the scene of his adventures, where his civilian friends, Aiken and Wardlaw, are carrying out the work of civilization among the natives, using methods that owed a great deal to the theories Francis Carey had spouted in *A Lodge in the Wilderness*.

This brief survey of the end results of successful quests for treasure illustrates that the industrial nature of British society in the nineteenth and twentieth centuries had not had a great deal of impact on the imperial writers. None of the returned heroes became captains of industry, or even showed signs of investing their riches in industrial enterprise so that through spin-off the nation would benefit from their adventures. Treasure hunters apparently lacked much interest in the countries from which their bounty had come, and felt that the exertions that they had undergone and the dangers that they had faced had fitted them for nothing much more exciting than an occasional reminiscence of their exploits. Only Buchan, fresh from writing his imperial propaganda work, could be struck with the idea that the finding of the treasure need not be the end of the story. Otherwise, the net result was that many writers wrote on a grand or exciting theme, one to stir the imagination, and then allowed their adventure to limp away to a tame, unheroic, and essentially unimperial conclusion.

To go hunting for gold in its raw state, not already conveniently collected, melted down, and hidden, awaiting the treasure seekers, was another exciting possibility of the adventurer's world. It called for the extremely arduous effort of getting to the site, and then involved sustained labor; anyone who carried away a fortune in gold really did earn it. Seeking for hidden treasure was an adventurer's lottery—the chances of finding something were so rare that the seeking was correspondingly more exciting, and more mythic. Finding treasure was like finding the pot of gold at the end of the rainbow; everyone wished that it was there to find, but to actually believe in it was difficult. Allan Quatermain, though he possessed a map to Solomon's treasure, and a copy of a letter of a Portuguese adventurer who had seen it, did not go seeking it himself because he considered it "a foolish story."[27] But a gold mine was real, and possible; gold mines were found, and hundreds of thousands of men had set out on their travels to California, to Australia, and to the Klondike to seek this reality, and some of them had become wealthy.

C. J. Hyne in *Stimson's Reef*[28] does not send his heroes prospecting for a new mine, but sends them to Brazil to reopen a mine that had been successfully operating, and then had been abandoned because of Indian attack. Jack Ellery and Nigel Dalton need money because Jack's father, who was also Nigel's uncle and guardian, had invested all their money in the Stimson's Reef Mine and had died when it collapsed. The two young men, raised to a different sort of life, do not much care for the sordid business of actually earning a living. Together with a friend, Tom Kingston, who owns a yacht and some small capital, and a Scottish seaman, Captain Malcolm, who owns the one-third of the shares of the mine that the boys do not, they set out for the Amazon on the yacht, taking care to arm it first with a machine gun and a two-inch gun.

G. A. Henty's plot for *In the Heart of the Rockies*[29] is much less complicated. Tom Wade, upon the death of his mother and the demise of the tiny pension she had as a naval officer's widow, decides that he should not be a burden upon his sisters who have resolved to keep a school, and he sets out for the western United States to join his Uncle Harry, a fur trapper and prospector in these regions for the past twenty years. Uncle Harry, aware of his responsibility to do something for the girls, takes his nephew and several friends into Indian territory prospecting for gold. After a considerable number of misadventures, they do find gold, and set up a regular mining operation to take it out.

The question of the ownership of the gold mines, even in a century less tolerant of the rights of "savages" over resources that they did not exploit, does cause some problems to the authors. Stimson's Reef Mine had been shut down because the Adira Indians in whose territory the mine was located had diverted a river over it and massacred all the miners. They react badly to the new party of gold seekers, especially when they find out their objective; though they themselves have no use for gold, they resent the intrusion into their territory.[30] Though the fire power of the adventurers makes mockery of the Indian's claim to all their own territory, and the heroes feel quite justified in their show of force, Hyne does indicate that there are arguments on the other side. Similarly, Henty sends his prospectors hunting through the territory of the Utes, and when they do find a rich gold strike and decide to bring in machinery to work the mine themselves, they come in a strong party of some forty well-armed men and build a fort to protect themselves. When a Ute war party shows up and the chief remonstrates on the clash that had occurred with the prospectors at the time the gold had been found, the conversational exchange does indicate that the Indians do have some rights in the matter.[31] A deal is struck, and the white men are able to proceed peacefully to extract several hundred thousand pounds worth of gold. As a transaction, it leaves something to be desired from the viewpoint of morality; an armed party has invaded territory clearly not its own, and has extracted an agreement that is based on a superior position and daunting force. Still, the concession is made that the land does belong to someone else, that the Indians do have some right over the gold, and that it is best to make some sort of agreement to be allowed to mine it unhindered, and to provide some compensation.

In contrast it is interesting to consider a gold-mining book written by one of the imperialist writers, but in an earlier period. R. M. Ballantyne's *The Golden Dream* published in 1860,[32] takes a much different view of the whole matter of gold seeking. It describes the plight of Ned Sinton, an eighteen-year-old on the verge of having to choose a career; the thought of becoming a lawyer as his uncle and guardian wished depresses him, especially in contrast to the dreams, golden dreams, that he has of adventuring to the new California goldfields. He is saved from a deskbound fate by a distant relative, a Captain Bunting, who wants Ned to accompany him on a trading enterprise to California. Their ship limps into San Francisco Bay, severely damaged in a storm, promptly loses most of its crew, who have deserted to the goldfields, and then is driven ashore in another squall. Renting out the hull of the ship, Captain Bunting, Ned, their two remaining crew, and Tom

Collins, a young Englishman that Ned has befriended, head for the goldfields themselves to find their fortunes.

The companions have varying success in the gold camps; sometimes they dig out or pan rich deposits, sometimes they work hard for little or nothing. In one camp where they are doing quite well, Ned announces that he is going to make "a tour through the country" because he is tired "'of grubbing in the mud.'"[33] Life was too short to spend it all searching for gold when there was so much that was beautiful to see.[34] So Ned and his friend Tom Collins go wandering in the mountains, finding many adventures. He supplements his income by selling watercolor sketches of the landscape, and by doing portraits for miners anxious to send something back home showing where they are and how they look.

When at last Ned returns to San Francisco, he has only a few hundred pounds in his possession. He gets considerably more money through the sale of a piece of real estate that had been left him by a dying man he had briefly cared for, but most of this he gives away to his friend Tom who has in the meantime married and is working in his father-in-law's mercantile concern. Summoned home by his uncle, Ned is quite happy to return, with only five hundred pounds to show for all his golden dreams, to settle down to the running of an estate that he had not known that his uncle possessed. To win a fortune abroad through finding a great deal of gold is only one of the paths to happiness, and in Ballantyne's mind it is not one of the most important.

There were, of course, other paths to sudden fortune open to imperial adventurers, and several writers did exploit these. Captain Marryat's heroes do not go seeking gold and diamonds. Yet on a number of occasions they did very well indeed, and this mainly through inheritance. Midshipman Easy, one of the most delightful of Marryat's creations,[35] inherits his father's fortune when his eccentric if not mad father experiments himself to death, and proceeds through judicious management to repair the damages his father has wrought on the property. The Campbell family, who have been forced to move to Canada because of a successful challenge to the inheritance of their British property,[36] reinherit the property when the owner dies after an accident. Peter Simple, having undergone terrific and sometimes horrific experiences, including being shut up in an insane asylum, finally inherits the extensive estates of his grandfather, Lord Privilege.[37] Frank Hargate, Henty's hero in *By Sheer Pluck*,[38] after many adventures in West Africa, inherits part of the property of his mentor, Mr. Goodenough, and with this solid base makes his way by training as a doctor and then buying a partnership "in an excellent west-end practice."[39]

Many of G. A. Henty's heroes, particularly those who had gone out to fight their country's wars in India, did very well by being given gifts in return for their excellent service, by winning prize money that resulted from the successful capture of enemy strongholds, and by investing wisely the proceeds of such gains. Charlie Marryat, having helped Robert Clive establish British dominion in India, is given more than twenty-five thousand pounds by a grateful rajah and shares extensively in the prize money from various campaigns; he is able to retire to England at a young age with a substantial fortune.[40] Harry Lindsay is given large gifts by Mahratta chieftains and retires to England, which he has never seen, having been born and raised in India, with some ninety thousand pounds.[41] Dick Holland, who goes on a successful hunt for his father held prisoner in Mysore by Tipu Sultan, brings home over twenty thousand pounds gained from gifts and investments and marries an heiress with at least as much.[42] The heiress herself is in a sense a prize won in India, since he has rescued her, when a fourteen-year-old girl, from the harem of Tipu. On the fringes of India, Stanley Brooke rescues a young Burmese bandit from certain death due to the unwelcome attentions of a leopard, and he is rewarded with bags of rubies.[43] The proceeds of the sale of the rubies, wisely invested in the mercantile business that Stanley's uncle runs in the eastern portion of the Indian Empire, result in the creation of substantial wealth for both men, and a London office for Stanley to manage the British side of the very prosperous business. The model for all these gains, of course, is Robert Clive and his associates as they developed British power in India, and any reader of these Henty novels would be aware that the windfall gains related in the stories were based on fact, and were actually a prospect, especially in the early days of the empire. If the possibility was more remote at the end of the nineteenth century, the exciting glow of the memory of what had been served to add profitable romance to the adventure tales.

More contemporary with the writers of the imperial novels was the prospect of another kind of windfall gain—loot. Rudyard Kipling pays his compliments to this soldier's friend:

Now remember when you're 'acking round a gilded Burma god
    That 'is eyes is very often precious stones;
An' if you treat a nigger to a dose o' cleanin'-rod
    'E's like to show you everything 'e owns.
When 'e won't prodooce no more, pour some water on the floor
    Where you 'ear it answer 'ollow to the boot
        (*Cornet*: Toot! Toot!)—
When the ground begins to sink, shove your baynick down the chink,
    An' you're sure to touch the—
    (*Chorus*) Loo! loo! Lulu! Loot! loot! loot!
        Ow the loot!
        Bloomin' loot
That's the thing to make the boys get up an' shoot![44]

Those who risk their lives in battle have the right to these little perquisites of battle.

Henty heroes were too pure to dig in like the common soldiers and despoil the people of a conquered city or fortress, but this did not mean that they had to let opportunity go to waste. The Warrener brothers, Ned and Dick, about to participate in the final ejection of the mutineers from Lucknow in 1857, clearly recognize an opportunity when they see one.[45] They borrow as much money in gold as they can from their father before the attack, explaining: "'They say that the palaces, the Kaiserbagh especially, are crowded with valuable things; and as they will be lawful loot for the troops, we shall be able to buy no end of things.'"[46] Such foresight has to be rewarded; they buy mainly jewelry and sell it in London for a hundred and thirty thousand pounds, which they share with their father, sister, and cousin. Rex Bateman, who is present at the storming of Peking at the culmination of the Boxer Rebellion in 1900, is less particular about what he buys.[47] His father has provided him with a considerable amount of money for the purpose, and Rex has bought furs and vases as well as jade and jewelry, and sends home three cartloads of his purchases. The value of these purchases will tide over the Bateman's mercantile concern until the restoration of the normal channels of trade. Again, the enterprise is based on fact. British officers did invest their pocket money in the aftermath of the storming of cities, and sometimes realized considerable profits.[48]

Making money is something of obvious concern to prospective emigrants. Given the lack of any compelling reason to move, such as religious and political persecution, or health broken down in the old occupation and the old locale, there is little point in making an often traumatic move to another part of the world unless there is an expectation of economic betterment; the actual achievement of wealth would be the perfect end to the enterprise. But this natural desire is not often a relevant one to the readers, usually quite young, of adventure stories and romances. A happy ending has its enticements, but an economic happy ending, especially an extravagant one, is not necessary to create satisfaction and the conclusion of a vicarious adventure.

Still, a considerable number of the writers of the imperial adventure stories did take care to leave their heroes in a satisfactory economic situation. Not all of them found diamond mines and treasure troves; quite often it was enough to end the stories with happy families on successful farms or plantations, or well on the way to a respected and reputable career. Only occasionally do the authors actually spell out the monetary details of what constituted the success that brought happiness, but all seemed to feel that the introduction of certain evidences of such success was necessary to reward the substantial displays of manly virtues exhibited by the heroes described in the preceding pages. A brief examination of the backgrounds of some of the writers suggests that the need to display evidences of success might come more from the preoccupations of the authors than from the needs of the plot—though indeed a book called *Treasure Island* does carry a self-fulfilling expectation of the actual discovery of treasure—to end the story with an empty hole and the treasure gone would be a sell indeed, and would belong to a more cynical genre of fiction, or perhaps reality.

Captain Marryat and G. A. Henty are probably the most persistent authors in ending all or most of their stories with substantial rewards accorded to the main characters. Marryat was a naval officer with an active, sometimes successful, naval career that essentially ended in 1830.[49] The economic situation of an unemployed post captain was not encouraging, especially a post captain of extravagant habits and with a family of young daughters to support. Though poverty is a relative term, and he was never destitute, money was a pressing concern and helped convert a literary career begun in his naval days as a pleasant, diverting pastime into a full-time occupation. The number of inheritances that settled the financial problems of many of his heroes suggests that this was a deus ex machina that Marryat himself would have found most welcome.

Henty had come, as had Marryat, from a prosperous middle-class family. His father was a stockbroker and mineowner, and young Henty was sent to Westminster and Cambridge, and was appointed to the Purveyor's Department of the army during the Crimean War.[50] For many years after his period in the army he followed an adventurous career as a war correspondent, satisfying to a healthy, physical man, but not especially rewarding financially, and he attempted various speculations, including gold-mining ventures in the Americas, all unsuccessful. When his health broke down, he turned finally to the writing of his boys' adventures to make his living, from all indications a comfortable one, but not substantial enough to establish him as a country squire, as so many of his young heroes ended up. Obviously he was projecting his own desires into the conclusion of the stories, creating endings that were often incongruent with the general tenor of the stories; a prime example is in *With Lee in Virginia*,[51] where the hero, Vincent Wingfield, born in America though attending school for a few years in England, at the end will probably sell his successful plantation and retire to England, referred to by the author as "home."[52]

Other writers had their financial problems as well. The failure of *Kingston's Magazine* sent William Kingston into financial difficulties and forced him to write numerous books and stories to make his living.[53] The collapse of the Ballantyne Press in 1826, with its adverse effect on the Ballantyne family fortunes,[54] and the death of his father in 1847, leaving a wife and five daughters with a limited income, helped propel Robert Ballantyne into a literary career. Neither author was affected to the extent of directing his heroes to enormous windfall gains, but both liked to leave their people in comfortable circumstances, suitable to their stations in life and their chosen occupations. After his newspaper and magazine failed in 1864, George Manville Fenn began to sell his writings, producing well over a hundred novels, some of them Henty-like in the successes accorded to his main characters.[55] Rider Haggard left South Africa after the failure of the Transvaal annexation with which he had been intimately connected.[56] Though his wife possessed an estate in England, and Haggard had an emotional attachment to farming—he had helped start an ostrich farm in Natal before he left—agricultural depression convinced him that a living could not be found there. He tried a writing career, at first unsuccessful, and trained for a legal career; the instant success of *King Solomon's Mines* finally diverted him to writing, at a time when money was beginning to be a problem. This story is one of the few he wrote that strongly concentrated on the successful achievement of wealth through treasure, and this may reflect his economic situation at the time that he wrote, or the fact that the success of *Treasure Island* was one of the inspirations for the writing of his own romance.[57] John Buchan did not dwell on the achievement of wealth—the conclusion of *Prester John* is almost incidental—but he was the son of a poor Scots minister, and he did have to make his way among the well-to-do. The hero of his first imperial novel, *The Half-Hearted*, was wealthy, and Francis Carey in *A Lodge in the Wilderness* was extremely wealthy. The main characters in the thrillers on which Buchan's later reputation, and a good deal of his income, rested were men to whom money was not a problem.

To be fair to the writers of the imperial stories, the economic themes are not uppermost. These are adventure stories, and the series of adventures unroll with what must have been a regularity satisfying to readers who could see themselves involved in similar circumstances. Beyond adventure, the themes are of character and imperial purpose, and these are emphasized. Still, success is the best argument for a course of action, and a book that presents the author's version of success satisfactorily rounds off a story.

NOTES

1. *Treasure Island* (London: Dean & Son, n.d.).

2. *King Solomon's Mines* (London: Collins, 1965).

3. See masters' theses by Derek Ferguson, "Robert Louis Stevenson and Samoa: A Reinterpretation" (University of Saskatchewan, 1980), and Kent Fedorowich, "H. Rider Haggard: The Spirit of Empire" (University of Saskatchewan, 1983).

4. F.M.L.Thompson, *The Rise of Respectable Society: A Social History of Victorian Britain, 1830–1900* (London: Fontana Press, 1988), 334.

5. The death of the woman, Foulata, and the trapping of the adventurers in the treasure chamber.

6. *The Treasure of the Incas: A Story of Adventure in Peru* (London: Blackie & Son, n.d. [1903]).

7. *The Golden Magnet: A Tale of the Land of the Incas* (London: Blackie & Son, n.d.).

8. *The Lost Island* (London: Henry Frowde Hodder & Stoughton, n.d.).

9. *Prester John* (London: T. Nelson & Sons, 1963 [1910]).

10. *The Lost Explorers: A Story of the Trackless Desert* (London: Blackie & Son, 1907).

11. Ibid., 12.

12. R. L. Stevenson, *Treasure Island*, 174.

13. Ibid., 179.

14. Ibid., 83. Is there an element of class distinction in this?

15. Allan Quatermain is the main character in eighteen books and short stories. D. S. Higgins, *Rider Haggard: The Great Storyteller* (London: Cassell, 1981), 71.

16. Ibid.

17. Ibid., 234.

18. Ibid., 235.

19. G. A. Henty, *The Treasure of the Incas*, 329.

20. Ibid.

21. G .M. Fenn, *The Golden Magnet*, 226.

22. Ibid., 330–31.

23. J. Buchan, *Prester John*, 233–34.

24. G. M. Fenn, *The Golden Magnet*, 352.

25. H. Rider Haggard, *King Solomon's Mines*, 223.

26. R. L. Stevenson, *Treasure Island*, 184.

27. H. Rider Haggard, *King Solomon's Mines*, 40.

28. *Stimson's Reef: A Tale of Adventure* (London: Blackie & Son, n.d. [1892]).

29. *In the Heart of the Rockies: A Story of Adventure in Colorado* (London: Blackie & Son, n.d. [1895]).

30. C. J. Hyne, *Stimson's Reef*, 157.

31. *In the Heart of the Rockies*, 338–39.

32. *The Golden Dream: Adventures in the Far West* (London: James Nisbet & Co., n.d.).

33. Ibid., 179.

34. Ibid., 179–80.

35. *Midshipman Easy,* first published in 1836.

36. Captain Frederick Marryat, *The Settlers in Canada.*

37. Captain Frederick Marryat, *Peter Simple*, (London: George Routledge & Sons, 1896 [1834]).

38. *By Sheer Pluck: A Tale of the Ashanti War* (London: Blackie & Son, n.d. [1884]).

39. Ibid., 352.

40. *With Clive in India, or The Beginnings of an Empire* (London: Blackie & Son, n.d. [1884]).

41. *At the Point of the Bayonet: A Tale of the Mahratta War* (London: Blackie & Son, n.d. [1902]).

42. *The Tiger of Mysore: A Story of the War with Tippoo Saib* (London: Blackie & Son, 1896).

43. *On the Irrawaddy: A Story of the First Burmese War* (London: Blackie & Son, n.d. [1897]).

44. "Loot," in *The Works of Rudyard Kipling* (Roslyn, N.Y.: Black's Readers Service Co., n.d.), 92–93.

45. *In Times of Peril,* 320.

46. Ibid.

47. *With the Allies to Pekin: A Story of the Relief of the Legations* (London: Blackie & Son, 1904).

48. Mrs. Muter, *My Recollections of the Sepoy Revolt(1857–58)* (London: John Long, 1911), 140. Mrs. Muter's husband, an army captain, was a prize agent after the fall of Delhi; the prizes, which were a form of legalized looting, were then offered for sale, and the proceeds distributed to the army. However, some soldiers, including officers, simply took what they could find, and Mrs. Muter was shocked that an officer should do this.

49. Oliver Warner, *Captain Marryat*, Chapter 6.

50. Guy Arnold, *Held Fast for England*, Chapter 1.

51. *With Lee in Virginia: A Story of the American Civil War* (London: Blackie & Son, n.d. [1890]).

52. Ibid., 384.

53. Rev. Maurice Kingsford, *William Henry Giles Kingston*, 190.

54. Eric Quayle, *Ballantyne the Brave: A Victorian Writer and His Family* (Chester Springs, Pa.: Dufour Editions, 1967), 14–19.

55. Brian Doyle, ed., *The Who's Who of Children's Literature* (London: Hugh Evelyn, 1971).

56. D. S. Higgins, *Rider Haggard*, 49–52.

57. Ibid., 70.

7

Humanity's Burden

The writers of imperial tales were convinced that there were many evils in the world and that it was their duty to try to do something about it. The whole imperial scene, consequently, was presented, usually in vague and general terms, as being morally good, and good not only for the British but also for the recipients of imperial attentions. Humanitarianism and imperialism were increasingly tied together. As Henty's hero, Harry Lindsay, explained to his Mahratta friend: "'Wherever their [the British] powers extend, the natives are far better off than they were under the rule of their own princes. Were the British masters, there would be no more wars, no more jealousies, and no more intrigues; the peasants would till their fields in peace, and the men who now take to soldiering would find more peaceful modes of earning a living.'"[1]

But Henty here had the advantage of speaking, not with total accuracy, with the advantage of hindsight, in that he was defending an imperial relationship that actually did occur—the British did conquer the Mahrattas. It was another matter to write a book advocating the flexing of imperial muscle in a situation in which conquest and annexation had not occurred—in other words, projecting the humanitarian imperial relationship into the real future. Although there was a humanitarian angle to so much of the imperial propaganda in the literature of the Victorian period, there was not a flood of books demanding the spread of Britain's beneficent power over larger portions of the globe—even on the scale envisioned by that imperial dreamer and doer, Cecil Rhodes, in his 1877 Confession of Faith: "It is our duty to seize every opportunity of acquiring more territory and we should keep this one idea steadily before our eyes that more territory simply means more of the Anglo-Saxon race more of the best the most human, most honourable race the world possesses."[2]

Robert Ballantyne did not have the same all-consuming interest in imperialism as Cecil Rhodes. But he was a humanitarian, and he was dedicated enough to the ideals of British imperialism to believe that to some extent Britain must be the keeper of the world's conscience. He set forth his clearest exposition of this point of view in *Black Ivory: A Tale of Adventure Among the Slavers of East Africa.*[3] It is a strongly worded diatribe against the slave trade of East Africa and on Britain's responsibility to bring it to an end. Though Ballantyne had never been in East Africa, he based the incidents in his novel on descriptions found in many sources, including David Livingstone's *Zambezia and its Tributaries*, the Reverend Henry Rowley's *The Story of the Universities Mission to Central Africa*, and Lyons McLeod's *Travels in Eastern Africa*, in which he found many accounts of the outrageous cruelties of the slave traders, and appalling statistics of the process of depopulation that the trade had set into operation.[4] He set out his purpose in the preface: "I began my tale in the hope that I might produce something to interest the young (perchance, also, the old) in a most momentous cause,—the total abolition of the African slave-trade, I close it with the prayer that God may make it a tooth in the file which shall eventually cut the chain of slavery, and set the black man free."[5] One of the curiosities of the book is that while it was being written, in 1873, Sir Bartle Frere with a small British fleet was busy pressuring the Sultan of Zanzibar into the abolition of the slave market in his state, one of the demands that Ballantyne was to make in the course of his narrative.

The hero of the story is Harold Seadrift,[6] aboard one of his father's ships to gain some business experience and do some sight-seeing and hunting in Africa. When the ship starts to sink off the coast of the East African coast, Harold refuses to abandon ship, preferring to stay on board with the one loyal sailor, Disco Lillihammer, to see if he could beach the ship and at least save the cargo. Instead, the ship struck a reef and the two men were flung overboard, eventually swimming to shore. They soon spot some natives coming to investigate the wreck and, in apprehension about their safety, take to the bush, where they find hidden in a creek a boat, an Arab dhow, with a number of armed men. The boat belongs to Yoosoof, an Arab slave trader, or dealer in "Black Ivory" as he prefers to call it. He agrees to take them to Zanzibar, but in the end he makes them prisoners and places them on a boatload of "damaged" slaves being used as a decoy to distract the British antislave cruiser while he takes his main cargo to market. The two Britons are rescued by the navy and taken to Zanzibar.

The experiences that Harold and Disco go through begin to enlighten their minds about slavery. They met a slave girl, Azinté, and Disco notices: "'I do honestly confess to 'ee that I think that's a *pretty* girl! . . . I mean *really* pretty, you know. I've always thought that all niggers had ugly flat noses an' thick blubber lips. But look at that one: her lips are scarce a bit thicker than those of many a good-looking lass in England, and they don't stick out at all, and her nose ain't flat a bit.'"[7] Ballantyne then presents a little lecture so that the reader will share the enlighten-ment: "It is but justice to Disco to say that he was right in his observations, and to explain that the various negro tribes in Africa differ very materially from each other; some of them, as we are told by Dr. Livingstone, possessing little of what, in our eyes, seems the characteristic ugliness of the negro—such as thick lips, flat noses, protruding heels, etc.,—but being in every sense handsome races of humanity."[8] By this, Ballantyne does not mean that the "ugly" races of humanity are less deserving of sympathy when they are enslaved, but he is trying to enlist the reader's sympathies by creating some sense of identity with the oppressed, through a common standard of beauty, even if this is European.

The second lesson on slavery and the slave trade comes when Harold and Disco are forced to sail aboard the decoy slave boat and first see the "cargo": "They were packed sitting on their haunches in rows, each with his knees close to his chin, and all jammed so tightly together that none could rise up or lie down. Men, women and little children sat in this position with an expression of indescribable hopelessness and apathy on their faces. The infants, of which there were several, lay motionless on their mothers' shrunken breasts."[9] When Harold taxes Yoosoof with the cruelty of it all, the slave dealer is indifferent. His father had done the same, and besides, the slaves were only "'brutes—cattle,'"[10] and had no feelings, so that they did not suffer.

Before he returns to England, Harold decides to travel deeper into East Africa, both to see more of the country and to investigate further the issue of the slave trade. With Disco, he sets off into the interior, eventually traveling in the slave trade-ravaged regions of Lake Nyassa. As the travelers proceed up river, they rescue a slave and return him to his wife and family. The joy with which Chimbolo, the freed slave, greets his restored wife and son prove to the English adventurers just how wrong Yoosoof had been; the blacks had feelings just as intense as the whites, and exhibited them in much the same way.

Much of the rest of the book concentrates on establishing the common humanity of white and black. The chieftain, Kambira, the husband of the slave girl, Azinté, that Harold and Disco had met at the beginning of their adventures, shows ingenuity in hunting wild beasts, and the blacks in general hunt with the same eager enthusiasm as the young Englishmen. Their hunting exploits, and their bravery, are presented in considerable detail. They are music loving and as full of merriment as Europeans. They show affection and steadfastness; Kambira has not taken another wife because of his love for Azinté, whom he has lost to the dreaded slave raiders. Strong individuals captured by the slavers continue to show defiance even though it means that they will be beaten or put to death in some other horrible way because of their lack of cooperation; even young boys prefer to die rather than to surrender their individuality. The staging of the reunion of Kambira, Azinté, and their young son could have come out of the pages of a melodrama, with its picture of joy raising a wasting boy from what appears to be his deathbed, a joy roused by the sudden and wild application of mother love.

Ballantyne knew that some of the objectives that he had in writing *Black Ivory* had been met by Sir Bartle Frere's intervention in the slave markets of Zanzibar, carried out before the book was finished. He was aware, however, that the catalog of iniquities he had presented to the reader had not yet been made obsolete; there was a great deal more to do before justice and humanity were restored to Central Africa, and it appeared that only Britain could adequately carry out the task. While Ballantyne tidies up a great many loose ends before he brings his narrative to a conclusion, the slave trader, Yoosoof, is still left at large to ply his villainies. The implication is obvious; the British must not be satisfied with what has been done so far because the serpent has not yet been stamped out. Ballantyne preaches another sermon, on "Prevention and Cure."

The closing of the Zanzibar slave marts has partially checked one of the three slave routes out of Africa, but Ballantyne points out, "It is vain to rest content with the stoppage of one leak in our ship if two other leaks are left open."[11] To firmly close the Zanzibar leak, British naval units still had to patrol the east coast of Africa. A second leak, through the Portuguese colonies, must be stanched. Ballantyne was not very happy with the Portuguese: "Domestic slavery remains untouched in the Portuguese dependencies, and Portugal has decreed that it shall remain untouched until the year 1878! It is well that we should be thoroughly impressed with the fact, that as long as slavery in any form is tolerated, the internal—we may say infernal—miseries and horrors which we have attempted to depict, will continue to blight the land and brutalize the people."[12] British consuls should be established in the colonies of the Portuguese to ensure that slavery and the slave trade in this part of the world stop. Further, the efforts of the khedive of Egypt to put down the slave trade through the services of Sir Samuel Baker[13] should be supported, and British consuls should again be appointed to see that the rulers of African territories remain steadfast to British reformist principles. All of this amounted to "Prevention," but the "Cure" for the maladies of the slave trade and slavery itself must be sought.

Britain must acquire territory on the African mainland to be "centers of refuge for the oppressed," and "there must be the introduction of the Bible":

> The first is essential to the second. Where anarchy, murder, injustice, and tyranny are rampant and triumphant, the advance of the missionary is either terribly slow or altogether impossible. The life-giving, soul-softening Word of God, is the only remedy for the woes of mankind, and, therefore, the only cure for Africa. To introduce it effectually, and along with it civilization and all the blessings that flow therefrom, it is indispensable that Great Britain should obtain, by treaty or by purchase, one or more small pieces of land, there to establish free Christian negro settlements, and there, with force sufficient to defend them from the savages, and worse than savages,—the Arab and Portuguese half-caste barbarians and lawless men who infest the land—hold out the hand of friendship to all natives who choose to claim her protection from the man-stealer, and offer to teach them the blessed truths of Christianity and the arts of civilization. . . . Three such centres would, if established, begin at once to dry up the slave trade at its three fountain-heads, while our cruisers would check it on the coast.[14]

As Ballantyne sums up his argument for intervention, he introduces a new element; not only will the slave trade be put down and the Africans be "saved," but this action will "materially increase the commerce, the riches, and the happiness of the world."[15] Earlier, Ballantyne's travelers have discussed the economic potentialities of the land through which they are passing: "'what a splendid cotton country it might be if properly cultivated!'" exclaimed Harold, and Disco added "'an' I shouldn't wonder if there was lots of gold too, if we only knew where to look for it.'"[16] Antonio, their cook, confirms the existence of gold, and of coal, iron, sugar cane, and ivory, all economic resources that were languishing because of the disruptions of the slave trade. Here Ballantyne is illustrating the arguments of David Livingstone that the introduction of legitimate commerce to Africa, commerce in goods that Africa could produce without resorting to man-stealing, is the only sure path to the destruction of the slave trade, by providing a viable alternative to the evils that are occurring.[17]

Though Ballantyne in *Black Ivory* is advocating a great deal of imperial intervention in African affairs, it is essentially an intervention more limited than the one presented by Buchan in *A Lodge in the Wilderness*. Buchan bases his recommendations on the holding of vast areas of East African territory, and on the provision of British settlers and administrators to keep the native population in line and to civilize and tame the chaos out of which so much of the human traffic had emerged. Buchan's picture portrays a colony with a regular colonial presence. Ballantyne's is much more restricted; missionaries would be located in isolated centers of civilization that would oversee the chaos and would through example and watchfulness, bid it cease, while compelling it through righteousness, and the judicious intervention of the British fleet, to retreat and disappear. This is imperial intervention of a different order; in theory, at least, all areas would remain self-governing, Britain would not be encumbered with the duties and costs of an imperial administration, and moral force would predominate. If the Gladstone government, which was essentially noninterventionist in philosophy, had yielded to such arguments, and had been willing to make the expenditures necessary for the form of minimum intervention Ballantyne had asked for, there is some question, of course, whether the intervention could have remained minimum. The centers of civilization would too obviously have been tempted to be impatient when savagery did not recede fast enough, or willingly enough; the land equivalent of gunboat diplomacy would have been difficult to avoid. And force sufficient to protect the missionaries might have been sufficient to increase defense through depth, involving the centers in natural extensions of boundaries.

In terms of quantity it is the West African transatlantic slave trade that attracted most attention from adventure story writers. The maintenance of an antislave fleet off the West African coast to intercept slavers, most often commanded, at least fictionally, by "evil" Spaniards, was regarded as a virtuous act of the highest order, especially since West Africa was such a dangerous field of operation because of disease. The danger of disease, storm, and battle is not minimized in the stories based on the antislave patrol—indeed the adventures of a Henty hero seem to be almost a picnic in comparison with the sufferings of one of Collingwood's young men on the Atlantic shores of Africa.[18]

Unlike Ballantyne's *Black Ivory*, the tales set in West Africa tend to be straight adventure stories, with little moralizing, even on the evils of the trade, or little special pleading for wholesale annexations to bring the scourge to an end. W.H.G. Kingston first published his very popular *The Three Midshipmen* in 1862. The three midshipmen of the title, Jack Rogers, Terence Adair, and Alick Murray, start their naval career in the Mediterranean, and then are appointed to ships on the antislave patrol. Jack Rogers has some trouble convincing his mother that this station is relatively safe, his mother having a well-founded prejudice against the area; in the course of his arguments he places no emphasis on the morality of a posting there, or on his duty to the poor enslaved; instead he concentrates on:

> There is, in the first place, plenty of work to be done there, which in these piping times of peace is a great consideration. Only think of the fun of capturing a slaver, and, what is more, of getting an independent command; or at least, that is, of a prize, you know, and being away from one's ship for weeks together. And then there is

cruising in open boats, and exploring rivers, and fights with pirates or slavers; perhaps a skirmish with the dependents of some nigger potentate, and fifty other sorts of adventures, not to speak of prize money, and all that sort of thing, you know. Oh, to my mind, the coast of Africa is one of the best stations in the world in spite of what is said against it.[19]

After describing military operations against slavers and their land base, and the African ruler in the locality, Kingston does bring in some humanitarian concepts as he describes a visit by a British delegation to the fortified town of the African ruler:

During a long palaver Hemming explained to him that if he persisted in carrying on the slave trade, the English would destroy his barracoons and injure and annoy him in every possible way; but that if he abandoned it, and refused to have anything to do with the slave-dealers, but would engage in commerce, encourage agriculture, well treat his people, and act like an honest man, they would assist and encourage him in every possible way; that the Queen of England would be friends with him, call him her well-beloved brother, and send him presents of far greater value than any he got from the Spaniards.[20]

The description of the capture of Lagos in 1851, the first overtly imperialistic action in West Africa in the Victorian period,[21] is a matter-of-fact depiction of military events. Only when the very difficult campaign is over does Kingston permit some moralizing, as one of the midshipmen, Alick Murray, who has a natural inclination to moralize, writes in a letter home:

it must be the consolation of the relations and friends of the gallant fellows who lost their lives, that a very important work has been performed, and that the capture of this stronghold of the slave trade will prove one of the severest blows that hateful traffic has ever experienced. It has done much also, I trust, to advance the cause of religion and civilization in Africa, and will help, I hope, to wipe away the dark stain which is attached to many of the so-called Christian nations of the world. Akitoye is now installed King of Lagos. He professes great friendship for the English, as well as for the people of Abeokuta. If he proves the stern enemy of the slave trade and the true friend of Christianity, we shall not have fought in vain.[22]

The equation of mid-Victorian religion with morality was perhaps so obvious that discussions of the bases of actions need be elaborated no further than this. Later novels, such as the sea stories of Harry Collingwood, hardly paused to discuss the slave trade beyond stock words of condemnation. The slaves are but a vehicle to provide a rationale for a series of rousing and deadly adventures, and, indeed, when slaves are rescued, as they are in *The Congo Rovers*, they could prove a nuisance. Eight hundred slaves rescued from a Spanish slaver are simply put ashore on a hostile coast, with the pious hope that though they are without weapons and with little food, their native wit would serve to rescue them and bring them to a better fate than what had awaited them had the slaving voyage continued.[23]

Humanitarianism and the cause of the blacks in Africa once again took a more serious and demanding turn in Herbert Strang's *Samba*.[24] Published in 1906, it was part of the concerted campaign being waged in England to totally discredit the disreputable regime of King Leopold in the Congo Free State, and to force major reforms.[25] In the preface, the work of E. D. Morel and the Congo Reform Association is called as witness to back up the grim picture presented in the book and justify the need for some type of intervention.

To the Congo comes Jack Challoner, a seventeen-year-old Rugby-educated Englishman, his wealthy American uncle, Mr. John Martindale, and their Irish servant, Barney O'Dowd. Mr. Martindale has received a concession to develop a gold mine that had been discovered by a friend, and he has brought along his nephew to begin the serious business of learning what life is really about. They make their way up the river with an African interpreter and a crew of unarmed canoe men, trying to reach the site of the gold find so that they can begin to set up an operational gold mine.

On the way, at the site of a village obviously destroyed by violence, they find Samba, a boy of about thirteen, semistarved and injured. Jack and Mr. Martindale now begin to learn something about Leopold's administration of the Congo. The servants of the Belgian king had come to Samba's village, seeking rubber from the forests. They were unlike the slave raiders, who were a "fierce tempest" that, once passed, allowed new and vigorous growth; the rubber hunters are "like a blight settling forever on the land. They came and stayed; none could escape them, none were spared, young or old."[26] Under their demands the village withers: "'It was not only rubber the men of Mpatu were bade to bring them, but so many goats, so many fowls, so many fish and cassava and bananas. How could they do it? The rubber vines near by were soon exhausted. Every week the men must go further into the forest. They had not enough time now to hunt and fish for their own families. How supply the strangers too?'"[27] Those who try to evade the task of rubber gathering, or cannot find their quota, are ruthlessly tracked down and whipped, or their hands cut off, or are killed. So it had happened in Samba's village. When the rubber collection had fallen short, the armed native servants of Bula Matadi (the native name for the Congo administration, after H. M. Stanley) had fired on the mass of villagers, there was a struggle, and the surviving villagers had fled into the jungle while their village was burned. Samba has survived the attack, but has lost track of his parents in the confusion and now is eager to find them; he travels along with the Martindale party for a few days, recovers his health, makes a great impression, and then disappears upon his quest for his parents.

In their further travels Mr. Martindale and his nephew fall in with the armed party of Monsieur Elbel, a representative of the Societé Cosmopolite du Commerce du Congo, one of the huge companies that holds concessions for the exploitation of the resources of the Congo. Monsieur Elbel is the villain of the story, and representative of the even greater villainy of the Congo administration. He is greedy, ruthless, and heartless; the sufferings of other human beings, whether black or white, do not move him. He is determined to find the source of the gold, the knowledge of which Mr. Martindale possesses, and intends to appropriate it for his own benefit and that of the company for which he works.

Jack Challoner, left behind in the native village near the location of the gold strike while Mr. Martindale goes off to collect the necessary material for setting up a mining camp, is the one who has to cope with the full force of Elbel's plots, and with the realization, as Elbel establishes himself in the village, of just what Belgian administration in the Congo entails. With the help of the Irish servant, Barney O'Dowd, Samba, who has returned with his mother and father, and a number of rifles that Mr. Martindale has managed to send up river, Jack builds a fort near the village, trains some men in the use of firearms, and begins a gradual resistance to the increasing atrocities of Elbel's men; this finally results in a confrontation and the expulsion of the Belgian force from the neighborhood. Knowing that Elbel will return with much greater force, Jack then builds a stronger and more extensive fort near the gold mine, large enough to withstand a siege and shelter a growing number of refugees fleeing Belgian oppression. The remainder of the book is a description of the successive campaigns, the defeat and death of Elbel, and the capture of the supplies of a Belgian army officer-led expedition. The number of firearms at Jack's command grows as he captures more and more rifles from the Belgians, and in the end he is also the proud possessor of a Maxim machine gun.

The evil Mr. Elbel, who at one point captures Mr. Martindale and allows him to die of fever, is killed following the storming of his camp by Jack's forces, a victim of the revenge sought by the Africans. Jack is fully aware that the death of Elbel does not solve the problem of the Congo. Elbel is simply a small portion of the larger evil. Though refugees keep coming to his fort, increasing his manpower, Jack is aware that he will not be able to hold out forever against an aroused Belgian administration bent on vengeance. On one of his expeditions through the forest he had found two Englishmen abandoned by most of their servants. One is the Honorable George Arlington, a politician of note but currently without a seat in Parliament, on a personal mission to study conditions in the Congo. His companion is Frank Dathan, a missionary on a tour of inspection of his society's missions in Central Africa. They had entered the Congo from Uganda, so as to be free from the interference of Congo officials in their investigations. Jack asks them to hurry back to England to present the case of the Congo natives to the British public. Mr. Arlington is to run for Parliament again, so that in parliament he can "'badger the Foreign Secretary'" and "'move the country until England moved the world.'"[28] Mr. Dathan would work through the missionary societies to achieve the same ends.

Jack meanwhile would remain in his fort to try to protect his little bit of the Congo from the terrible evil, and to wait for public opinion to change the system and relieve him of his awesome responsibility. It is a sorrowful task, for not only is his uncle dead, but the heroic Samba, who had saved his life, himself lay dying from the effects of the tortures he had undergone. On his deathbed he lay: "The blithe spirit was departing, the poor body done to death by the greed of a Christian King. 'Botofé bo le iwa! Rubber is death!' The words rang in Jack's ears; would they were the knell of this despotism, this monstrous 'system' that bought wealth with the price of blood!"[29] Soon the poor boy dies, another victim of rubber, and the greedy exploitation of men without conscience.

Samba has all the earmarks of a boys' adventure story. A young man, at seventeen just old enough so that his exploits might be credible, with a few faithful companions, fights successfully against enormous odds, and by courage, steadfastness, and resourcefulness, wins through. The major part of the book is a detailed description of a campaign, or rather, a series of campaigns, in the jungle, and the intelligent stratagems that Jack uses under adverse circumstances to achieve his purposes. At this level it is a typical "Strang" book, celebrating the capabilities of the British Boy, and suggesting to the readers that they too, should they be placed in similar circumstances, could reach into the resources of their character and carry out similar exploits. But the book also came at an opportune time, at the high point of the British propaganda campaign against the Congo atrocities, and humanized the problem in a way that statistics, or anecdotes, of piles of hands, could not. Samba was a boy like any boy, though wise in the ways of the jungle. He laughed and played and sang. He loved his grandfather and was deeply loyal to his parents. When the tragedy of the rubber collectors hit him, it was a human tragedy, not an awful event that happened to poor unfortunate blacks in a distant land. It is an effective piece of propaganda for the times.

When Rudyard Kipling published the poem "The White Man's Burden" in 1899[30] to encourage the United States to take up its imperial burden in the Philippines, he likely little thought that he was writing something that would be cordially hated by anti-imperialists, for whom the work epitomizes all that is arrogant and evil about the imperialism of the late nineteenth century.[31] Phrases like "new-caught, sullen peoples / Half-devil and half-child" are emotive of racial prejudice, as is the whole title—the *White* Man's Burden. Stripped of its words loaded with imperialist concepts, the poem is a humanitarian plea to aid those who need aid, and it does not matter whether they want the aid or not. It is a paternalistic humanitarianism—people who do not know they need help, who perhaps can say, "'Why brought ye us from bondage, / Our beloved Egyptian Night?'" are like children, and must be treated like children. It is everyone's duty to help children to reach the skills and self-sufficiencies of adulthood.

The concept of duty enters widely into many of Kipling's stories, and it would be redundant to dwell on them all. One story that illustrates well Kipling's coupling of humanitarianism and duty is "William the Conqueror,"[32] the story of a famine in India and the efforts that had to be undergone to bring it under control.

William is the sister of Jack Martyn, a superintendent of police. She has been in India for four years and is roughing it because her brother does not make enough money to send her to a hill station for the hot weather. She probably would not have gone, anyhow, since she believes in sharing hardships with her brother, enjoying both the dangers of his life as well as the pleasures. She goes through a cholera epidemic and suffers through six weeks of fever, and rightly has a high opinion of her ability to cope. Consequently, when famine breaks out in the Madras province and the famine relief administrator, Sir James Hawkins, an ex-Punjabi official himself, begins raiding the Punjab for officials—"'Every man who isn't doing two men's work seems to have been called upon'"[33]—and drafts Jack for duty, William insists on coming with him, despite all his efforts to dissuade her; she would find work aiding the wife of Sir James, who is already on the scene.

Also drafted from the same station is Scott, an engineer in the Irrigation Department and an official whose potential is highly thought of by Sir James. Scott is immediately placed in charge of a wagon train of bullock carts carrying grain into the most hard-hit areas, feeding people on the way and doing whatever he can to help. Scott initially finds two major problems; the people of the south are rice eaters and most seemed to be willing to starve rather than eat the unfamiliar wheat, millet, and barley from the north; this problem is soon rectified when adequate supplies of rice begin to arrive, leaving Scott with the necessity of getting them to the distribution depots. The second problem concerns the young children, many of them babies, left in his care all along the route by starving mothers in a last desperate effort to save their lives. Scott's servant, Faiz Ullah, begins feeding the unwanted grain to goats he has picked up along the road, and feeding the goat's milk to the starving children. Soon Scott is deeply immersed in this process, along with all the other duties he has, and begins milking the goats directly into the mouths of the children, saving time and saving lives. At the end of a round-trip of his bullock train he leaves behind, at the base camp under the care of William and Mrs. Jim, the administrator's wife, such children as have not been claimed by death or reclaimed by their mothers. Scott teaches William his method of feeding infants.

The rest of the story chronicles the growing love between Scott and William, a love that blossoms in the very small spaces allowed by the overwhelming duty in which each are immersed. William stays at the base, looking after countless infants collected by Scott, suffering through fever, the horrendous workloads, worry for her brother, and growing concern for Scott, who is obviously overworking. Scott drives himself as he was being driven by Hawkins, because he is a good man and the job has to be done. Finally, Scott wears himself down into a deadly fever, which he barely survives, but the back of the famine has already been broken, and he can look forward to his reward—Sir James's appreciation and recommendation, a good position in the Punjab, full of hard work and responsibility, and William.

The story "William the Conqueror," written slightly earlier than "The White Man's Burden," is a less offensively phrased version of the concept. Famine is a breakdown in the structure of life and causes chaos, misery, and death. Unchecked, it will go on and on, augmented by disease and crime, until a large portion of the population of an affected area will be wiped out. Relief of famine is more than a mechanical matter, the ordering of surplus supplies from one area and redistributing them to a region where they are needed. Because life has broken down in a famine region, it is the duty of the rulers of a people to leave their places of safety and security and get down among all the scenes of misery and devastation, and, shorthanded though they might be, drive themselves and the people until order begins to form out of chaos, and relief from disaster is in sight. They must do this even though some of them will die of diseases caught in the affected areas, or from the cumulative effect of stress and overwork. They must:

> Fill full the mouth of Famine
> And bid the sickness cease;

and then pass on to their ordinary backbreaking duty of making the ordinary lives of their charges more enlightened than before.

Most of G. A. Henty's novels do not dwell on humanitarian issues. The hero has duties and obligations to his country and, in a vague, general way, if there is an imperial setting, to the people of a colony or a potential colony. But these obligations to the natives of an imperialized area are seldom spelled out in detail, beyond the statement that British peace, order, and good government will greatly benefit any less fortunate peoples, no matter what competence they have shown in this area on their own—"'Wherever their powers extend, the natives are far better off than they were under the rule of their own princes.'"[34] In one of his "adult" novels,[35] *Rujub, the Juggler,*[36] Henty does present as his main character a man, Ralph Bathurst, who has shouldered the white man's burden.

Bathurst had been an officer in the Indian Army, but had resigned his commission because a prenatal commotion had left him with a terrible fear of loud noises,[37] a severe handicap for a soldier. He has returned to India as a civilian official, and a very hardworking and conscientious one indeed, who often plagues his superiors with lengthy reports recommending major reforms. He explains to a young lady he has recently met, and who is destined to be the love of his life: "'I wish I had an army of ten thousand English ladies all speaking the language well to go about the women and make friends with them; there would be more good done in that way than by all the officials in India. They might not be able to emancipate themselves from all their restrictions, but they might influence their children, and in time pave the way for a moral revolution.'"[38] The paths of love and humanitarian duty do not lie smooth, however, and the budding lovers are soon caught up in the Indian Mutiny, and the turmoil of a sepoy attack on their cantonment; after a great many dangers they escape and arrive at a place of safety. Having brought his principals through all the excitement and placed them in a position where, at the end of the Mutiny, the two could, hand in hand, take up the cause of humanitarian reform, Henty could not resist a return to the formula of his boys' fiction. Bathurst, in the course of numerous clashes, has rid himself of his psychological disability with respect to loud noises, has won a Victoria Cross in battle, and has laid to rest any imputations on his physical courage. And so, at the end of the Mutiny he resigns both his wartime military commission and his civilian commission, and returns to England, married to his Isobel, to live there on his substantial inherited fortune. The cause of the poor benighted Indian people had been forgotten, fallen victim to the conventions of a Henty success story.

A great deal of imperial literature has an undercurrent theme of humanitarian endeavor. It is clearly the purpose of the heroes of the British Empire to do good not only for the British people themselves, and they certainly must do that, but for all the many millions who would so clearly be impoverished by the lack of their fertilizing touch. Considering the importance of the theme, and it is of premier importance in providing what to Buchan was an unequivocal justification for British imperialism, it is a theme that is not too often explicitly dealt with, as it is in the poem "The White Man's Burden." Detailed descriptions of doing good for the less fortunate peoples of the world would undoubtedly be uplifting and moral reading, almost in the category of books of sermons. For the markets for which most of the imperial writers wrote, however, humanitarianism as the major theme had its limitations. It less often lent itself to the type of hair-raising adventure and relentless pursuit of the picturesque and informative for which the young and young-minded readers apparently had an untiring appetite. So for the most part the humanitarian theme had to be implicit, part of the fabric or preconceptions of a tale, rather than the major moving force. Just the same, the humanitarianism is almost always there, lending a warm glow to the background of the enterprise. This concern for the welfare of humanity was also intimately related in the minds of the writers of the imperial adventure stories to the Christian beliefs that they felt had an important impact on imperialism.

NOTES

1. *At the Point of the Bayonet*, 103.

2. John Flint, *Cecil Rhodes*, 250.

3. *Black Ivory: A Tale of Adventure Among the Slavers of East Africa* (London: James Nisbet & Co., n.d. [1873]).

4. *Black Ivory* is extensively footnoted to sources, which is unusual in a work of fiction, but this gave it greater authority as a propaganda work that was well received by the reading public. Eric Quayle, *Ballantyne the Brave*, 263.

5. R. M. Ballantyne, *Black Ivory*, iv.

6. It would be tempting to see in the name Seadrift a deeper meaning, with Harold as a naive Candide about to experience the harsh realities of life in East Africa, but, in fact, he is not naive—he is simply an inexperienced young man willing and capable of learning from his experiences.

7. *Black Ivory*, 19–20.

8. Ibid., 20.

9. Ibid., 56–57.

10. Ibid., 58.

11. Ibid., 387.

12. Ibid., 388. Ballantyne's attack on the Portuguese represented a standard British view of the Portuguese in Africa.

13. Sir Samuel Baker was governor of the Sudanese province of Equatoria, 1869–73, charged with extending Egypt's empire and with putting down the slave trade in the area. See Michael Brander, *The Perfect Victorian Hero: The Life and Times of Sir Samuel White Baker* (Edinburgh: Mainstream Publishing Co., 1982), Chapters 8 and 9.

14. R. M. Ballantyne, *Black Ivory*, 389–90.

15. Ibid., 391.

16. Ibid., 258.

17. Tim Jeal, *Livingstone* (London: Heinemann, 1973), 142–43.

18. See for example, *The Congo Rovers: A Story of the Slave Squadron* (New York: Worthington Co., n.d.).

19. *The Three Midshipmen*, 110–11.

20. Ibid., 227–28.

21. Robert S. Smith, *The Lagos Consulate, 1851–1861* (London: Macmillan Press, 1973), 18–33.

22. W.H.G. Kingston, *The Three Midshipmen*, 316.

23. *The Congo Rovers*, 346.

24. *Samba: A Story of the Rubber Slaves of the Congo* (London: Hodder & Stoughton, 1906).

25. For brief discussions of this campaign, see Jean Stengers, "The Congo Free State and the Belgian Congo before 1914," in L. H. Gann and Peter Duignan, eds., *Colonialism in Africa, 1870–1960 Vol. 1* (Cambridge: Cambridge University Press, 1981), 261–87, and Thomas Pakenham, *The Scramble for Africa: White Man's Conquest of the Dark Continent from 1876 to 1912* (New York: Avon Books, 1991), Chapters 32 and 37.

26. Herbert Strang, *Samba*, 54.

27. Ibid., 57.

28. Ibid., 334.

29. Ibid., 341.

30. In *The Times*, on February 4, 1899.

31. Much critical commentary has been expended on this little poem, which probably would have surprised Kipling, but is a measure of the importance of Kipling as a writer.

32. "William the Conqueror," Parts I and II, from *The Day's Work* (London: Macmillan & Co., 1964 [1898]).

33. Ibid., 151.

34. G. A. Henty, *At the Point of the Bayonet,* 103.

35. Henty had a great ambition to write for the adult market but was not successful with the novels that he wrote for this market. Guy Arnold, *Held Fast for England*, 87.

36. *Rujub, The Juggler* (New York: Hurst & Co., 1901).

37. His mother, while pregnant, was badly frightened by shots fired during a burglary.

38. *Rujub,* 88.

8

Christianity, Faith, and the Imperial Adventure

John Buchan, the son of a minister of the Free Church of Scotland, was bound to bring some religion into his imperial plans put forward in *A Lodge in the Wilderness*. There is a missionary, the Reverend Alexander Macdowall, of the Scottish Mission, in charge of a mission station supported by Francis Carey, and in general much approved of. But there is very little talk about religious ideas; it is agreed that Carey, though "'lamentably unsound in the faith,'" is still "'a profoundly religious man'"[1] but the details of religious positions are not spelled out. Even the missionary's assessment of his achievement in East Africa before Carey's arrival is not couched in religious terms—"'Our work had been much blessed—not in the ordinary sense, ye understand, for there were few converts of the real sort, but we had driven some habits of industry and decency into the people.'"[2] With the arrival of Carey's aid it is made clear that the progress—industries have been started—is more along the lines of the white man's burden, rather than the Christianization of the people, and Carey approves of this because he finds "spirituality" unintelligible to the native mind.[3] The summing up of the various imperial arguments is often done in a theological manner, and Carey makes it clear that to him imperialism is a religion, but it is also clear that it is a secular faith despite any talk of prayers and thanksgiving.

In much of the imperial literature that preceded Buchan, there is even less explicit presence of religion. It is obvious that the writers are Christian, that their heroes are Christian, that their opponents are not only savages, but heathen savages, and that Christian moral principles are being presented to the readers, but most of this is implicit rather than explicit. The terms of this Christianity are seldom spelled out, and even the moral principles that are there are often presented as springing as much from racial instinct or from class—true breeding—as from specific religious views. Missionaries, when they appear, are respected, but more likely for their civilizing activities, or even their military qualities,[4] than for their specific religious contributions.[5] The problem is that religion and imperial adventure coexisted uneasily within a single book, as becomes evident when several of the best-known books with religious content are examined.

Captain Frederick Marryat wrote a number of novels of the sea aimed at adults, such as *Peter Simple* and *Midshipman Easy*. These contain a great deal of adventure, much humor, some moralizing on politics and social behavior, and virtually no discussion of or involvement in religious topics. He wrote several novels specifically for a juvenile audience, and one of these, *Masterman Ready*, has both imperial adventure content and a very strong explicit religious content.

In the preface to his book Marryat explains that he wrote the book for his own children, who had wanted him to write a continuation of *Swiss Family Robinson*;[6] rather than do this he chose to write a completely new book because he considered the original to have far too many errors, not only in seamanship, but in geographical probability, and he preferred to write a more realistic tale. It is also clear that he intends to inform, and to make children think, not only about the great deal of information that he presents on all sorts of natural phenomena, but also about moral principles and how they are based on religious principles. The book was to educate and to guide his children, and all children who should read the work in the future.

Like *Swiss Family Robinson*, *Masterman Ready* is a story of a shipwreck on a deserted tropical island. Buried within the book is an interesting little adventure story. The Seagrave family is returning to Australia, where Mr. Seagrave had been for a number of years a successful government official and is now a considerable landholder. He is Marryat's "theoretical" man,[7] and on the evidence presented in the book, it is hard to see that he could have been a hardheaded successful engineer and agriculturalist, for he appears throughout as a moralizing wimp. Mrs. Seagrave is a liability to any red-blooded adventure story, being weak, with a distinct tendency to weep and to retire to her tent while all about her are busy trying to repair damages. William, the twelve-year-old, is a good boy, ready to work hard, and always willing to ask the right questions to start flowing the fountains of information both moral and practical. Caroline, who is seven, and Albert, the infant, play very little part in the story; she is always good, and he cries lustily at appropriate times and has to be cared for. Thomas is the only realistically drawn member of the family; he is six, a bundle of concentrated mischief who has a profound interest in his food. He pokes at lions in their cages, billy goats not in cages, and lands himself and his family in serious trouble. Traveling with the family is a black girl, Juno, who is a strong and faithful servant with, fortunately for her, a hardy constitution. The ship on which they are traveling, after leaving the Cape of Good Hope, runs into a series of severe storms, is badly damaged, and begins to take on water. The surviving crew members, led by the first mate, the captain having been knocked unconscious, determine to take to the single surviving boat, leaving the Seagraves behind, since the boat is not large enough for them. The second mate, Masterman Ready, refuses to leave and is determined to see what he can do, since the ship is still afloat, to save the family. The ship in fact does stay afloat long enough to be beached on a coral island, and the adventure begins.

Masterman Ready is an old man, already in his mid-sixties, with a long seafaring career behind him. He is Marryat's "practical" man.[8] He had run off to sea as a young boy, and over the years he has acquired a great deal of practical knowledge, seafaring experience, and religious tranquillity. Though a "practical" man as opposed to Mr. Seagrave's "theoretical" man, he is just as willing as Mr. Seagrave to launch on extended sermonettes to guide young William, his favorite among the Seagraves. He is realistically drawn to the extent that as an old man, he is portrayed with an old man's limitations in strength and physical endurance. He has a strong sense of duty and loyalty.

Ready leads the Seagraves into settling as comfortably as they might on a coral island; from tents they progress to log cabins built in shady groves, protected from the storms of the rainy season. Together they discover and make use of such plants and animals as might be found on a tropical coral island; there were no elephants, ostriches, lions, tigers, buffalo, jackals, or other beasts that abound in *Swiss Family Robinson*. Apart from the animals that they brought off the wreck, sheep, goats, dogs, pigs, and chickens, they caught giant turtles, fish, crayfish, oysters, and parrots. They discovered coconuts, yams, bananas, guava, pepper, eggplant, and wild grapes. Before they have made full use of their resources, they spot a ship that becomes aware of them but is forced to retreat in a storm, to their great disappointment. Two island women in a canoe are cast on their shore, aided to recover, and steal off with a large number of nails and pieces of iron, throwing Ready into apprehension about a future visit from "savages," come in force to appropriate all the good things to be found on the island. A residence is quickly fortified, and a barrel full of water is provided inside the stockade, just in time for the expected attack by masses of natives, who, for reasons not explained, are instantly hostile and obviously have come to make war and not to trade. Their attacks are beaten off, but to the defending party's great consternation, Tommy has previously emptied the barrel of water, and the besieged are left parched in the summer heat. The desperation of the young children becomes so great that Ready slips out at night with a small barrel to get water from the spring, returns with the water, but has been mortally wounded in a struggle with a native. The natives launch another attack, which threatens to overwhelm the stockade, when at the last moment they are beaten off by the crew of a ship brought from Australia to the Seagrave's rescue by the captain of their previous ship. Ready dies, and the Seagraves go on to Australia, to success and prosperity.

The religious emphasis begins in the midst of the description of a storm; the masts have been blown down, and several of the crew have been killed, and Ready's judgment is that "'it is God's will.'"[9] There is a strong indication of a belief in an almost minute-to-minute intervention of the supernatural in the affairs of men—"'I do wish that Mr. Mackintosh would not swear so; I always think that the winds blow harder, as if angry that their Divine Master should be defied by such poor worms as we are.'"[10] Mr. Seagrave comes with his son William onto the deck and immediately renders judgment: "'See how the pride of man is humbled before the elements of the great Jehovah,'"[11] though what particular sin of pride was being punished in such drastic fashion is not discussed. Indeed, throughout the book, it is easy to get the impression that Marryat's God is capricious and vengeful, and that it is ever necessary to be fearful and prepared to meet one's end. But of course, Marryat does not mean this at all, for Ready's God is "'a merciful God . . . who will dispose of us as He thinks fit,'"[12] and it is not for mere mortals to question his judgment; all, even disaster, must be accepted passively as right in the eyes of God, and even merciful, though the extent of the mercy is not immediately obvious. Mr.

Seagrave needs to be reminded of this often by the practical Ready, to still "his doubts of the goodness of Providence."[13] God uses nature for his purposes; "'lightning and thunder are as the eyes and voice of the Eternal in His wrath,'" and "'it is through the elements that God speaks to man, and that we feel his power.'"[14] It is a natural philosophy of religion for seamen exposed in the sailing ships of Marryat's time to the vagaries of the winds and the powerful surging waters of the limitless oceans.

There is, however, another element to Marryat's religion, most often presented by Mr. Seagrave, concerning the benevolent nature of God and the care taken in creation. In examining a "minute insect," probably a centipede, crawling on his finger, he points out the lesson to his son: "There is nothing which points out to us the immensity and the omniscience of the Almighty more than the careful provision which has been made by Him for the smallest and most insignificant of created beings.'"[15] Throughout this world and the infinite universe, which is composed of suns and planets such as Earth, the complex power of God is shown—the "'visible works of the Creator prove beyond all doubt His stupendous power and His overpowering love,'" though the achievement of salvation is, after all, an "'incomprehensible mystery.'"[16]

Masterman Ready often stops its action for these little sermons about divine wrath or the divine goodness as evidenced in creation, or for lessons in history, natural phenomena, or the place of instinct and thought in the lives of lower animals. That the book has remained in print into the twentieth century is an indication of either the tolerance of young British readers to be lectured at at length, or their ability to skip through such passages in order to get to the meat of the book, the adventure story with all its excitements, the imagination stirred by storms and shipwrecks, sharks and exploration, and the desperate conflict with masses of hostile natives.

What Marryat and *Masterman Ready* do not do is tie the religious content of the book to the imperial message. The Seagrave family were on their way to a colony in Australia; their enforced stay on the coral island was an interlude that leads to no announced imperial consequence. The island at the end is merely deserted, with the building and some animals left behind for the benefit of future unfortunates wrecked upon its shores. Despite its attractions, it is not colonized. The stalwart qualities of William and Ready are not related to the qualities that gained the British Empire, and the religious principles that Marryat pounds into the reader are held to be universal—the black girl, Juno, struck by lightning and, recovering, discovered by Ready deep in thoughtful prayer, is commented upon: "'There's more good under that dark skin than many a white one, and her prayers are acceptable to the Most High as those of kings and princes.'"[17] The Christian qualities that Marryat preaches are not specifically British ones, and certainly at this point in the emergence of imperial literature, they are not ones that are specifically tied to the qualities that were winning for the British their empire, and were justifying their rule over other peoples of the world.

W.H.G. Kingston was a religious man; at least part of his work on behalf of the emigration of the poor to the colonies was religiously motivated,[18] and he managed to get the Society for the Propagation of the Gospel and the Society for the

Propagation of Christian Knowledge interested in the work. Many of the fiction works that he produced had strong religious elements in them and were, like *The Gilpins and Their Fortunes*, tracts to point out the relationship between true Christian belief and success. In the first of his sea stories for boys, *Peter the Whaler*, published in 1851,[19] Kingston presents the evolution of the character of a young man, Peter Lefroy, who at the beginning is willful and disobedient; when he is caught poaching, as a punishment, he is sent to sea to mend his ways. He passes rapidly through the hands of a bad captain, on a ship that catches fire while at sea, and almost dies of thirst and the fire, and then from fever after he is rescued. Offered a chance to redeem himself, he still willfully prefers to go hunting and literally misses his boat, is captured by a pirate in the Caribbean and is impressed into service, barely escapes hanging when the pirate is captured by the American navy, and is forced into the American naval service. The American ship is wrecked on an iceberg in the north, and Peter and some friends are rescued by a whaler. After a series of whaling adventures, Peter and a portion of the crew are separated from their ship and have to rely on their resourcefulness in order to survive. Rescued by a French ship, Peter is once more shipwrecked, this time on the coast of Ireland, from which point, barely clothed and fed, he makes his way to Dublin where he rejoins his family, and a dear, sweet girl he has met along the way. When his father remarks that he has returned poorer, he answers: "'No, father . . . I have come back infinitely richer. I have learned to fear God, and to trust to his infinite mercy. I have also learned to know myself, and to take advice and counsel from my superiors in wisdom and goodness.'"[20] The development of his character makes this book rare among boys' adventure stories, since in most of them character is fully formed at the beginning, and the boys learn how to do *things* rather than learn how to become better people. Much more typical, and with a stronger religious message, is Kingston's next book, *Mark Seaworth*.[21]

There are two religious messages in *Mark Seaworth*, sometimes given separately and sometimes together. The first is that "God is everywhere"[22] and the second is "that whatever apparent misfortunes may occur to us, He orders them for our ultimate and permanent benefit."[23] The message that all things happen for the best is at time so strong that the book reads like an unconscious parody of Voltaire's *Candide*.

Mark and Eva Seaworth are two very young children who are found adrift by an East Indiaman; in the boat are two dead sailors and a dying native nurse, who has sacrificed her life, and the last of the water, to feed the two children with moistened biscuits. There are few clues as to their identities, apart from their initials on their clothes, and from these they are named by the passengers, and taken up and raised, Mark by Sir Charles Plowden, an East India Company civil servant, and Eva by Captain and Mrs. Clayton, a childless couple, the husband serving in the Company's armed forces. Shortly after the children are taken from the sea, a storm arose which would surely have destroyed them, thus prompting the comment of the narrator, Mark himself, that "God is everywhere." Curiously, he does not seem to have noticed that God's intervention had arrived too late for the two sailors or the nurse.

In the course of the story Sir Charles Plowden and Captain Clayton die, and Mrs. Clayton and little Eva disappear while traveling from Canton aboard the brig *Emu*. Very likely they have been the victims of the crew of the *Emu* turning pirate and holding them in the hope of extracting money. Young Mark, taking his inheritance from Sir Charles, sets out to track down his sister in the pirate-infested waters of the South Seas. He takes passage in a Dutch ship, which strikes a reef, sending the crew and passengers into boats for survival; on his boat Charles meets the mate, Fairburn, a very useful companion in the troubles to come. The boats are captured by Malay pirates, and these in turn are attacked by a Dutch warship, and most of Mark's former companions are killed. Fortunately surviving are Fairburn and a young Malay, Hassan, whose life Fairburn had saved on a previous occasion. As Mark lay safely in a berth on the Dutch ship, knowing that so many of his companions have died, he hears a comforting whisper in his ear, "'God is great—God is everywhere.'"[24] These disasters are all for the best because he is collecting useful companions for his quest.

This quest continues by means of a schooner, *The Fraulein*, that Mark has purchased and outfitted in Batavia. Another disaster at sea brings him the companionship of an old school chum, who also gives him news of the pirate chieftain of the *Emu*. When at last this awesome personality is tracked down, he has been marooned by his own crew; he tells Mark that his sister has been carried off by natives and gives him information on the origins of brother and sister. Richard Kidd, the pirate, who had gone to the bad as a young man, had been hired by the relatives of the two infants—whose names are now revealed to be Marmaduke and Ellen Seaton, and who were orphans on the way to a rich inheritance in England—to see that they should be lost at sea. It was his arrangement that had landed them in the boat from which they had been rescued by the East Indiaman. Chance, or God, had once more brought young Eva into his hands, but the pricking of a remorseless conscience determined that he try in some way to right the wrong. Dying as he is, however, the best that he can do is make a statement before witnesses and give Mark further documentary proof of his birth and inheritance.

Storm and chance, in fairly rapid succession, lead to Mark's separation from his comrades, capture by natives, the finding of his sister (a captive of the same tribe), rescue by another old school friend when a different tribe attacks and destroys his captors, and eventual rescue by Hassan and another native that Mark had befriended. Shipwreck and storm, disasters in themselves, progressively lead them into a situation from which they are rescued by Fairburn, commanding Mark's own schooner. All the catastrophes have led, through the inexorable hand of God, to the reuniting of Mark with his sister, and their eventual return to England and their rightful position in life. The lesson is pointed out by Fairburn when, in a discussion of the question of whether a desperate position could possibly be worse, he insists that there was always a worse alternative to every seemingly bad thing that had happened to them.[25] It is a comforting philosophy for the narrator and his friend, but again, unfortunately, of little value to the majority of passengers and crew who failed to survive the adventure.

But Kingston's Christianity is not simply a religion devoted to the survival and betterment of the heroes of his stories. Mark, in the midst of what he would call scenes of savagery among the head-hunting Dyaks, expresses his feeling that his Christianity and that of his sister should be turned to useful purposes, such as attempting to convert and civilize the natives.[26] Nevertheless, they escape at the first opportunity, and at the end of the book, restored to name and fortune, they show no sign of returning to the South Seas to carry out their valiant, virtuous, and dangerous project.

Still, the religious elements in Kingston represent a change from those in Marryat. Though in both the religious doctrine is intended for the moral edification of the principals of the stories, and, of course, the readers, Kingston is able to take a step forward into the political ramifications that could result from his religious principles. Mark, enslaved by a native tribe in Borneo, can universalize his experience using his religious ideals: "Those who have once tasted the bitterness of slavery will know how to compassionate [sic] their fellow-creatures, whatever the hue of their skin, reduced to a like condition. Surely the heart of the white and black man is the same: yet such is the fate of thousands and thousands of human beings, not only of the sons of Africa, but of the inhabitants of these magnificent islands I am describing."[27] To Mark as to Kingston the logical next step is obvious: "To what nobler purpose could the power and influence of Great Britain be turned, than by putting a stop to such atrocities, and by bringing the blessings of Christianity and civilization among a people capable of benefiting by them."[28] This does not necessarily and automatically lead to imperial expansion, but in much more religiously loaded terms Kingston is already expressing the connection between the British Empire and the Christian religion that is so casually assumed by the end of the century.

While Kingston in his future books often combined religious sentiment with the adventures his young men went through, a prosaic style, a lack of a sense of humor, and the sheer volumes of information on natural phenomena lessen considerably the attractiveness of his stories. R. M. Ballantyne was almost equally religious in tone, and had Marryat's and Kingston's tendency to stop midnarrative to deliver little sermonettes on religion or morality, but he had a greater talent for storytelling and a much more good-humored tone of delivery. The religious element in Ballantyne's stories is often connected to the activities of missionaries, though occasionally a young man is moved to play the role of religious teacher to a black sinner. This is the case with the book that has perhaps the longest lasting popularity of Ballantyne's adventures, *Coral Island*.[29]

Coral Island is a classic tale of adventure. Three boys, Jack Martin, about eighteen, Peterkin Gay, about fourteen, and the narrator, Ralph Rover, somewhere in between in age, are cast upon the shores of a deserted coral island when their ship is wrecked in a gale, and the crew depart without them. They had been plunged into the raging sea with only the clothes on their backs, an oar they were clutching into which Jack had stuck an ax, and a telescope that was partially broken, but which did provide them with one burning glass. Therefore, unlike the Swiss Family Robinson, Marryat's Seagrave family, or even Robinson Crusoe, they arrive at their place of adventure practically destitute. Significantly, Ballantyne immediately misses the opportunity to sermonize on divine intervention leading to their safe arrival on shore, and perhaps more surprisingly, given Ballantyne's religious bent, he does not have the boys kneel in prayer to give thanks for their safe delivery. With their limited means the boys fashion shelter, weapons, an adequate supply of provisions, a sailboat, and a great variety of adventures calculated to convince the three young men and the readers of their adventures that what had happened to them was a lark rather than a disaster.

Into this paradise come two sets of intruders. The first are South Sea natives, with one lot chasing another, catching and defeating it. The victors then set out, in the standard nineteenth-century fictional view of these people as being inveterate cannibals, to be beastly to the lost souls. A baby is tossed into the sea, and a pretty young girl is in imminent danger of being clubbed; this of course unleashes the chivalrous instincts of Jack Martin, the eldest of the boys, and in a furious attack with his club, with the other boys freeing the bound prisoners to come to their aid, he firmly turns the tables. The dead are now equally firmly *buried*, and the natives are allowed to recover, and to depart, with the newly defeated survivors now as prisoners, though to face what fate when out of the reach of Jack's moral wrath is not clear.

The second set of intruders are pirates, and in the course of events, poor Ralph is tricked and caught by the pirate captain, and carried off the island. Here Ralph is exposed to men depraved almost to an extent that matched the "savages" that he had fought earlier ("almost" simply because the pirates did not eat people). He is lied to by the captain, who says that the pirate vessel is a trading schooner and sandalwood gatherer (which it is, in part) and tells him that he will be released later if he wants. But Ralph soon sees the viciousness of the crew members as they massacre a group of natives who are opposing the schooner's watering party, and he realizes that the crew are black-hearted and without moral or religious scruples. There is one exception; Bloody Bill has some spark of decency left, enough to convince him to plan Ralph's escape, and later to foil the massacre of the natives at a sandalwood island. This latter action results in the death of the pirate crew, and the schooner barely escapes with Ralph and Bloody Bill, who has been badly wounded by the captain.

Ralph is primarily an observer, and a thoughtful boy, brought up in a Christian home, enjoined by his mother when he took to a seafaring life to read his Bible every day. The Bible that his mother had given him had been left aboard his ship, and he had none on Coral Island, and showed no sign of missing it. Now, among the pirates, and among the South Sea natives with whom the pirates traded, he sees sights that recall him to his religious upbringing: "At last, in my feeling of utter helplessness, I prayed fervently to the Almighty that he would deliver me out of my miserable condition; and when I had done so I felt some degree of comfort."[30] The prayer is answered by the killing of the pirate crew and a great many of their opponents, and the bare escape of Ralph and the now bloody Bloody Bill.

When it becomes clear that Bloody Bill is dying aboard the fleeing schooner, Ralph sees that the blackened soul of his companion is in dire need of saving and, despite the pirate's protests that he is doomed in any case, racks his brains for some vestige of his former religious training that could have some relevance in this situation, finally arriving at "'Bill,'" said I, in a low voice, "'Believe in the Lord Jesus Christ, and thou shalt be saved.'"[31] The pirate has some difficulty believing that it is all so simple, and so Ralph emerges with "'Though your sins be red like crimson, they shall be white as snow.' 'Only believe.'"[32] Again Bill returns with quite an able philosophical demur, considering the circumstances, but finally asks to hear the two quotations again. He dies during a sudden squall, still leaving in the air the matter of his salvation.

The greatest part of the religious portion of *Coral Island*, however, does not concern this essay in personal conversion, but involves Ballantyne's attitude to and reverence for missionaries. Already, in his first successful published book, *The Young Fur Traders*, based on his experiences as an employee of the Hudson's Bay Company in what is now western Canada, a minor role is assigned to a very favorably portrayed missionary working among the Indians. The importance that the missionaries are going to assume is evidenced early in Ralph's cruise aboard the pirate ship, when the pirates overhaul a trading schooner crewed entirely by natives. To Ralph's surprise, the ship is not looted, and instead the pirate captain is very cordial when he finds out that the schooner is a missionary ship. One crew member explains to a newer member of the pirate club: "'The captain cares as much for the gospel as you do (an' that's precious little), but he knows, and everybody knows, that the only place among the southern islands where a ship can put in and get what she wants in comfort is where the gospel has been sent to.'"[33] Missionaries evidently are very valuable commodities in the South Seas, valuable even to the ruffian element of society.

When Ralph, alone since the death of Bloody Bill, returns to Coral Island with the pirate ship, the three boys decide not only to cruise the islands, but to see what they can do on behalf of the young native woman Avatea, whose distress had helped precipitate Jack's wild charge against the victorious natives in their earlier adventure. She is being held by the chief, Tararo, who had also been rescued by the boys, and faces the alternative of either marrying a powerful heathen chief or death. Since she is a Christian, and in love with a Christian chief, this choice is not palatable. The boys from Coral Island decide to see how far gratitude could operate in the South Sea islands in effecting her release.

When the adventurers arrive at the island of Mango, they make contact with the native missionary teacher who has successfully converted a small tribe on one side of the island, and they are impressed by his grave demeanor and fund of knowledge. He presents the boys to Tararo as part of their initial plan, unsuccessful, to get him to free Avatea, and then arranges the equally unsuccessful attempt to spirit her away by canoe to the island of her Christian lover. Imprisoned by the wrathful Tararo, and threatened with death, the boys spend an uncomfortable month shut up in a cavern, isolated from contact with other human beings, and giving way to a sense of desolation. From this they are suddenly released. A huge and destructive storm that has devastated the village of Tararo at the beginning of their imprisonment has also brought to the island a white missionary. So effectively has he worked that in a few short weeks he has converted Tararo, and the chief has helped convert his people; the boys are released just in time to see the burning of a great pile of wooden idols. They also see the marriage of Avatea to her Christian chief, and her departure in peace from the island. What the boys had failed to accomplish through their physical heroics, the missionary has easily achieved through his moral heroics. The boys leave the island to return home on their pirate schooner, convinced at heart that the value of missionaries in "heathen" lands was inestimable.

Many of Ballantyne's future books were to have a missionary or missionary-like person within them, playing usually a minor role within the story, but setting the moral tone of the book, and making the strong suggestion that European missionaries were essential to tame wild lands and wild people. These books are like tracts promoting a useful and virtuous activity, and as such they are in keeping with the substantial number of Ballantyne books that were "missionary" in the sense that they commended to the British public the activities of ordinary people in Britain, such as firemen, railway workers, lighthouse keepers, miners, and those heroic individuals who manned the lifeboats to rescue people from the stormy seas.[34] A book that combines commendation of a moral and useful activity with religion and adventure on the frontiers of empire is *Blue Lights*.[35] The crusade that is promoted is that of Mrs. Sarah Robinson and the Soldiers' Institute of Portsmouth; the morality is that of the Blue Lights, who have taken the pledge to abstain from the consumption of alcohol, and the guiding force is Christianity.

The plot of *Blue Lights* comes close to achieving a rarity in Victorian boys' adventure stories—it promises character development in the main character, who is to start out bad and end up good. In the end it produces development of the mildest sort; Miles Milton is hotheaded, somewhat stubborn, and does not always listen to his parents. At the end of the book he is humbly submissive to his surviving parent, and has become a Blue Light, not a great change since he drank little in the first place. Among the other main characters, even the drinkers are courageous and sound at heart, and the road to religion and sobriety is not a long one. Only the minor characters, Mrs. Flynn and Mr. Soper, have any distance to travel, and they are witnesses of power as well as comic relief.

Miles Milton quarrels with his father over his desire to enter the army, and leaves home in a fit of temper; he might have returned when he cooled down, except that a stupid detective has mistaken him for a wanted swindler and attempts to arrest him. In his flight he makes his way to Portsmouth, meets a number of interesting persons, including volunteers working with the Soldiers' Institute, and joins the army. He attempts to write to his mother to confess that he had been wrong to leave home in anger, but does not successfully complete the letter before he is shipped out with the reinforcements for the small British garrison at the Red Sea port of Suakim, all that is left of Egypt's empire in the Sudan, and constantly besieged by the Mahdist forces of Osman Digna. It was one of those hot hellholes of empire, where strategic interests, this time the protection of the Suez Canal route to India, kept numbers of British troops pinned down in miserable, unhealthy, and dangerous surroundings. It was an area where the weak soldier or sailor could easily succumb to the lure of strong drink to make bearable the miseries of daily existence. Aboard ship, Miles falls in love with a sweet, demure sixteen-year-old daughter of a missionary, who teaches him to think that a soldier's first thought should be Duty—and sets him further along the path to developing a sense of responsibility.

In the course of campaigning in and around Suakim, Miles is captured, along with five of his friends, is taken prisoner to Khartoum, meets the Mahdi, and is enslaved. Eventually they are all secretly released by a Mahdist chieftain whose life Miles had earlier saved, and they set out to walk across the desert to Suakim. When almost there they become part of a general battle, heroically defending a hillock that they have occupied until the tide of battle has passed over them; they are all then rescued, though Miles is in desperate shape, with serious wounds including the loss of his left hand. Only the love for a good woman keeps the spark of life burning within him. Eventually Miles and his friends return to Portsmouth, where Miles finds that a legacy left to him by a friend will amply support a wife, his widowed mother, and his best friend.

Religious references are copiously scattered throughout the book, and though there is a good deal of humor, adventure, and even romance, the moral purpose of the writing is never far from the surface. Miles Milton, "our hero, at the age of nineteen, stood at the dividing ridge of his life. If the oscillating spirit, trembling between right and wrong, had decided to lean to the right, what might have been his fate no one can tell. He paused on the balance a short time, then he leaned over to the left, and what his fate was is the purpose of this volume to disclose. At the onset, we may remark that it was not unmixed good. Neither was it unmitigated evil."[36] By leaning to the left (and right and left are not political terms for Ballantyne) Miles does arrive at the end of the story in a situation of almost unmixed good. But he does start out with a hot hasty temper, quarreling with his father, ignoring the scriptural lesson "Children obey your parents in the Lord."[37] The consequence of this evil act was much heartache and sorrow to himself, and to his gentle, timid mother, and he never sees his father alive again. It has led him to an adventure that almost costs him his life and did cost him his left hand, points which Ballantyne makes abundantly clear throughout the book. The moral he does not point out, however, is that without this hasty act he would not have ended up with a beautiful and sweet-tempered wife, the inheritance that made him comfortable after his father had died bankrupt, and the friendship of a great many stalwart men who had been his companions in the Sudan campaign.

Religion is presented as the comfort of the afflicted. When a young woman comes to the harbor to meet the troopship on which she expects to find her husband, and does not find him, she is taken in charge by workers for the Soldiers' Institute. They take her to the Institute and break it to her gently that her husband has died in Alexandria. The poor woman, who had previously revealed about her son that "'God took him home when he was two years old,'"[38] breaks down, takes to bed, and dies of a broken heart; but in her last hours she informs her helpers "that her Fred had been stationed in Alexandria, and while there he had been led to put his trust in the Savior," but she did not know how. With her last words, "'But he will tell me about it soon, thank God!'"[39] she dies, putting her trust in a God who for purposes she did not know had caused her so much agony. The Christian beliefs of the British are presented as the most appropriate support in times of stress, though, interestingly enough, since Ballantyne and Kingston are near contemporaries, there is little indication in Ballantyne that God therefore on a sustained basis interferes in the lives of individuals, and orchestrates triumph and tragedy on their behalf. Rather, Ballantyne teaches acceptance no matter what the previous course of a person's life has been, and that acceptance of God will see a person through to death as well as in life. This is perhaps a sustaining belief for adventurers who are frequently likely to be facing death, and are not too concerned with the puzzlement of figuring out God's role in it.

Most of the boys' adventure stories talk very little directly about God and religious belief; they simply form the background that is commonly accepted, and from which the boy heroes have emerged. More important than the direct religious beliefs in these books is the impact that religion has had, or presumably had, in the forming of the characters of the heroic youngsters. Character played a major role in the stories, because it carried the whole load of right and wrong, and the proper behavior under all circumstances that a Victorian would find acceptable.

NOTES

1. John Buchan, *A Lodge*, 136.

2. Ibid., 132.

3. Ibid., 139.

4. See the missionary, Mr. Mackenzie, in H. Rider Haggard, *Allan Quatermain*, Chapters 3–9.

5. Ballantyne is an exception to this observation. In a number of his books, the activities of a missionary are presented as having profound religious significance.

6. Johann David Wyss, *The Swiss Family Robinson* (New York: Grosset & Dunlop, 1949 [1812–13]). Since Wyss's son collected and published his father's stories in 1812–13, there have been many variations. The above version comes from the publication of W.H.G. Kingston in 1889.

7. *Masterman Ready*, ii.

8. Ibid.

9. Ibid., 32.

10. Ibid.

11. Ibid., 33.

12. Ibid., 41.

13. Ibid., 49.

14. Ibid., 181.

15. Ibid., 193.

16. Ibid., 196–97.

17. Ibid., 190.

18. Rev. Maurice Kingsford, *The Life of William Henry Giles Kingston*, 64–66.

19. *Peter the Whaler* (London: W. Foulsham & Co., n.d.).

20. Ibid., 160.

21. *Mark Seaworth: A Tale of the Indian Ocean* (London: Henry Frowde, Hodder & Stoughton, 1912 [1852]).

22. Ibid., 18, 40.

23. Ibid., 384.

24. Ibid., 154.

25. Ibid., 135.

26. Ibid., 344.

27. Ibid., 320.

28. Ibid.

29. *The Coral Island* (London: T. Nelson & Sons, n.d. [1857]).

30. Ibid., 172.

31. Ibid., 184.

32. Ibid., 185.

33. Ibid., 151.

34. *Fighting the Flames: A Tale of the London Fire Brigade; The Iron Horse or Life on the Line: A Tale of the Grand National Trunk Railway; The Lighthouse: The Story of a Great Fight Between Man and the Sea; Deep Down: A Tale of the Cornish Mines;* and *The Lifeboat: A Tale of Our Coast Heroes.*

35. *Blue Lights: or Hot Work in the Soudan* (London: James Nisbet & Co., n.d. [1888]).

36. Ibid., 2.

37. Ibid.

38. Ibid., 62–63.

39. Ibid., 73.

9

Facing Death

John Buchan did not like Cecil Rhodes,[1] but the South African millionaire had so dominated South African politics with his "big idea"[2] that he became the inevitable model for the host of *A Lodge in the Wilderness*. Rhodes did have characteristics that had to be admired by anyone who believed that it took special qualities to build and hold an empire. Very prominent was Rhodes's courage in the face of a deadly situation, where even the slightest error could lead to destruction.

In 1896, with many of his imperial schemes collapsing around him in the aftermath of the Jameson Raid, Rhodes was faced with the uprisings of first the Ndebele and then the Shona in his northern colony of "Rhodesia."[3] Not only did these uprisings bring death and destruction to the white colonists, but also, because the imperial government quickly sent imperial troops to quell the rebellions, they brought the suffering of heavy expenses by Rhodes's Chartered Company and the subsequent loss of the area it had previously administered. Rhodes accompanied the imperial troops as an unofficial participant and led charges into dangerous situations, armed, apparently, only with a whip.[4] When the defeated Ndebele abandoned the open field and took to the hill terrain of the Matoppos, from which it would take a long and costly campaign to extract them, Rhodes, still with no official position, developed a new strategy to end the war quickly and cheaply. He made contact with the Ndebele chieftains, and with a handful of companions rode unarmed into the Matoppos to talk peace with the elders of the tribe. The first meeting contained touchy moments when anger could result in the annihilation of the small group of white men, but Rhodes was able to convince the elders then, and in a following series of equally delicate meetings, that peace was essential and in their best interests; he had greater trouble convincing the more warlike of the imperial troops who resented his interference. The almost fatalistic courage shown by Rhodes, a man known to have an intense aversion to physical pain,[5] was rightly very impressive, and Buchan would not only admire but would make use of the adventure in his own writings.

Near the end of *Prester John*, with the Reverend John Laputa's conspiracy for an uprising in tatters through the intervention of the young hero, David Crawfurd, and John himself dead, the white troops are still facing a long and costly campaign to mop up the remnants of the rebellious tribes. Captain John Arcoll, the British intelligence agent in charge of foiling Laputa's conspiracy, and David Crawfurd arrange an indaba with the leading chiefs, ride into their midst, hand over their revolvers to one of the chiefs—"'We come in peace,' he [Arcoll] said. 'We give you our lives.'"[6]—and begin their parley. It is David's impassioned speech about John Laputa's last moments, which he had witnessed, and his words that "'the Rising was over'"[7] that turn the tide in favor of peace. David has faced the whole ordeal with perfect calmness: "It was a very bright, hot winter's day, and try as I might, I could not bring myself to think of any danger. I believe that in this way most temerarious deeds are done; the doer has become insensible to danger, and his imagination is clouded with some engrossing purpose."[8] There is no way of knowing what Cecil Rhodes actually felt at the time of his ordeal, whether there were tremors of fear that he had to swallow, but fiction writers would be in no doubt about how such a moment must be faced; there must be calmness and the absence of any manifestations of fear, outwardly or inwardly. Character was all-important, and events which served to highlight the good points of character were often the centerpieces of imperial and adventure fiction, as well as the numerous "school stories" that had become so popular in the second half of the nineteenth century.

Facing death was a supreme test of character, because to the Victorians, death was a scary, somber and ever-present reality.[9] Death could strike individuals with sudden finality, or wipe out successive members of families when epidemics that could still ravage "modern" industrialized England struck. Death was tragic and mournful, and no amount of evangelical moralization about the departed soul achieving a better existence could provide more than bare solace to those who were left behind. Comfort had to be sought in the ceremonial of the funeral, the gathering of mourners, the solemnity of the music and the sermons, and the wearing of dark clothing and black armbands. Excessive mourning might be regarded as being not quite British. In the ideal, death had to be faced stoically, with supreme courage; the agony of grief must be muted.

Death was a frequent visitor in the imperial adventure stories because, of necessity, they occupied violent settings in violent times, and war and skirmishes of war, and criminal activities and the vagaries of nature so often carried death as the inevitable passenger that the presence of death seldom needed comment. Many of the deaths occurred off center, with a mother or father, or both, dying and setting free a youth for a career of adventure; these deaths are simply enabling and are not dwelt upon. Death was often impersonal; faceless soldiers in the ranks keeled over as the enemy attacked, or equally faceless savages were mowed down as they sought to overcome the forces of right, or, more particularly, the hero of the piece; this latter death could come in bloody batches. Rex Bateman, a sixteen-year-old in Henty's *With the Allies to Pekin*, and his Chinese companion, Ah Lo, intercepted by a dozen Boxers, promptly shoot eight of them, batter in the heads of two more, and possibly kill the other two.[10] Harry Collingwood's heroes often see ships sink beneath them, smashed to pieces by storms, with a loss of all but a handful of companions; the survivors barely have time to lament the loss before they are plunged into further desperate adventures.

In a sense, all the adventure stories were about facing death, and about how heroic youth, British youth, reacted to the challenge, but most often very little was made by the authors of the act itself. Facing death was one of the challenges in life, and the books were very much about fast-moving life. Only occasionally did an author take some time to examine a scene of death or potential death in some detail and consider some of the ramifications of it, including some slight analysis of the hero's reaction to the prospect of imminent demise. G. A. Henty, in one of his nonimperial, nonhistorical boys' novels, *Facing Death: A Tale of the Coal Mines,*[11] places his young hero in such a situation on a number of occasions.

Jack Simpson, son of a coal miner, lost his parents while an infant and is raised by Bill and Jane Haden. Henty quickly establishes Jack as a strong, silent type. At the age of six he requests of his adoptive father, a rough hard-drinking miner: "'And look 'ee here, dad, I've been a thinking, doant lift I oop by my ears no more, not yet. They are boath main sore. I doant believe neither Juno nor Bess [two bulldogs] would stand bein lifted oop by their ears, not if they were sore. I be game enough, I be, but till my ears be well you must try some other part. I expect the cheek would hurt just as bad, so you can try that.'"[12] The reader instinctively knows that any boy who asks merely for a recess from being lifted by his ears will deserve the nickname "Bulldog" and will be in an advantageous position when it comes to dangerous situations.

Sure enough, when he is twelve years old Jack goes down an old abandoned well, clinging to a rusted chain that might break at any moment, to rescue a friend, sends the friend up first, and clutches a projecting stone while immersed in cold water, foul air, and oppressive darkness, waiting for the chain to be sent down again. Is he afraid? His thoughts are:

> He wondered vaguely whether it [the unconscious body of his friend] would ever reach the top; he wondered whether the arm would pull out of the socket, and the body plump down into the water; he wondered how long he could hold on, and why his clothes seemed so heavy. He wondered whether, if his strength went before the chain came down again, his hand would hold on as Harry's had done, or whether he should go down to the bottom of the shaft. How far was it! Fifty fathoms, three hundred feet; he was fifty below the mouth, two hundred and fifty to sink; how long would his body be getting to the bottom? What would his mother and Bill Haden say? Would they ever try to get his body up?[13]

But there are no fears or regrets. Again, when Jack is sixteen, he stops striking coal miners from flooding the mines by turning a steam hose upon them; he keeps his identity a secret because he knows that he would be killed if the miners find out who has foiled them, but no fear of death had stopped him for a moment from doing what he considered to be his duty to the mine owner and even the striking miners.

At the climax of his adventures young Jack, still in his early twenties, but self-educated as a mining engineer, is caught underground in a gas explosion and is trapped with a small group of survivors, which include his father and the mine owner; they desperately try to escape certain death, from gas, fire, explosion, or starvation. Jack never wavers, but puts his knowledge and coolness to work to evolve a plan that sees the miners dig their way into a neighboring abandoned mine, and safety. Rightly, he becomes mine manager, part owner, and later, with his wife, sole owner of the mine.

Actually, very few authors had their heroes face certain death; to end a book on the note of the destruction of the main character would have a demoralizing effect, and perhaps carry the wrong message, especially to young readers. It was all very well to promote the concept that in the interests of building a greater empire, or certainly a greater Britain, a heroic young man should be prepared to face the possibility of death, but certain martyrdom might inhibit volunteers for the great cause. One author who experimented with a destructible hero was John Buchan, in *The Half-Hearted*, one of his early novels, and not written for boys. In this book Lewis Haystoun, in many ways the stuff of adventure heroes, but with a flaw, a lack of a sense of final commitment, which makes him "half-hearted," redeems himself at the end by his final sacrifice. With two rifles and a revolver, alone in the night on the northern borders of India, atop a narrow pass, he meets an invading army of Russians and wild frontiersmen and stops them, though his purpose has been merely to delay them long enough so that the Indian stations in the path of the invasion can prepare their defense. In the end he dies, as "twenty bayonets pierced him,"[14] but he has had time to exult his fate:

> He was alone in a very strange place, cut off by a great gulf from youth and home and pleasure. For an instant the extreme loneliness of an exile's death smote him, but in a little he comforted himself. The heritage of his land and his people was his in this ultimate moment a hundredfold more than ever. The sounding tale of his people's wars—one against a host, a foray in the mist, a last stand among the mountain snows—sang in his heart like a tune. The fierce northern exultation which glories in hardships and the forlorn came upon him with such a keenness and delight that, as he looked onto the night and the black unknown, he felt the joy of a greater kinship. He was kin to men lordlier than himself, the true-hearted who had ridden the King's path and trampled a little world under foot. To the old fighters in the border wars, the religionists of the South, the Highland gentlemen of the Cause, he cried greeting over the abyss of time. He had lost no inch of his inheritance. . . . Whenever the English flag was planted anew, wherever the last stand was made in the march of Western progress, wherever men did their duty faithfully and with hope of little reward—there was the true land of the true patriot.[15]

Buchan was enamored enough of the fate of this self-sacrificing hero that he repeated an aspect of his adventure in *A Lodge in the Wilderness*, in Considine's story of Lacey, an "'ordinary stupid fellow who fought because he liked it'"[16] and defended his border fort with his dozen soldiers against overwhelming odds, and though offered his life, chose to die fighting, not out of stubbornness, but because it was his duty to create a moral effect upon the savages of the frontier. To Buchan, the existence of such men as Haystoun and Lacey was essential to the creation of an empire, and indeed the legend of the forlorn hope had had a fairly recent reinforcement in Matabeleland in the fate of the Shangani Patrol.

In 1893 relationships between the Ndebele and Rhodes's pioneers in Mashonaland had broken down, and an unequal conflict broke down. However, occasionally the outgunned Ndebele had their successes.[17] A small patrol operating out of a column sent to capture Lobengula, the Ndebele chieftain, decided to exceed its orders and carry out the spectacular coup of effecting the capture by itself. The fifteen men of the patrol were pinned down in gathering darkness and sent for help; the commander of the main column, rather than making the sensible decision of withdrawing the patrol, sent a small reinforcement of twenty-one men. This enlarged patrol of thirty-six men was then wiped out in an Ndebele attack; legend had it that the men sang the National Anthem as they waited to die, their ammunition expended. It was a foolish action precipitated by wrongheaded decisions by several officers, and did little if any good in affecting the outcome of the war, but it became part of the mythology of the white Rhodesians. Facing death bravely, whether with Scott in the Antarctic, or among the icebergs of the North Atlantic on the Titanic, seemed to encapsulate the ultimate character strength of the British,[18] to invigorate and enthuse those left behind, who showed a resolute capacity for ignoring the stupidity and inefficiency that brought about such deaths. A nation that wanted to ensure that its national spirit remained high could not afford to ask too many introspective questions about intelligence levels.

Facing *apparently* hopeless odds and *apparently* certain death was a much more attractive proposition for authors, for it created an opportunity to display what the authors considered to be true British character without creating at the same time a depressing conclusion. Almost all true adventurers from these adventure stories at one time or another faced overwhelming odds, and survived, often unscathed, or with a quickly healing wound or two. Most of the authors tended to follow the same policy as Henty had in *Facing Death*, making the hero react to the situation without a quiver of fear, or a question or a doubt. But occasionally the question of courage and fear, as well as ultimate death, is faced, if not with a great deal of depth.

Henty, whose boys are generally so fearless in their exploits that they constitute something of a menace to their companions—always suggesting as they do new and dangerous exploits, such as spiking inconvenient guns located in the midst of a non-sleeping army[19]—does, in one of his attempts to write an adult novel, deal with a form of fear in the face of great danger on the field of battle.[20] Ralph Bathurst is a poor unfortunate because, before he was born, his mother had been frightened during an attempted burglary in which shots were fired, and this makes Ralph constitutionally afraid of any loud noises, a serious handicap since he follows in his father's footsteps and becomes an officer in the army. As a result of his problem, Bathurst freezes while leading his men in a charge in a battle during the Sikh Wars, and consequently he resigns his commission and returns to India in the civilian service instead. His handicap makes him feel terrible: "'It is an awful curse that I am not as other men, and that I tremble and shake like a girl at the sound of firearms. It would have been better if I had been killed by the first shot fired in the Punjab eight years ago, or if I had blown my brains out at the end of the day. Good Heavens! what I have suffered since.'"[21] He counts himself a coward even though he has the courage to beat off a man-eating tiger with a whip, an action that could be accomplished with relatively little noise.

The curse of Ralph Bathurst achieves serious proportions when the sepoys of his station mutiny and besiege a small group of white officers and officials and their dependants; although he exposes himself to the fire of the enemy, he turns pale and becomes paralyzed into inactivity. This polarizes the station, even though acts of silent courage are duly noted, and most concerned is Isobel Hannay, who has fallen in love with him, and whose mind and heart are now torn:

> But the big thing is to be brave in battle, Doctor! You would not call a man a coward simply because he was afraid of a rat, but you would call a man a coward who was afraid in battle. To be a coward there seems to me to be a coward all round. I have always thought the one virtue in man I really envied was bravery, and that a coward was the most despicable creature living. It might not be his actual fault, but one can't help that. It is not anyone's fault if he is fearfully ugly or born an idiot, for example. But cowardice seems somehow different. Not to be brave when he is strong seems to put a man below the level of a woman.[22]

Questions of courage aside, Bathurst does leap into the midst of a mass of sepoys pouring into a breach in the defensive wall, and armed only with an iron mace he wreaks dreadful execution on the attackers. Further along in the story he is creased in the head by a piece of shrapnel, recovers sufficiently to rescue his Isobel from the dreaded garden at Cawnpore where later all the women and children are massacred, joins a troop of cavalry, and wins the Victoria Cross; the blow on the head has worked wonders for his tolerance level for loud noises. But when handicapped with his strange affliction, and when not, he constantly places himself in positions where he courts death. An Englishman must be expected to do that. Only his ability to perform effectively in such situations has been affected by his prenatal trauma; Henty would say that the instincts of the race and of a gentleman always remained the same, no matter what the situation.

An interesting contrast in the story, to show that Henty had actually done some thinking about questions of courage and facing death in dangerous corners, is the case of Captain Forster, also caught in the siege. Forster is a dashing cavalry officer and a ladies' man, always ready to lead a charge, to plunge into battle, to launch even a forlorn hope. And yet Forster finds it almost intolerable to remain besieged, passively waiting to be attacked; he is the first to volunteer to break out, to ride through the enemy lines to seek help. Under siege, he muses, "I have felt like a rat in a cage with a terrier watching me for the last month, and long to be on horseback again, with the chance of making a fight for my life."[23] His departure does not meet with universal praise. The lovely Isobel Hannay, somewhat attracted by this handsome and dashing cavalier, absolutely refuses to go with him; she sees it as her duty to stay and to share the fate of the other members of the besieged garrison.

G. Manville Fenn, a contemporary and friend of G. A. Henty, often wrote boys' fiction in much the same mode as his friend, though with a somewhat livelier style, and occasionally brought some interesting observations and contemplations into his stories. In *Gil the Gunner*[24] he actually considered the questions of depression and even fear in the face of death. Gil Vincent, a very young subaltern in a horse artillery unit in India, contemplating the extent of the sepoy rebellion, the atrocities that have been committed at his own station, the friends killed, and the possibility that his father, mother, and sister might meet the same fate at another station, becomes "horribly troubled"[25] and even allows himself to have doubts about whether the English can succeed with so much treachery around them. He needs to be rallied by an older officer, Captain Brace: "'The rebellion is widespread, but what of it? We must put it down. England is not going to have her great conquests wrenched from her hands like this.'"[26]

An earlier conversation between Brace and Gil centers on the issue of fear. After the rising at the station, the horse artillery has been carried off by an ambitious native prince, and Captain Brace is determined to get it back. With the European survivors, including Gil and another officer, he tracks down the artillery and finds the Indians drilling with the guns, using the procedures they had witnessed at the station. An elaborate plan is worked out, which involves Gil, Brace, and a trumpeter, to literally hijack the horse artillery while on maneuvers, relying on the automatic response of the well-drilled horses to the command calls of the bugle. While waiting for the proper moment, which involves exposing themselves at that point to overwhelming odds and certain death if the plan fails, they converse:

> "We may succeed even now, Gil," said my companion; "but once more, while there is still time, speak out frankly to me as if I were your brother; the trumpeter cannot hear. Do you feel—well, to be plain—frightened?"
> "I suppose so," I said. "It's a curious nervous situation."
> "Then give it up, and follow the men, and I'll go alone."
> "You said I was to speak to you as if you were my brother," I said.
> "Yes."
> "Then I will speak," I said through my teeth. "It is to my brother, and not to my commanding-officer. I won't. I'll go with you now if I die for it."
> And all the time the feeling of dread I felt was horrible, and worse than all was that the feeling grew.
> Brace caught my hand and wrung it.
> "Well done!" he said in a low voice. "I can see. I know the sensation; but that's the way. Fight it down."
> "I'm trying," I said huskily; "but I wish I was not such a coward."
> "I don't, Gil," he said, smiling.[27]

Fear of death, of course, should not prevent one from doing brave deeds, but at least some authors acknowledged that it was legitimate to feel some fear.

Death had to be faced in situations other than the battlefield. Kingston, in his *My First Voyage to Southern Seas*,[28] presents a considerable number of hunting stories set in Ceylon. Young Ralph Marsden, looking to meet his grandfather, whom he had never seen, somewhere in the interior of Ceylon, travels along with a "sporting party." Caught in the path of a wounded and charging buffalo, he admits some sensation of the "full horror" of his situation, and having been rescued, comments, "I had enough of buffalo-shooting for the day. Even then I felt what a senseless sport I had been engaged in."[29] Despite this, he is soon hunting elephants, and after shooting a great number, he finds himself charged by a huge rogue, into whom he fires the only shot in his rifle an instant before he is hurled some distance by the trunk of the beast. Lying still in the grass while the wounded elephant searches for him, Ralph allows that "It is impossible to describe my sensations."[30] Not too long after, he is leaped upon by a bear just as he fires both barrels of his rifle into its chest; this little adventure gives him a "horrid fright,"[31] the first time he clearly admits such a sensation. Hunting is evidently a dangerous pastime, and after his companion is killed by an elephant, Ralph has to comment:

> I need not further dwell on Mr. Fordyce's grief; but I cannot leave the subject without reminding those of my readers who may some day be inclined carelessly to risk their lives as Nowell and I had been doing ours, first, that they have no right to do so—that they are committing a great sin by the act; and then, also, that though they may be careless of the consequences, that they have mothers and sisters, fathers and brothers at home, to whose loving hearts their untimely fate will bring many a bitter pang of grief. It is a soldier's duty to be ready to die fighting for his country; and though those at home mourn, and mourn deeply, their grief is not bitter or full of anguish as it would be if those they have lost had died in consequence of their own folly or wickedness.[32]

Such moralizing perhaps sounds a little strange from a hero who earlier, when charged by another buffalo, could boast "I never felt more cool and composed. I really believe that I could have taken a pinch of snuff if I had had one."[33]

Robert Ballantyne, in what amounts to a singularly bloodthirsty hunting book, *The Gorilla Hunters*, has two out of his three hunters reacting with coolness in all hunting situations, but the narrator, Ralph Rover, does have problems in his first crisis. As an enraged, wounded buffalo bull charges down on his friend, who was caught in some thorns while trying to escape, Ralph finds it difficult to function:

> Horror almost overwhelmed me as I gazed with a stare of fascination at the frightful brute, which with flashing eyes and bloody foam dripping from its mouth charged into the thicket, and crashed through the tough boughs and bushes as if they were grass. A film came over my eyes. I tried to reload my rifle, but my trembling hand refused to act, and I groaned with mingled shame and despair on finding myself thus incapable of action in the hour of extreme peril.[34]

This may appear to be fear at work, but not at all. Ballantyne, in a lengthy sermon that follows is careful, to point out that growing boys should accustom themselves to taking chances, whether jumping from heights or leaping across rivers, so that they will become well acquainted with their own capabilities and be able to act quickly and confidently in an emergency. After he has been hunting for some time, when next a friend is in peril, this time with a foot caught in the path of a rampaging elephant, Ralph reacts differently:

> To this day I have never been able to account for the remarkable condition of mind and body that ensued on this occasion. Instead of being paralyzed as I had been when Peterkin was in imminent danger, all sensation of fear or hesitancy seemed to vanish on the instant. I felt my nerves and muscles strung, as it were, and rendered firm as

a rock, and with calm deliberation, yet with the utmost rapidity of which I was capable, I turned round, sprang between Jack and the enraged beast, and presented my piece at his head.[35]

Coolness in hunting and in battle was the mark of a gentleman and of the adventurer whose deeds built the empire. It was always made clear, however, that it was in battle that death-defying nerves were essential. Fear in such a circumstance was for women and little children. Mrs. Seagrave in *Masterman Ready* suffers from the yells of the savages, which "struck terror into the heart," and the children "cling around her neck with terror in their faces,"[36] but calm courage and resignation to their possible fate is the only course of emotion open to the men of the little group.

A glorious death might be an inspiration to aspiring young imperialists, but the writers of adventure stories were usually astute enough not to dwell on the act of dying and extended deathbed scenes. So there are only a limited number of such scenes to show how a true adventurer should die. The most spectacular concerns the death of the Zulu adventurer, Umslopogaas, in *Allan Quatermain*.[37]

To Rider Haggard, a stalwart Zulu warrior must have at times appeared to embody the many qualities that were essential to an English gentleman.[38] Certainly Umslopogaas is painted with greater care and affection than his English counterpart, Sir Henry Curtis, who, in this sequel to *King Solomon's Mines*, still has not shed his essentially wooden image. In the climactic battle scene of *Allan Quatermain*, Umslopogaas stands, finally alone, on the steps of the sanctuary to which Queen Nyleptha has withdrawn, and defends her against those who would assassinate her. Before help can arrive he kills the chief of the queen's enemies, but is severely wounded. In true mythic fashion he staggers, trailing blood, to the sacred stone of the Zu-Vendis, addresses his old friend, Allan Quatermain, the narrator, addresses his battle-ax, and brings the ax down in one mighty blow on the sacred stone, shattering it and fulfilling an ancient prophecy; "And thus Umslopogaas the hero died."[39] In contrast, Allan Quatermain, the grizzled old hunter who has many of the virtues of a true imperialist, and who also was severely injured in the final battles, simply sinks and extinguishes slowly over a period of weeks—but then he has the epilogue of the story to narrate.

Masterman Ready, as befitting the hero of Marryat's pious book, dies an appropriate death to drive home the religious lessons; in this, Marryat is much closer to the evangelical writers of the century than to the imperialist. Ready prays, decides where he should be buried, and dictates that the young scamp Tommy, whose actions had indirectly caused his death, should never be told of the consequences of his ill-considered acts. Then he kisses all his friends goodbye and dies.

The question of facing death naturally leads on to the consideration of courage, and the courage to face death was only one of the types of courage that the writers had decided must be developed in young men who would be useful to Britain and the British Empire. The discussion of courage that takes place in most of the adventure novels is not of a very sophisticated type, and it seldom occurs to an author to wonder whether the hero who has no fear in a situation where there is great danger, is showing real courage in facing the danger. Perhaps he is simply too emotionally dense to be sufficiently awake to the peril he faces. This is certainly true of Henty's Jack Simpson in *Facing Death*, who has a young village girl trailing him constantly, even into adulthood, without having the slightest inkling that she is in love with him; he is obviously so narrowly self-centered that he would be incapable of seeing that in a situation of great danger there is reason to have fear, a fear that a brave man faces and overcomes, and then he acts. Most of Henty's heroes appear to be in the same category as Jack.

In some of his novels Henty does try to explore other issues besides mindless courage and endless adventure. In *With Cochrane the Dauntless* he considers loyalty, party politics, and how a nation can mistreat one of its heroes.[40] In *With Wolfe in Canada* he makes the rare admission that a weak-willed villain is capable of redemption;[41] *The Curse of Carne's Hold* explores the problem of hereditary madness, and its impact on a young man who is feared to have inherited the family malady.[42] The pervasive issue that runs through *Rujub, the Juggler* is the nature of courage.

Ralph Bathurst is a mixed bag when it comes to manifestations of courage. Because of the prenatal incident when his mother was frightened by burglars, Ralph is paralyzed by loud noises. He is aware of this shortcoming, but does not have the moral courage to withstand his father's pressure that he enter the army. Following his disastrous performance at the Battle of Chilianwala, he resigns his commission and returns to England, to the intense disgust of his father, a retired general. Upon his father's death Ralph inherits enough money to stay home to live the life of a gentleman, who, because he did not hunt, would seldom have to confront his disability. Instead, he returns to India as a civilian, a district officer, where he shows a great deal of moral courage, if somewhat less common sense and sense of proportion, in constantly badgering his superiors with lengthy proposals for reforms. He could face a tiger with a whip or spear, but not with a rifle. Thrown into battle again, he freezes when the firing starts, but excels in hand-to-hand combat and in carrying out prodigious tunneling while trying to create an escape route from the besieged residence. His friend, Dr. Wade, could understand the problem, and considers Ralph a brave man, but Ralph sees himself as a useless coward and sympathizes with the ambivalent attitude of his beloved Isobel toward him. In the end Henty can only resolve this dilemma of courage with a piece of shrapnel, which, properly applied to Ralph's head, cures him of his prenatal encumbrance and allows him to show courage in all aspects of manly behavior, including noisy battle; he had become only now a whole man.

G. M. Fenn, also, though many of his stories cover the same adventure territory as those of Henty, occasionally puts in some more realistic emotional elements that allow the possibility of fear, and courage springing out of that fear. In *Ching, the Chinaman*[43] two young midshipmen, Fred Murray and Bob Riches, serve on a gunboat on a river in China. Murray is a thoughtful boy, not given to bloodthirsty thoughts or to feigning eagerness to do battle. In a conversation with a senior officer he is asked:

"How do you feel about going into action for the first time?"

"Not very eager, sir," said the boy bluntly.

"Humph! That's frank. Neither did I, my lad. You will not mind it by and by. It's the thought of it more than anything."[44]

Later the officer asks Fred whether he would rather stay back from an excursion to spy out a Chinese fort, and though somewhat apprehensive the boy certainly wants to go and help. In the same way, once the fort is captured, he volunteers to hold a lantern for the boatswain, who is laying a train of gunpowder from the powder-house, in preparation for blowing up the fort. It dawns on him, in middle of the operation:

> the terrible risk of the task he had undertaken, and [he] began to suffer from a sharp attack of the peculiar trouble known as "gooseskin." It was as if the whole of his surface beneath his clothes had become closely sown over with tiny pimples, all of which were creeping upward towards his cap and amongst his short crisp hair as if to make it rise up on end.
>
> But that did not last long, for the idea struck him that he ought to back away a little, in case the overturned powder should send up a tiny cloud of dust.
>
> "But if I go back," thought the lad, "old Beane will not be able to see. I must stand still." And he did.[45]

It was perhaps a subversive doctrine to give to schoolboys that brave deeds must be performed not without fear but in spite of fear.

In *Gil the Gunner* Fenn also briefly deals with the question of moral courage. Captain Brace severely tells off Lieutenant Barton for bullying the Hindu servants and the young ensign, Gil Vincent, and then refuses Barton's challenge to a fight. Vincent, though admiring the senior officer, is much concerned with this, and thinks: "'He is a coward! . . . and I have been gradually growing to like him, and think of him as being patient and manly and noble. Why, I would have tried to knock Barton down, if he had killed me for it.'"[46] Yet Barton is murdered by the natives for his mistreatment of them, and Brace goes on to prove his courage in the face of dreadful odds, in battle.

The schoolboy hero, of course, was expected to "duel." Boys fought at school, then and now, and in the stories of boys' adventures they were expected to, but usually in a good cause. When schools appeared in these stories, they were either public schools or modeled on public schools, very much in the manner of *Tom Brown's Schooldays*.[47] Thomas Hughes's sturdy hero, Tom Brown, fought the bullies of his school, and G. A. Henty's boys often became involved in such noble conflicts. Henty himself took up boxing to build up his physique, and in his books he advocated that his boys, and all boys, learn this useful art. Dick Holland's mother encouraged him to fight, though not on his own account; "'but whenever you see a boy bullying a smaller one, take the opportunity of giving him a lesson while learning one yourself. In days of old, you know, the first duty of a true knight was to succour the oppressed, and I want you to be a true knight.'"[48] This would make him fit to go to India to find his lost father. Charlie Marryat was a good boxer and fought often in the battles between the schoolboys and the "fisher lads."[49] James Walsham fought and beat an older and bigger boy who pushed a little girl into the water, and covered him with scorn to boot: "'I thought you weren't any good; a fellow who would bully a little girl is sure to be a coward.'"[50] Reuben Whitney often fought heavier village boys and earned the reputation of being a tough customer.[51] Considering the careers into which the author proceeded to send his boys, a sense of pugnaciousness, and the ability to fight, proved to be useful. Edgar Clinton, who ran away from home because of a misunderstanding, joined the army as a trumpeter and did himself a lot of good by rescuing two ladies from two tramps.[52] The grateful officer-husband of one of the ladies was to promote his interests in the future. He later earned the respect of the common soldiers of his battalion by taking on and defeating a bullying older soldier, relying upon superior conditioning to beat the larger man.

On the other hand, some authors do not present these schoolboy squabbles in the best possible light. Fenn's Gil Vincent fought often, but too often out of sheer bad temper, and he had a tendency to feel sorry for himself.[53] And Rudyard Kipling, whose work is in a different category than that of most of the writers considered here, occasionally portrays his schoolboy heroes in *Stalky & Co.*[54] as less than perfect. Instead of an old-fashioned one-on-one fight as would be favored by the other authors, the three chums from Number Five study trick two bullies into being bound and then put them through an ordeal that included torture.[55]

The boys were expected, and Kipling is explicit about this,[56] to carry their love of schoolboy conflict into the world of military endeavor. No one shirks battle, and almost everyone, with the exception of one or two of Fenn's characters, appears to enjoy both the prospect and the actuality of battle. W.H.G. Kingston was a peaceable man who spent a great deal of his time promoting the settlement of the lower classes in the colonies, yet in his *The Three Midshipmen* he notes that "Their conversation was cut short by that rolling sound of a drum, which makes the heart of every true man-of-war's man leap with joy."[57] There are no qualms, no fears, no "butterflies in the stomach" at the prospect of battle, or what battle might bring for the individual or for the ship. Furthermore, there is not here, or elsewhere, any consideration of what impact battle might have on young boys or men engaged in their first successful conflict. They kill, and this does not worry their minds at all; there is no agonizing over the fact that human life has been destroyed. There are no nightmares featuring the faces of the dead; the deed is done in all righteousness, and there is no indication that the boys will ever be bothered by it.[58] Pity is reserved for your own dead, and there is seldom any left over for the dead of the enemy. There is some concern when:

> Two thousand pounds of education
> 　　Drops to a ten-rupee jezail—
> The Crammer's boast, the Squadron's pride,
> 　　Shot like a rabbit in a ride![59]

but there is not much evidence that the wailing in the huts of the losing side is recorded.

Roland Graves, inviting his nephew Percy to come out to India and share with him the pleasures, profits, and dangers of a princely estate in the Sikh kingdom of the Punjab, writes:

> Think it over yourself, Percy. Can you trash most fellows your own age? Can you run as far and as fast as most of them? Can you take a caning without whimpering over it? Do you feel, in fact, that you are able to go through fully as much as any of your companions? Are you good at planning a piece of mischief, and ready to take the lead in carrying it out? For though such gifts as these do not recommend a boy to the favour of his schoolmaster, they are worth more out here than a knowledge of all the dead languages. It is pluck and endurance, and a downright love of adventure and danger, that have made us the masters of the greater part of India, and will ere long make us the rulers of the whole of it; and it is no use anyone coming out here, especially to take service with one of the native princes, unless he is disposed to love danger for its own sake, and to feel that he is willing and ready to meet it from whatever quarter it may come.[60]

Given the content of Henty's novel, it is obvious that this is Henty himself speaking, outlining the admirable characteristics, especially strength of body and strength of mind, that would be of essential service to a young empire builder. Most of the other authors would have agreed with him.

There would be less agreement on the role of stratagem in the character of a gentleman and an imperialist. Gentlemen did not lie. An English gentleman would not tell a lie to another English gentleman, or to a gentleman of any nation; he would be reluctant to lie to any Englishman or European. Perhaps to a limited extent a gentleman might lie to one of these people if he was an enemy, but this was touchy. Henty's Vincent Wingfield, in *With Lee in Virginia*, when caught in disguise spying out Yankee positions, considered that "while in disguise, and doing important service for his country, he was justified in using deceit; but merely for the purpose of saving his own life, and that perhaps uselessly, he would not lie."[61] The "merely" shows a very nice sensitivity.

It was, however, acceptable to lie to natives in order to save lives, even those of the heroes themselves. Allan Quatermain, Sir Henry Curtis, and Captain Good, discovered by the natives of Kukuanaland while searching for King Solomon's mines, did not hesitate to let their involuntary hosts, who proposed to kill them, believe that they were wizards who had come from the stars, using Good's removable teeth and Quatermain's skill with a rifle to prove their point. Furthermore, in order to save the native girl, Foulata, and incidentally to give the sign of their power to the chiefs thinking of joining them in Ignosi's attempt to regain the throne of Kukuanaland, they pretended during an eclipse to be able to control the sun. In order to save the life of another intended sacrifice victim, a woman, Ballantyne's heroes from *The Gorilla Hunters* were willing to lie about their activities, though the narrator does admit to "some probings of conscience at the thought of the double part we were compelled to play."[62] These qualms are quieted when he recalled the probable fate of the girl if they had failed to act to save her.

Disguise, of course, is a form of lying. All the writers were willing to concede that disguise was legitimate in times of war. Kipling could see its value for the purpose of playing The Great Game, a quasi war with Russia on the northern frontiers of India; but he also saw it as useful for the maintenance of order within India itself, to keep under control the turbulent internal factions and bad characters. Learning another language could be justified on the grounds that it made perfect a disguise adopted for spying out the land, or saving life, whether that of the hero or someone else, a lost father perhaps, or a damsel in distress.

There is more difficulty over a disguise of a different sort, a disguise of scene, so to speak, or an ambush. For G. A. Henty an ambush was a natural form of warfare, and his young warriors were adept at setting them up and merciless at carrying them out. Firing from his hiding place, beginning without warning, Nat Glover killed eight blacks and mulattoes who threatened the security of himself and the women he was protecting; the last man had merely broken his leg in a fall, but Nat put a pistol to his head and fired to ensure that no one lived to reveal their hiding place.[63] On the other hand, some authors were leery about letting their heroes fire on an enemy without warning, and there were conversations in these stories that would amaze practical soldiers. Lt. Colonel F. S. Brereton does have some claim to a military background, and yet his One of the Fighting Scouts contains the following passage:

"Another point which we must not lose sight of is, that at present they do not know whether you are here or not, and certainly do not suspect that you have a companion. That will give us the advantage of a surprise if we wish to take it; but it becomes a question whether we have a right to shoot down some of these fellows without warning. Of course, ours is a kind of ambush, and I am sure that the Boers themselves would have no scruples. Still, it isn't quite the thing that an Englishman likes to do. He would rather face his enemy on more equal terms, and if he must shoot him, would rather warn him first."

"You're quite right there, George," exclaimed Cyril heartily, "and I'm with you in what you say. Mind you, I know very well that our enemies will laugh at us for our trouble, but then we shall have the satisfaction of having done the right thing. Supposing I sing out to them as they start to climb up. Then they'll have their warning, and will still be ignorant that I have someone to help me."[64]

It is hard to believe that they are discussing a prospective attack by fifty men on two. Earlier in the same book, while George is shrinking from the killing of a Boer who is about to discover him and a friend, the Boer blunders into a sleeping horse, and solves the problem by getting himself kicked in the head. All the action takes place in the dark, and the horse at least had no scruples about striking from ambush.

There was nothing very complicated about the virtues of the Victorian period as taught primarily to its boys with the intention that they should hold and observe these lessons for the rest of their lives. Honesty, truth telling, friendship, loyalty, purity, and family cohesiveness were the basic precepts provided by both evangelical literature and chivalry. If the imperial adventure stories placed more emphasis on courage and a defiant attitude toward danger and death, they did not therefore repudiate any of the other virtues; it was simply because exhibitions of courage oiled the wheels of the all-out action adventures. By including all the virtues in the catalogs of their heroes' qualities the imperial authors made their works comfortable and nonthreatening; they fit into the mores of that society, and, fitting in, they were accepted as suitable moral tales for the generations growing up in the imperial age; and imperialism itself became for a time one of the virtues.

NOTES

1. J. A. Smith, *John Buchan,* 136.

2. R. I. Rotberg, *The Founder,* 73.

3. A good description of these events can be found in Arthur Keppel-Jones, *Rhodes and Rhodesia: The White Conquest of Zimbabwe, 1884–1902* (Kingston and Montreal: McGill-Queen's University Press, 1983), Chapters 11 and 12.

4. R. I. Rotberg, *The Founder,* 560–62.

5. Ibid., 561.

6. John Buchan, *Prester John,* 228.

7. Ibid., 229.

8. Ibid., 227.

9. See John Morley, *Death, Heaven and the Victorians* (Pittsburgh: University of Pittsburgh Press, 1971).

10. *With the Allies to Pekin,* 81–84.

11. *Facing Death: A Tale of the Coal Mines* (London: Blackie & Son, n.d. [1882]).

12. Ibid., 17.

13. Ibid., 58–59.

14. *The Half-Hearted,* 315.

15. Ibid., 308–09.

16. *A Lodge,* 100.

17. Robert Blake, *A History of Rhodesia* (London: Eyre Methuen, 1977), 109.

18. Mark Girouard, *The Return to Camelot,* 7.

19. As in *With the Allies to Pekin,* 187–91.

20. This is in *Rujub, the Juggler.*

21. Ibid., 16.

22. Ibid., 149.

23. Ibid., 268.

24. *Gil the Gunner, or The Youngest Officer in the East* (London: S.P.C.K., n.d.).

25. Ibid., 247.

26. Ibid., 245.

27. Ibid., 215.

28. *My First Voyage to the Southern Seas* (London: T. Nelson & Sons, n.d.).

29. Ibid., 230.

30. Ibid., 275.

31. Ibid., 293.

32. Ibid., 344.

33. Ibid., 326.

34. *The Gorilla Hunters,* 47.

35. Ibid., 82.

36. Frederick Marryat, *Masterman Ready,* 348.

37. H. Rider Haggard, *Allan Quatermain,* Chapter 22.

38. Kent Fedorowich, "H. Rider Haggard: The Spirit of Empire," 84.

39. *Allan Quatermain,* 258.

40. *With Cochrane the Dauntless: A Tale of the Exploits of Lord Cochrane in South American Waters* (London: Blackie & Son, 1909 [1897]).

41. *With Wolfe in Canada, or The Winning of a Continent* (London: Blackie & Son, n.d. [1887]).

42. *The Curse of Carne's Hold* (New York: Hurst & Co., n.d. [1889]). This is one of his adult novels.

43. *Ching, The Chinaman and His Middy Friends* (London: S.P.C.K., n.d.).

44. Ibid., 69–70.

45. Ibid., 178.

46. Ibid., 89.

47. Thomas Hughes, *Tom Brown's Schooldays* (London: George C. Harrap & Co., 1927 [1856]). Chapter 5 of Part II is dedicated to "The Fight."

48. *The Tiger of Mysore,* 17.

49. *With Clive in India,* 11.

50. *With Wolfe in Canada,* 40.

51. *A Final Reckoning,* 18.

52. *The Dash for Khartoum,* 101–02.

53. *Gil the Gunner,* 3–4.

54. *Stalky & Co.* (Oxford: Oxford University Press, 1987 [1899]).

55. Ibid., "The Moral Reformers," 117–38.

56. Ibid., "The Flag of Their Country," 202–21.

57. *The Three Midshipmen,* 67.

58. In contrast are poems written by soldiers in the Boer War, such as:

> The Empire's poets and the Empire's priests
> Make out my deed was fine,
> But they can't stop the eyes of the man I killed
> From starin' into mine.

Quoted in M. Van Wyck Smith, *Drummer Hodge: The Poetry of the Anglo-Boer War (1899–1902)* (Oxford: Clarendon Press, 1978), 152.

59. Rudyard Kipling, "Arithmetic on the Frontier."

60. *Through the Sikh War,* 19.

61. *With Lee in Virginia,* 341.

62. *The Gorilla Hunters,* 102.

63. *A Roving Commission, or Through the Black Insurrection of Hayti* (London: Blackie & Son, 1900), 175.

64. *One of the Fighting Scouts: A Tale of Guerrilla Warfare in South Africa* (London: Blackie & Son, n.d.), 192–193.

10

Heroes and Imperialists

Who and what is an imperialist? Buchan's gathering in *A Lodge in the Wilderness* is a gathering of imperialists. They are all in this instance people who would be acceptable in high society of Edwardian England, well-educated, well-connected with family and friends, and well-off financially; the men, at least, follow a variety of professions, and the women are married to or are related to men in a variety of professions. There are two financiers, several politicians, a journalist, a soldier, an ex-bureaucrat, and an explorer and big-game hunter who is also a part-time politician; several of the wives were related to politicians, ex-politicians, and bureaucrats. Only the journalist can be called a writer of any sort, and he plays a minor role in the proceedings. As wide-ranging a group as they are, they obviously cannot represent the sum total of the types of people who could be called imperialists; the missionary, Mr. Macdowall, who appears later in the book, is also a dedicated imperialist. Most of the types of imperialists who appear in this colloquium on imperialism do not appear in the books on adventure and imperial topics that had appeared in the century previous to the publication of *A Lodge*, and they were not to appear in most books published in the decades to follow. There are two, however, who are closely related to the raw material of the adventure imperial novels of the period. These, as described in the list of characters,[1] are Sir Edward Considine, "An Explorer and famous Big-game Hunter," and Colonel Alastair Graham, "A Soldier and Traveller; now of the Intelligence Department."

John Buchan had already described in an early novel, *The Half-Hearted*, how an adventurer, Lewis Haystoun, had redeemed certain domestic shortcomings and deficiencies in his soul by dying alone on the frontiers of India, in defense of the empire. In Considine and Graham he has two men who are intended to be more complete adventurers, though, of course, in a novel devoted to talk this could not be adequately illustrated. Considine, however, is the philosopher of the relationship between adventurers and empire. An adventurer is a simple man, whose yearning for the wild places is the proper ambition for a real man, in contrast to the ambitions of an "'ordinary industrious citizen'" who "'wants to "get on" in his beastly trade, and to have a house in Mayfair and a place in the country, and marry his daughters well, and get into Parliament and have a title to clap on to his squalid name. Or perhaps he wants to be applauded in the papers and be treated as a personage wherever he goes.'"[2] "'I ask you,' Considine sneers, 'if these are ambitions for a white man?'"[3] The ordinary life of an English gentleman really ruined a useful imperialist. In an unconscious parody of Henty and Henty's conclusions to the careers of the bulk of his young heroes, Considine gives the object lesson of the career of Lord Thirlstone: "'I used to know him long ago in the service, and he was the hardest-bitten devil I have ever struck. He was in Tibet with Alastair, and he and I once had a try at getting into Kafiristan. Then his uncle died, and he became an enormously rich peer and had to come home and attend to his affairs.'"[4] At home he marries, is tamed, and has lately become an under-secretary. At a social gathering, which Considine characterizes as a meeting of chattering caged monkeys, Considine asks his former companion "'if he liked his new life. He said he did, talked a lot of rot about doing his duty in the sphere to which it had pleased God to call him, and about the fun of being at the centre of things; but there was not much conviction in his tone.'"[5] He quickly falls into the argot of the explorers until plucked away by his wife and political boss and brought back to his "'gilt cage.'" When one of his listeners questions Considine's judgment in this case: "'And yet,' said Hugh, 'What good is the *wanderlust* in itself? You may have all manner of dreams, but you spend your strength in futility. I dare say Thirlstone sitting chafing in Parliament is playing a better part in the solid work of the world than Thirlstone gallivanting about the Hindu Kush.'"[6]

Considine objects, "'That's where you are wrong, my dear. . . . We are the advanced guard, . . . unless we had gone before no one would have come after.'"[7] From this reasonably solid argument Considine leaps into poetic philosophizing and a good deal of fantasy about the adventurer being "'the electric force in civilization'"[8] whose failure is his success. This was the case with General Charles Gordon, regarded by many Victorians as martyred at Khartoum, who was, according to Considine, very necessary to the mental health of imperial Britain: "'You may tell me that he was mad and a fanatic, that he ran his own head into the noose, that he had flaws in his character, that he was impossible as a colleague or a subordinate. I daresay that is all true, and I don't care. His failure and the manner of it were worth a dozen successful wars and a whole regiment of impeccable statesmen. It put new faith into the race, and screwed us up for another century.'"[9] Apart from the fact that this was a remarkably poor piece of forecasting, it stands as a clear statement by Buchan on the importance of the individual in achieving what was necessary for the creation of the solid foundations of the British Empire. This being the case, unless the Thirlstones of political society specifically targeted their political careers to further the interests that they pursued as adventurers, they are really sellouts who fear to make the ultimate sacrifice for the ideals they held sacred as youths. The Henty concept of the young man who had done "enough" for Britain and the empire, and deserved the reward and leisure of sitting back and enjoying himself while others took up the struggle was quite foreign to Buchan's official imperial philosophy. Henty's imperialism, as important as it was to the individual as well as to Britain, was a way of life; Buchan had already passed on to an imperial theology.

Sitting on the fringes of this imperial theology, especially as it concerned the individual and the adventurer, and occasionally crossing fully into it, was Rudyard Kipling. It is necessary to say "occasionally" because as mystical and mythical as Kipling becomes in many of his poems and stories, Kipling is usually much more grounded in reality than Buchan; romantic reality perhaps, but reality all the same— "what do they know of England who only England know"[10] is not a *theological* phrase. It is only because Kipling's prose and poetry is often so steeped in emotion, so capable of being sensed rather than reasoned, that the impression is left that he is presenting a religious faith rather than an imperial philosophy based on experience.

Stalky & Co. is certainly based on experience, Kipling's own, and very little of it could be accepted as religious dogma. But it does set forward Kipling's adventurers' canon, and bit by bit it weaves a picture of the place of the adventurer in the larger scheme of the British Empire. What appears on the surface to be the story of a boys' school soon converts into something different, not just because so many of the schoolboy sentiments described within it would be alien to the typical schoolboy story of the time,[11] but because a series of phrases, almost asides, constantly remind the reader that the author is talking about the raw material of empire. Young Hogan, three years later, would die "in the Burmese sunlight outside Minhla Fort,"[12] and Wake minor would become "a bimbashi of the Egyptian Army."[13] M'Turk had a wooden West African war-drum, "a gift . . . from a naval uncle."[14] His face would later be "tanned blue-black with the suns of the Telegraph Department"[15] in India. To the young readers of these stories, these phrases were instant reminders of both the glamour of the empire and the fact that the schoolboys in the stories would soon be adventurers on a worldwide basis.

Stalky is the hero of the stories and is an adventurer clear through; he is not a thoughtless adventurer, but one who places a great deal of effort into the planning of his epics. This was what makes him the most useful type of adventurer for the empire to have; this fact helps distinguish Buchan's and Kipling's adventurers, because Buchan allowed some animal, almost mindless, adventuring as being useful. Kipling is careful to establish Stalky's academic qualifications; he is not a grind. He does well in his French, for example, but needs some help in his mathematics from M'Turk and Beetle. In contrast to the heroes of Buchan's later thrillers, he is not superhuman. What Stalky is, as indicated by his nickname, is clever, and able to see the potentialities of a situation and exploit them to the maximum extent.

The important illustrations of Stalky's stalkiness are found in many of the stories, but two of the most imperially connected are in the stories "Slaves of the Lamp (Part I)" and "Slaves of the Lamp (Part II)." They are really variations of the same plot, one sketched out and implemented by a schoolboy to get the better of a teacher, and the second brilliantly developed by an adult army officer to get his men out of a very sticky situation *and* to establish dominance over his opponents.

In the first story the three boys of Number Five study, Stalky, M'Turk, and Beetle, have been insulted by King, one of the masters, and vow vengeance. The plan and execution is mainly Stalky's as the boys first of all get themselves thrown out of their study in order to provide themselves with alibis for subsequent events. Stalky, who has hidden in the study when it has been locked up, proceeds to assault with his catapult and buckshot "Rabbit Eggs," a carrier on his way home, roaring drunk, in such a way as to make the man believe that the pellets are coming from the window of Mr. King's study. In retaliation he begins to hurl rocks through that window, to King's consternation, and the delight of Beetle, who is in the study being "jawed at" and who improves on the confusion to augment the damage. In the end the study is wrecked and King blames all on Rabbit Eggs; it is a cleverly executed maneuver that has gained the boys their vengeance without drawing punishment upon them.

In the second story Stalky applies the lessons that he has learned in the course of this boyhood lark, this time in an imperial setting, on the frontiers of British India, an area that fascinated Kipling. Stalky now is the commander of Sikh troops who revere his name, and on whose emotions and sentiments he can play if necessary to achieve what he wants. If the Indian Civil Service man is the philosopher king of the administration of India,[16] Stalky is the ideal commandant of native troops. In the course of the intricacies of frontier policy, which is always badly handled by the central government, Stalky and two other officers from the old school are trapped with their detachments of Sikhs and Pathans in a remote fort on the frontier and besieged by two hostile tribes of frontiersmen, the Khye-Kheens and the Malôts. The two tribes have been deadly enemies in the past, and have joined for the specific purpose of wiping out the Imperial troops who were apparently helpless in their midst, but they do not trust each other. Consequently, and also because Stalky has put up a stout defense before the other British officers had arrived with their Pathans, the attack was not being pushed with a great deal of vigor. Stalky proceeds to improve on their reluctance, by killing a couple of the outposts of one tribe while he is out patrolling, and leaving the tribal mark of the other tribe cut on their bodies. After a somewhat hostile conference, the two tribes decide to launch a combined attack, something that Stalky, of course, has foreseen. In the night he takes his Sikhs out of the fort and into the hills into a position from which they can lob shots at one tribe in such a way that the shots appear to be coming from the other tribe. The aggrieved tribe stops its attack to retaliate against its supposedly treacherous allies. This development is aided by an attack from the fort by the British-led Pathans, who fire only on one tribe, and soon the two tribes are busily engaged fighting one another and ignoring the British force. In the end the alliance is broken up and the British retreat, with a prisoner, an influential chieftain. Up to this point, the affair has been the schoolboy adventure replayed on an imperial field—any crafty adventurer could have duplicated it. Stalky proceeds to improve on it in an imperial sense.

Stalky returns to the frontier with his Sikhs and his prisoner, sets the frontier tribes to the road building that had been interrupted by the hostilities, creates a semiprotectorate over the area, which is beyond the official frontier, earns himself the wrath of the central government, and produces able Pathan recruits for the frontier forces of the empire. Of course he is reprimanded, but only with words and with a lenient hand, and he returns to help to reinforce Britain's hold on the fringes of empire.

The above tale is narrated to a gathering of the "old College," and one of the listeners concludes "'There's nobody like Stalky.'" Kipling as narrator replies:

> "That's where you make the mistake. . . . India's full of Stalkies—Cheltenham and Haileybury and Marlborough chaps—that we don't know anything about, and the surprises will begin when there is a big row on."
>
> "Who will be surprised?" said Dick Four.
>
> "The other side. The gentlemen who go to the front in first-class carriages. Just imagine Stalky let loose on the south side of Europe with a sufficiency of Sikhs and a reasonable prospect of loot. Consider it quietly."[17]

The lesson was obvious; it would have appealed to more than just Kipling's boyish imagination. The adventurer not only was a fun companion (though somewhat trying to his opponents) but was of positive use both to England and to her empire. The defense of the homeland ultimately depended on those boys who carried their well-developed sense of fun and adventure into the adult world and used it to punish (as did Stalky) all those who were foolish enough to provoke England, or in some way threaten parts of her empire.

To a certain extent Stalky is merely a cleverer, more witty (in a schoolboyish mode) version of G. A. Henty's adventurer heroes; the major difference is that Stalky is eternal—the reader gets the impression that Stalky will be irrepressibly Stalky no matter what age. A sixty-year-old Stalky would still be ready to lead his sufficiency of Sikhs rampaging through the Balkans in the service of the empire. The Henty hero on the other hand is an adventurer only in his youth; it is hard to imagine him past the age of thirty, tearing himself away from his wife, children, friends, and country estate to go adventuring anywhere—that sort of stuff was best to be left to the really young. Henty's heroes belong to a more complacent age, an age of security in which there were always enough young men to serve England. Stalky comes in an age that is changing, a period of greater anxiety about the future and the challenges that Britain would have to meet.

The Henty heroes did not meet the criteria for imperial adventurer as set out by Buchan, where the adventurer is a restless soul, rooted only in his love for Britain and his ideal of service for the empire. The Henty hero goes adventuring strictly from necessity. Will Gale started his adventurous career because the fishing boat he was on was run down by a Dutch ship heading for the East; Harry Prendergast had to find a great deal of money in a hurry in order to be able to marry his sweetheart; Frank Hargate's mother and father were dead and he had to make his way in the world with very little money; Reuben Whitney needed a fresh start in a new land because he had been falsely accused of theft in the old; Edgar Clinton was being blackmailed by the woman he supposed was his mother; Dick Holland went seeking his lost father in India.[18] Less idealistically than Buchan and Kipling, but more realistically, and reflecting Henty's own concern with stabilizing his finances, many of the boys, like Yorke Haberton,[19] went adventuring out of sheer economic necessity. This is not the stuff of romance, perhaps, but could set young male readers to thinking about the advantages of a career in the empire.

One of the few exceptions to Henty's predilection for necessity being the mother of adventure is found in *Maori and Settler*, where indeed the boy hero, Wilfrid Renshaw, is forced to migrate to New Zealand with his family because a bank has failed, wiping out most of the Renshaw family fortune. But the real hero/adventurer of the story is an adult, Mr. Atherton, and he is a restless dilettante. Overweight, and feeling a misfit in English society, he is much more at home as the perpetual tourist in the rougher parts of the world, cracking heads and fighting off savages with his enormous strength and expert marksmanship. Though he does not exactly push back the frontiers of European penetration, he, so to speak, shows the English flag in his person, as the stalwart, dogged Englishman who is not afraid to go anywhere, do anything, and impress his worth upon the natives. But in the end, love and marriage tame even him, and with less distress than that felt by Buchan's Lord Thirlstone: "Mr. Atherton entirely gave up his wanderings abroad, and by dint of devotion to racquets and tennis in summer, and of hunting and shooting in winter, he kept down his tendency towards corpulence. He was an energetic magistrate, and one of the most popular men in the county."[20] Perhaps in his case his wandering has been less a service to the empire and more a form of weight control, and as soon as he finds suitable alternatives, amply pointed out to him by his wife, he happily gives up his duty to the empire and becomes one with the rest of the Henty heroes.

If he does tend to be prosaic, the Henty hero is still adventuresome enough to employ stratagem to deal with his own or his country's enemies. He is clever enough to make plans to take advantage of his opponents' weaknesses. In *The Dash for Khartoum*, for example, Edgar positions a defensive fortification for his by now friendly captors in such a way that the attacking force quickly feels the lack of access to water. He also has no scruples about an ambush, and sends a force to deal with that portion of the enemy that has been detached to go back to a water hole for supplies. Unlike Captain Brereton's heroes, who are so suffocated by sense of honor that they would place themselves in extra danger to avoid unfairness to the enemy, the Henty hero sees ambush as well as disguise as legitimate tactics to be used against the opposition.

The Henty hero is a man/boy of action, seldom engaged in intellectual activity, which to Henty would mean a long period of sedentary life, probably in administration. He tends to move almost directly from a life of danger and action to one of retirement, often at a very young age. The task of governing the empire was to be left to different types of young men. Because Henty, unlike Kipling, had very little to do with, and little experience of, India, he was never bitten by the Punjabi bug of admiration for the soldier/adventurer/administrator into whose capable hands the cause of the maintenance of empire could so confidently be placed. For Henty adventure was not a career or duty, but an interesting and useful occurrence on the way to financial competence and independence; there is little sign, apart from his messages to "his boys" in the prefaces of some of his novels which indicate the long-term significance of the actions in which his heroes have been involved, that Henty saw his heroes as the lonely forerunners paving the way for more prosaic settlers, merchants, and administrators.

R. M. Ballantyne could never make up his mind just what his boys were, whether adventurers pure and simple, or plain working boys to whom adventures occurred. Sometimes they were both. His trio from *Coral Island* were ordinary, hard-working sailors-in-training who were catapulted through shipwreck into the dream adventure of their lives, as castaways on a deserted island that was a miniparadise, though complete with a skeleton to show that without outside contact it was possible to die alone, even in paradise. The same trio, transformed into hunters in *The Gorilla Hunters*, are three young men voluntarily satisfying their lust for adventure, under the thin veneer of being on the frontiers of scientific knowledge in seeking out and slaughtering a considerable number of gorillas. The young men Charlie Kennedy and Harry Somerville seemed destined to fill seats behind desks in the Fort Garry headquarters of the Hudson's Bay Company, but then go adventuring as fur traders all over the Company's territories of the Northwest. Harold Seadrift, seriously learning his trade as supercargo on one of his father's ships, and shipwrecked off the coast of East Africa, turns to adventuring with a vengeance and becomes a crusader against the slave trade.[21] There appears to be no philosophy of imperialism linking empire and adventure in any of these cases. Instead, these are stories of romance into which convenient maxims of morality are worked; education and entertainment are linked together in such a way as to leave imperial messages implicit rather than explicit. Much the same combination was to be found in the numerous stories produced by W.H.G. Kingston.

One of the curiosities of the stories of Kingston, Ballantyne, and Henty is that, apart from the historical romances of Henty, their adventurers do not become involved in the acquisition of territory; not a single acre is added to the British Empire as a result of their activities, and what is more, the authors do not really seem to be advocating that the empire should be extended in this way. Henty might lament the inefficiencies to be found in former Spanish-ruled territories in the Americas,[22] and comment on how much they would benefit from some British tutelage, but he is not really advocating the wholesale annexation of these areas. The *Coral Island* is not left with a British flag floating over it when its three inhabitants sail away, and the island of Marryat's Seagrave family is left garrisoned only by the grave of Masterman Ready. The slave trade of East Africa is to be controlled by the purchase of a few areas as "centres of refuge," and occupied mainly by consuls, missionaries, and free Christian blacks, but with a small force to protect them against "the savages, and worse than savages,—the Arab and Portuguese half-caste barbarians and lawless men who infest the land."[23] It is easy now to recognize in "centres of refuge" centers of future imperial expansion, because savagery of any type would not be that easily quelled by a few missionaries, but less easy to see the young merchants and treasure seekers as the thin edge of empire, because in fact they were not always followed by the imperial factor. Perhaps this was not important to nineteenth-century writers who saw their adventurers operating not within the finite boundaries of a British empire, not in the parts of the world already painted red; they were expounding a broader, more universal doctrine that the whole world was really Britain's empire, that their adventurers everywhere served to strengthen this "informal empire," and that the young Britishers could operate anywhere with impunity in the security of the Pax Britannica, but even more surely in the security of their own native intelligence and resourcefulness.

Allan Quatermain, in Rider Haggard's first two novels about him,[24] is a wanderer and adventurer for whom civilization has little attraction. It is his contention that he is a simple hunter, and that he hunts lions and elephants merely for a living; he wanders southern Africa as a trader in between hunting expeditions to supplement the uncertain earnings of his profession. It is clear, however, from the loving descriptions of his hunting exploits and adventures that he chose a footloose existence as an economic venture precisely because of its freedom from the ordinary restraints of civilization and of earning a living. To Quatermain "Civilization is only savagery silver gilt,"[25] and on the whole he prefers the savages. Though he becomes enormously wealthy as a result of his adventures with King Solomon's mines, when his son dies he finds that he cannot stand a civilized life on a country estate, a Henty-type life, and very soon proposes to be off: "The thirst for the wilderness was on me; I could tolerate this place no more; I will go and die as I have lived, among the wild game and the savages."[26] And so he sets out for the veldt, and the wild animals, this time in East Africa, chasing a rumor of a white tribe lost in the interior of Africa.

Of his two white companions in his lengthy odysseys into the interior of Africa, very little background information is given about Sir Henry Curtis. He is, in the first book, thirty years old, large, powerful, handsome, and reminds Allan Quatermain of an ancient Danish warrior. He is also rich and a gentleman, but what he actually does remains vague; perhaps he hunts and travels. He appears to have no other useful preoccupation, not even that of pushing back the frontiers of knowledge. It is a search for his brother, whom he feels he has wronged, that brings him to southern Africa to start the adventure of *King Solomon's Mines*, and not some even vague concept of duty to the empire. In *Allan Quatermain,* boredom and restlessness, and the need to distract the mind of his friend from the recent death of his son, send him on his last trek to Africa.

Captain John Good is somewhat better provided with respect to a background. He is a naval officer, reduced, after seventeen years, to the ranks of the unemployed officers trying to exist on half pay: "shot out into the cold world to find a living just when they are beginning really to understand their work, and to reach the prime of life."[27] He is well-built, though inclined to stoutness, brave, and nice, which last two characteristics appear to Quatermain to be typical of Royal Navy officers: "I fancy it is just the wide seas and the breath of God's winds that wash their hearts and blow the bitterness out of their minds and make them what men ought to be."[28] He accompanies his friend Curtis to southern Africa out of sheer companionship, and to East Africa because he fears that he is getting too fat and lazy living a life of wealth and leisure in England.

Since Rider Haggard was a dedicated imperialist, and in his later career got involved in such schemes as soldier settlement in various parts of the empire, it is interesting to note the extent of imperial advancement advocated by the three adventurers of two of his most popular novels. In *King Solomon's Mines* the travelers arrive at the land of the Kukuana, a Zulu-like people, though somewhat more formally organized, who inhabit a remote area of Central Africa, substantially free from contact with the outside world. Here they assist Umbopa, one of their servants, and a Kukuana in exile, to regain his rightful position as ruler of Kukuanaland. In *Allan Quatermain* the remote region they penetrate to is that of the Zu-Vendis, a warlike, civilized white people who also have had little contact with the outside world, perhaps for a longer period than the Kukuana. Sir Henry Curtis marries Nyleptha and becomes King-Consort of the Zu-Vendis. Having reached these out-of-the-way places, the adventurers do not open them up to the world, not even to the glories of the British Empire. Umbopa/Ignosi, grateful though he has been for the intervention of his white friends, announces that:

No other white men shall cross the mountains, even if any man live to come so far. I will see no traders with their guns and gin. My people shall fight with the spear, and drink water, like their forefathers before them. I will have no praying-men to put the fear of death into men's hearts, to stir them up against the law of the king, and make a path for the white folks who follow to run on. If a white man comes to my gates I will send him back; if a hundred come I will push them back; if armies come I will make war on them with all my strength, and they shall not prevail against me. None shall ever seek for the shining stones; no, not an army, for if they come I will send a regiment and fill up the pit, and break down the white columns in the caves and choke them with rocks."[29]

This was a verdict on white civilization, even one dominated by the British Empire, by an African native who has grown up in the midst of it.

Similarly, Sir Henry Curtis, now ruler of Zu-Vendis, announces his plans:

There is one more thing that I intend to devote myself to, and that is the total exclusion of all foreigners from Zu-Vendis. . . . I do not say this from any sense of inhospitality, but I am convinced of the sacred duty that rests upon me of preserving to this, on the whole, upright and generous-hearted people the blessings of comparative barbarism. Where would all my brave army be if some enterprising rascal were to attack us with field-guns and Martini-Henrys? I cannot see that gunpowder, telegraphs, steam, daily newspapers, universal suffrage, etc., etc., have made mankind one whit the happier than they used to be, and I am certain that they have brought many evils in their train. I have no fancy for handing over this beautiful country to be torn and fought for by speculators, tourists, politicians and teachers, whose voice is the voice of Babel, . . . nor will I endow it with the greed, drunkenness, new diseases, gunpowder, and general demoralization which chiefly mark the progress of civilization among unsophisticated peoples.[30]

Thus did an English gentleman react to the blessings of civilization that could come in the train of British administrators fulfilling the white-man's burden.

So if Rider Haggard's adventurers are not the pioneers of civilization as most imperialists would envision it, what advances did they bring to Kukuanaland and Zu-Vendis? From Ignosi they got the promise that he would "'rule justly,'" "'respect the law,'" and "'put none to death without a cause,'"[31] aspects of what Rider Haggard would consider the best of what Britain had to offer to the world.[32] Sir Henry Curtis and Captain Good were left to create a navy in Zu-Vendis, which would tame the warlike tribes by introducing the calming effects of commerce. Sir

Henry would attempt to centralize the government, thereby ending the factional strife that had often led to civil war in the past; he would also suppress as much as possible the indigenous priesthood, a constant "source of political danger" the removal of which "will pave the road for the introduction of true religion in the place of this senseless Sun worship."[33] Since he proposed to isolate the country, it is hard to see how he would recruit the missionaries to Christianize his country. Civilization, as Haggard envisioned it brought to these remote places, would be stripped of its modern technological accretions, and reduced to a few basic principles, which, if properly applied, would re-create a type of Garden of Eden, from which the serpent must assiduously be excluded. This is, of course, one of the dangers of imperialism as brought by Buchan's breed of adventurers; they are so isolated from the delights of civilization by the inclination that sends them into the wilderness that they might not desire to be the pathfinders for a lifestyle that they themselves have scorned.

Herbert Strang was a composite author, being the two writers George Herbert Ely and James L'Estrange, who collaborated for more than thirty years, beginning in 1903. In many ways Strang's heroes exhibited the best qualities demanded in Buchan from an adventurer/hero/imperialist. A leading example of such a sterling creation is found in *Tom Burnaby*, first published in 1903.[34]

Tom Burnaby is eighteen years old, recently orphaned, with the ambition of entering the army as an officer, but because of a lack of money, he ends up in an engineering office. When he learns that an uncle has been appointed to command an expedition in Uganda, his military ambitions revive, and he takes passage to East Africa, only to find that Uncle Jack is not at all pleased to see him and insists that he return to his job. Before Tom can return, however, he learns from a young African, Mbutu, that his uncle's expedition is marching into an Arab-led ambush. Though his uncle has several days head start, Tom pursues the expedition and catches it in time to warn his uncle and participate in the battle that destroys the ambush.

At the end of the battle Tom is wounded, captured by the Arabs, and finally rescued by Mbutu. They escape into the forest, evade Arab pursuers and the deadly pygmies, and fight starvation and fever. In the course of their wanderings, they rescue a chieftain fleeing from slavers, and the chieftain takes them eventually to his village, where Tom slowly recovers from the effects of his wound, fever, and deprivation, only to find that it is a case of out of the frying pan into the fire. The village is threatened by an attack of numerous, well-armed Arab slavers and their African allies. Tom, out of a sense of gratitude, and also out of a sense of that noblesse oblige that is a characteristic of the adventurer hero of the fiction of the period (but not just fiction; Eldred Pottinger had stopped in Herat to help thwart an invasion by the Persians[35]) undertakes to organize the defense. Stockades and trenches are built, and pits dug. When the attack comes, Tom personally leads a section of the defenders in defeating the initial attempt to overwhelm the village; when the Arabs settle down to a siege, Tom cleverly engineers the diversion of a large reservoir of water to destroy the Arab camp, and repulses and disperses the attackers.

Unfortunately, in the last skirmish the chieftain of the village is killed. The villagers now turn to the young man whom they acknowledge as their savior to take the place of their dead leader, and to save them once again from the vengeance that the Arabs were sure to seek. Tom, for his part, is eager to return to civilization, to assure his uncle and his friends that he is not dead, and to resume whatever career that fate has in store for him. What were his obligations? After "serious thought" he decided that the villagers really needed him, despite his limited military experience.[36] He stays, but not as chief; he would hold office in the name of the young brother of the previous chief, and relinquish it as soon as the crisis was over.

In true hero/adventurer style, Tom now undertakes to reorganize an African society to meet an external threat. This time it is not simply a matter of building stockades. He drills the warriors into disciplined regiments—a portion of them are trained in the use of firearms as they are captured from the enemy; he learns how to make gunpowder and to manufacture grenades. He persuades most of the neighboring villages that unity against the Arabs is required, and then incorporates their men into his defense system. All in all, he performs an impressive amount of military organization for an eighteen-year-old boy whose previous military experience had been in the cadet corps of his school. With the forces that he has organized Tom not only beats back and destroys the attacking forces as they come, but counterattacks and captures and destroys the stronghold from which the slavers had terrorized their neighbors for so long. He now has the total adulation of the people he has saved. As the katikiro of the tribe, Msala, explained to Tom's uncle once Tom had returned to civilization: "'He will be to us a Good Spirit, to hearten us against Magaso, and Irungo, and all the other evil spirits who blight our crops and steal our cattle. He will be even as the Buchwezi, the spirits of our ancestors, whom we do not see, but who nevertheless see us and watch our doings and maybe help us in our hour of need.'"[37] Unlike the hero/adventurers of Rider Haggard, Tom Burnaby has not sought to isolate his Africans but has begun bringing them into the modern life of the twentieth century, and his memory would be sure to bring them even farther down the road. In the meantime, Tom returns to Britain, not to the engineering works, but to contemplate his future as an imperialist, with offers from Rhodesia, from Nigeria, and from King Leopold of the Congo Free State. And though he has fallen in love, it is obvious that love will not keep him safe in England, because adventure will send him to the frontiers of Africa, where he will once again risk his life in the service of people whose simplicity would insist that even a very young Englishman was a decided asset to have in their midst to assist in the very grim business of survival.

In 1910, John Buchan published *Prester John*, his first novel after *A Lodge in the Wilderness*. The hero of this story is David Crawfurd, who abandons his studies at the University of Edinburgh at the death of his father because the lack of money makes it necessary that he immediately set about making his living. Even this necessity does not immediately turn David's inclinations toward the colonies; an uncle takes him in hand and tells him that with his training he can only hope in Britain for the position of a lowly clerk, but in the colonies great possibilities existed. This useful uncle secures for him a position as assistant storekeeper in Blauwildebeestefontein in southern Africa. Launched by this on the great adventure of his life, David "felt the loneliness of an exile,"[38] and suffers from acute homesickness, hardly the sentiments that Buchan had touted for the adventurer/imperialist of his earlier book. And, in fact, David Crawfurd never does become such an adventurer.

In the adventure related in *Prester John* David is presented as being alert, curious, and intelligent, especially when he finds himself in the midst of the conspiracy that was to result in a great black rebellion centered around the Reverend John Laputa. He is also adventuresome and brave, and when recruited by the army intelligence officer, Captain Arcoll, he is willing to take dangerous risks, eavesdropping on conspirators and even attending a secret meeting of the rebels in a cave where Laputa accepts the mantle of Prester John in his effort to free the black population from European domination. He then sets in motion the events that ultimately lead to the thwarting of Prester John, his death, and the defeat of his rebellion. Having accomplished all this, David does not turn into a Sir Edward Considine, or a Colonel Alastair Graham, dedicating his life to adventure in the cause of empire, or even a Tom Burnaby, dedicated to preserve and better those that needed to be weaned from following false prophets such as Prester John. Instead, the now wealthy David returns to the University of Edinburgh to finish his education, and when invited by a friend to see the fruits of civilization working among the black population in whose lives he had so dramatically intervened, he does not leap at the chance, but merely, gravely, records "I am thinking seriously of taking Wardlaw's advice."[39]

The imperialists of the Victorian and Edwardian period felt that it was they who defined their age. If the necessity for the British Empire was not as clear to everyone as it was to them, it was because too much fuzzy thinking was abroad in the land, and it was the job of the imperial writers to sharpen the focus and to create images that were irrefutable. Basically, anybody could be an imperialist; with all the optimism of the philosophers of the Age of Enlightenment who believed that progress would result from reason and knowledge, the imperial propagandists were convinced that knowledge and reason would create imperialists. Though an analysis of the adventurer/hero/imperialist as presented by individual writers reveals some basic differences in the images of these providers of the engine power of the empire, there are very substantial similarities. They are mainly young, vigorous, and carefree. They are all doers of things. Like Kipling's Stalky, they are meant to be emulated. Many of the authors, from Marryat to Buchan, were frequently reprinted, often in cheaper editions, and their books were given as prizes and gifts to the boys who were expected to value the examples set by such role models of Britain and the British Empire. And no matter what these boys ended up doing with their lives, when they expressed their imperialism, perhaps in their minds they were the adventurers whose exploits they had so closely followed.

NOTES

1. *A Lodge*, vii.
2. Ibid., 101.
3. Ibid.
4. Ibid., 102.

5. Ibid., 103.

6. Ibid.

7. Ibid.

8. Ibid., 104.

9. Ibid.

10. Rudyard Kipling, "The English Flag."

11.For example, the young heroes have a total lack of reverence for the games that had become so large a part of public school life.

12. *Stalky & Co.*, 208.

13. Ibid.

14. Ibid., 60.

15. Ibid., 280.

16. Philip Woodruff [Philip Mason], *The Men Who Ruled India*, Vol. 2, *The Guardians* (London: Jonathan Cape, 1963), 75–76.

17. *Stalky & Co.,* 296.

18. In *For Name and Fame, The Treasure of the Incas, By Sheer Pluck, A Final Reckoning, The Dash for Khartoum*, and *The Tiger of Mysore.*

19. *With Roberts to Pretoria: A Tale of the South African War* (London: Blackie & Son, 1902).

20. *Maori and Settler*, 351.

21. *The Young Fur Traders* and *Black Ivory.*

22. *With Cochrane the Dauntless,* 308–10.

23. R. M Ballantyne, *Black Ivory*, 389–90.

24. *King Solomon's Mines* and *Allan Quatermain.*

25. *Allan Quatermain*, 5.

26. Ibid., 3.

27. *King Solomon's Mines*, 26.

28. Ibid.

29. Ibid., 244.

30. *Allan Quatermain*, 276–77.

31. *King Solomon's Mines*, 243.

32. Kent Fedorowich, "H. Rider Haggard: The Spirit of Empire," 57.

33. *Allan Quatermain*, 276.

34. *Tom Burnaby* (London: Oxford University Press, 1929).

35. George Pottinger, *The Afghan Connection: The Extraordinary Adventures of Major Eldred Pottinger* (Edinburgh: Scottish Academic Press, 1983), Chapters 3 and 4.

36. *Tom Burnaby*, 223–24.

37. Ibid., 354.

38. *Prester John,* 32.

39. Ibid., 237.

11

Conclusion: The Rose-Colored Vision

The world of imperial fiction writers had very few stylists whose prose sparkled with wit, innovation, and flair. Ballantyne could manage brief passages, Rider Haggard occasionally whole books. Buchan, as long as he stuck to the narrow path of his thrillers, was entertaining; his most stylish book was not imperialist.[1] Kipling was almost always good, and, from time to time, he was outstanding—very few writers could equal his ability to stimulate the imagination with a few evocative phrases or passages.[2] On the other hand, writers like Kingston and Henty wrote bland and uninspiring prose—the inspiration in their books came from content, not style. Despite this, for a long period the pedestrian efforts of imperialist writers met with considerable success, and adults continuously bought them as gifts for their youth. This is because these works, as well as the more stylish productions of their imperialist contemporaries, with their rose-colored images gave comfort for the minds of young and old alike in an age of aggressive imperialism.

Both the principle and the process of imperialism can be disturbing, even to the imperial power. Would someone question the right of one people to rule over another—the absolute moral right? Would someone, after the euphoria of victory had passed, question the statistics of the victory? Eleven thousand Dervishes died at the Battle of Omdurman in 1899, compared with a mere handful of British and Egyptians.[3] Did anyone want to think seriously about the morality of taking pride in a victory so one-sided? In an age of increasing literacy a greater proportion of the population either knew about such problems of being an imperial power, or had the possibility of knowing. This literacy both created the potential uneasiness and provided the potential antidote. The literature of imperialism, with its endlessly repeated themes about the value and the rightness of what was happening on the world scene, met the desire to feel comfortable with the circumstances, in the same way that Ian Fleming's James Bond stories sorted out the good guys and the bad guys of the Cold War period and showed that the good guys, after many tribulations, could emerge on top.

Victorian writers in general, especially those who can be judged as producing literature of a high quality, cannot be accused of constantly wearing rose-colored spectacles when they looked at their world. Many of their works were not designed for comfort and are full of the expressions of human weaknesses—jealousy, greed, overweening ambition, spite, and pettiness—to name a few. They produced even darker visions, of disease, degeneracy, and madness. The author of *Treasure Island*, Robert Louis Stevenson, also wrote *The Strange Case of Dr. Jekyll and Mr. Hyde*. Arthur Conan Doyle, who wrote a boys' book of rousing historical adventure, *The White Company*, also wrote the extremely popular Sherlock Holmes stories, with their frequent themes of insanity, degeneracy, and pure evil. Bram Stoker's *Dracula* thrilled and frightened Victorians as much as movies based on the novel have excited twentieth-century moviegoers. So if the writers of imperial novels presented their images of empire at a different end of the light spectrum, they felt they had ample reason for doing so.

First of all, they were writing, usually, about the young and for the young. Their stories might be violent, but life was violent, and otherwise they hit upon all the right themes—faith, courage, comradeship, duty, honor, truth, and all the other virtues that the young were to be taught to admire and emulate. In the process they succeeded, for a time, in tying these virtues to British imperialism. This was deliberate, but it was not hypocrisy. The conjunction appeared to be overwhelmingly appropriate.

British imperialism did appear to many as the apotheosis of the happy ending to human endeavor. Britain might, at home, be suffering from all the effects, bad and good, of the industrial revolution, the emergence of a class struggle, changes in political power balances, and real crises of faith, of which the reaction to the theories of Charles Darwin is but one example. But, at least on the surface, the British did seem to be doing something right in the world, and that was in their empire. The writers of the twentieth century, including colonials and postcolonials, might see this as a delusion, and treat it as scathingly as Charles Dickens had often flayed the British middle class, but there is every indication that the imperial writers believed in what they wrote, to the extent that much of their image of imperialism was not only comfortable, but was presented almost casually, as a given, and not needing further explanation.

John Buchan's *A Lodge in the Wilderness* is one of the few books from this period that is overtly imperialist, in that most of it concentrates on an apology for imperialism and schemes for strengthening the existing empire. It, however, is not a book that would end up in the Christmas stockings of the young, or even on the must-read lists of ordinary purchasers of novels—it is not a gripping tale of adventure. What it does is provide some mental comforts to serious intellectuals of Buchan's own ilk, people who were parlor imperialists rather than those who got their hands dirty poking around the corners of the world and serving the role of pathfinders that Buchan so admired. There are from this period a number of far better representatives of an imperialist adventure genre that presented the sometimes questionable activities of the imperialists in a palatable light.

Rider Haggard's *King Solomon's Mines*, which has retained its appeal for more than a century since its publication, is not an example of "gung-ho let's expand the empire" literature. In fact, at the end, one of the principal characters, Ignosi, explicitly rejects future contact with the British Empire,[4] and Rider Haggard is so much in agreement with this sentiment that he repeats it in the sequel, *Allan Quatermain*, though this time it is expressed by an Englishman, Sir Henry Curtis, the new king of Zu-Vendis.[5] It does, however, contain many of the elements that made the imperial adventure stories so popular.

Rider Haggard wrote *King Solomon's Mines*, his first successful novel, under the inspiration of the recently published best-seller *Treasure Island*.[6] And so his book is ultimately, despite deviations into all sorts of vigorous and warlike adventures, the story of a hunt for treasure, and what a treasure it is! Piles of ivory, boxes of gold, and chests of diamonds amaze and pale the adventurers. When the treasure chamber becomes a death trap sprung by the ancient witch Gagool, the treasure loses a great deal of its luster, but when a chance of escape presents itself, the ever prudent Allan Quatermain fills his pockets and a picnic basket with diamonds, most of which, delivered to a London jeweler, are declared to be "'of the finest water, and equal in every way to the best Brazilian stones.'"[7] They are of a quantity and quality that makes three men enormously wealthy.[8] The book, being written in such an authentic and authoritative manner, solidified the reputation of the "Dark Continent" as a treasure house waiting to be plundered. *King Solomon's Mines* also illustrates the humanitarian aspects of much of this type of literature, with heroic Englishmen helping those less fortunate than they. In this case, the adventuresome trio save the maiden Foulata from ritual sacrifice, and are duly rewarded when she gives her life trying to save theirs in the treasure cavern.[9] More to the point, when they leave the Kukuanas, having helped their former servant gain his rightful position as king, Quatermain reminds Ignosi of the promise he has made "'to rule justly, to respect the law, and to put none to death without a cause.'"[10] Other peoples have admirable characteristics, but the British had an instinct for helping all sorts of people who so obviously needed the help.

Like all imperial heroes, Quatermain, Curtis, and Good face death many times, but none so impressively as in the great civil war for control of Kukuanaland. Not only do they actively participate in this struggle of armies numbering in the thousands, numbers so great that the firearms the Englishmen carry make little if any difference to the outcome, but Curtis becomes a Viking warrior, fighting in the forefront of the elite Greys regiment, using the weapons of the Kukuana. And in the last act of this drama, taunted by the defeated king Twala, Curtis proves his courage in single, victorious combat against a formidable opponent who could attack recklessly because he has nothing to lose and vengeance to gain. The illustration of courage is more impressive in that Quatermain, Curtis, and Good are three different physical types; courage is a obviously a characteristic of Englishmen in general, and not of Englishmen of particular physical endowments, a comforting concept to the subscribers of imperial doctrine. In the sequel, *Allan Quatermain*, Haggard enhances the portrayal of their courage even further by making the trio the leaders, rather than simply co-fighters, in a similar civil war in Zu-Vendis. Taking the courageous responsibility of leadership, in fact, became in imperial literature the typical response of battling Englishmen to crises, and is illustrated in such books as Henty's *The Dash for Khartoum* and Strang's *Tom Burnaby*.

King Solomon's Mines was an imaginative adventure story, full of ingenuity, and the illustration of the most positive aspects of the careers of the pathfinders that carried the British name into the remote regions of the world. It provided a comforting justification for the presence of the British in places like southern Africa, and left the suggestion that the emerging imperial dogma had valuable substance. By the time that John Buchan found himself in South Africa, in the aftermath of the Boer War, such suggestions and such comfort proved to be more necessary than ever, a necessity emphasized by the now more frequent outbursts of anti-imperialism by talented writers.

Robert Ballantyne's *Coral Island* is another book from this period that is not only written with style and wit, but has an endearing plot that has made it a perennial favorite. Unlike *King Solomon's Mines*, it does not have the central lure of great wealth within its pages—the three young middle-class sailors who are its heroes emerge from their adventure having gained only the pirate schooner on which they sail home to England at the end—but it does have at its heart the almost idyllic life on a coral island. As the narrator, "Ralph Rover," notes in the preface, it was a "wonderful adventure,"[11] the type to be constantly revisited in nostalgic recollection, and the type to continually stimulate the imaginations of young readers who could identify with the ingenuity of three boys surviving, and surviving very well, on a "desert island." It was not overtly an imperial adventure in that no territory was acquired for the British Empire—when the boys sailed away from their coral island, they were never to return. What the novel did instead was illustrate the characteristics that would be assumed by the heroes of the more frankly imperial stories.

Very important is the quality of leadership. Jack Martin is a leader not only because he is older and stronger than the other two, but because he has common sense and a fund of knowledge accorded to him by his education. He also has reckless courage; he is fully prepared to lead the charge on behalf of the weaker side of the two parties of natives that landed on the island, and he suggests that the boys sail off to rescue the girl Avatea from an unwanted marriage, just like "true knights."[12] The pirate captain is also a leader, one of the few examples in imperial boys' fiction of an Englishman who is strong, courageous, a leader, and evil as well. His men followed him because "he was a lion-like villain, totally devoid of personal fear, and utterly reckless of consequences, and therefore a terror to his men, who individually hated him, but unitedly felt it to be to their advantage to have him at their head."[13] But to Ballantyne, undoubtedly the most impressive leader is the English missionary who almost single-handedly converts an island tribe and rescues the boys from dark and dangerous confinement. He is "an English gentleman. . . . The expression of his countenance was the most winning I ever saw, and his clear gray eye beamed with a look that was frank, fearless, loving, and truthful."[14] With men such as these it was no wonder that the British were making such a major impact on the Pacific islanders.

Rudyard Kipling's *Kim* is one of the best of the imperial novels and there is no doubt about its pro-Empire message. It is a story, or more accurately a series of stories surrounding the central character, that is dominated by mood and memorable characters and incidents. Kim is an Irish orphan, an imp thoroughly acquainted with the Indian milieu in which he has been raised; of the major persona, most of the other effective and finely drawn characters, the lama, Mahbub Ali, the Sahiba, and Hurree Babu, are Asiatics. Only Colonel Creighton and the shadowy Strickland play the roles normally assigned to the English in this type of adventure novel. Because the majority of the participants in this action drama are well worked out, *Kim* has an air of reality; it appears to be a story about real people who are also almost overwhelmingly exotic, a combination that helps to explain the lasting appeal of this book. Kipling also surrounds his people with a series of mood-portraying descriptions that bring the reader into complete involvement with the action.

Kim illustrates the positive aspects of the imperial story, in contrast to the novel published almost at the same time, Joseph Conrad's *Lord Jim*.[15] Conrad sets the mood of his novel with passages such as the one that begins Chapter Three: "A marvellous stillness pervaded the world, and the stars, together with the serenity of their rays, seemed to shed upon the earth the assurance of ever-lasting security."[16] Throughout the novel the stillness becomes almost oppressive, and illustrates profoundly Conrad's resolute conviction that imperialism in the real world, as opposed to the world of fiction, is not exciting.[17] Kipling on the other hand fills his landscape with life and enhances his descriptions with the "magic" of his language, which, in *Something of Myself*, he acknowledges as special,[18] particularly in relation to his account of the journey of Kim and the lama along the Grand Trunk Road, the "broad, smiling river of life."[19] The description is so authentic in detail, and the sense that Kipling is writing about reality is so fully realized, that the impact begins to cross the borders of such reality into the realm of magic.

To use the word "magic" when speaking about an imperial adventure novel may seem to be out of place, but it is an accurate depiction of the experience of *Kim,* and by analogy, of much of the image created by the literature of imperialism late in the Victorian period. Magic depends on creating an illusion, and sustaining it in a way that will convince the viewer that what is being seen is reality. It does not bear deep thinking about because any systematic examination will at least suggest the misdirection; reason and logic are often so hostile to magic. Kipling critic Martin Seymour-Smith says that *Kim* "tends to lose its appeal . . . the more it is *thought* about."[20] That, of course, is the point of the book and why it has been so popular; a book dominated by magic and mood is not meant to be *thought* about. It is meant to be felt, and in this particular case the predominant feeling is of the rightness of the situation in which an Irish waif raised in India undergoes a series of adventures ultimately dedicated to the preservation of the British connection with India on the grounds of its value to the Indians.

If *Kim* does not have a prominent character who exhibits the heroic, and British, qualities of the boys in most imperial stories, it still does not lack some reinforcement of the main themes of such stories. Most prominent is the humanitarian aspect, where, apart from the general emphasis of the value of "the Great Game," in which Kim was trained to participate, for the stability and well-being of the Indian population, Kim performs individual humanitarian acts such as his treatment of the feverish Jat child. It is true that Kim's motives are mixed and that he is showing off his abilities and training to the lama, but the important thing is that he has the training and ability to do good, to bear "The White Man's Burden" of Kipling's earlier, less fortunate terminology.[21] In addition there are the numerous illustrations of courage, in the natives as well as in the whites. Hurree Babu, despite his disclaimers, is obviously a very brave man, as revealed in a depiction that goes against the stereotyped image of the Bengali which existed not only generally among the British, but more specifically in a number of Kipling's own earlier poems and stories. Kim has the thoughtless bravery of the very young, but in his first night in the establishment of the mysterious Lurgan Sahib he exhibits a courage of a higher level when in the darkness he is presented with an unknown phenomenon that "for a moment lifted the short hairs in his neck,"[22] but which he then relentlessly tracks down and destroys. Imperial heroes need this kind of courage to face the unknowns of the world; it is an excellent type of courage for young readers to identify with.

Kim is about The Great Game, and it is itself full of games, such as the game that Kim learns in Lurgan's shop—the memory game with trays of gems and collections of other articles; there is also the game in which the desperate agent hounded by his enemies is disguised and rescued by the neophyte agent, Kim, and the game played by Hurree Babu with the enemy agents on the mountain paths. These games are so distractive and attractive that it is easy to forget that Kim is one of the few imperial heroes of fiction for whom the British Isles are not "home." Home for Kim is the streets of the cities of the Punjab, and later the highways of exotic India. Home is life itself, and the exuberance of life that is so much the trademark mood of this book. All of this is evocative of the romance of Empire and casts a warm glow over an area that writers such as George Orwell and Evelyn Waugh, in a more somber age, were to bathe in harsher tones.

Rider Haggard, Ballantyne, and Kipling were the best of the imperialist writers as far as style of presentation and even plot are concerned, until the twentieth century when Buchan's *Prester John, Thirty-Nine Steps,* and *Greenmantle* established him as a writer of imperial thrillers that were the equal of the earlier writers. But the less stylish writers were still popular and even influential, and of these, G. A. Henty was perhaps the most prominent.

At first glance the Henty canon does not appear to have a great deal to recommend it. The books have numerous shortcomings as literature. The style is stiff and stilted, the humor is often ponderous, and the plot a thin thread weaving its way through extensive tracks of historical narrative. There is very little real characterization; it can be said of the various Henty boys that they are very much alike—one might be tempted to say that the same boy roams through each of the stories, with merely a change of name and some minor changes in physical appearance.[23] This might appear to be a serious drawback, and yet in fact, given Henty's other shortcomings in literary skill, it is a strength that goes a long way toward explaining Henty's popularity and the influence his books had on the imperial image.

Henty placed his boys into romantic situations that were intrinsically interesting to a generation raised in an age which saw the revival of the concepts of chivalry,[24] when deeds of bravery were much admired and to be honored. Since the boys are stereotyped, with their characteristics as individuals little more than sketched in, they can be any boy, and any boy can identify with them—become them for the period of the adventure—and be left with a memory and a sense of nostalgia for the activities the boys were engaged in. If the fictional boy is too vividly individualistic, there is a danger that the identification might not take place—it takes a writer of Kipling's exceptional skill to make Kim nevertheless a universal boy—and if the identification fails, the whole message of the book can be lost. The Henty boy/boys therefore proved to be a very useful tool in the dissemination of the ideas that were to create the image of the empire so prevalent at the end of the Victorian age. If the Henty boy can engage in such wonderful and patriotic adventures, then anyone—the twelve-year-old who got the book for Christmas or for his birthday or as a Sunday School prize—could do it. Or at least he could imagine that he could do it; print always makes the fantastic feat more feasible because only the imagination and not the eye is in play. When the imagination takes over, the reader can do things and not think too deeply about them. There need be little musing on life, on good and evil, on moral choices. Of course he will act in this way or that way, it has all been comfortably prescribed in the imperial mythology and the reader can simply tap into what he already is convinced is the moral choice; and having vicariously participated in the action, the reader can retain an affection for the institution that he has been instrumental—almost—in creating.

As realistic as many accounts of imperial actions, especially the conflicts, might have appeared to Victorian readers, they were not very graphic in comparison to the pictures of war that have become commonplace in the second half of the twentieth century through the use of motion picture and video cameras. A Henty hero might dispose of his enemies by the half-dozen, but, though death lies all around, there is not much bloodshed in the accounts. There is also very little that is personal about the deaths; unknown people die and there is little or no portrayal of the indignity of their demise.

The Victorians, of course, did have paintings, and the story-pictures of the time often portrayed scenes out of the imperial experience, including depictions of warfare and death. Though some of the pictures dwell on tragic scenes, as does Alfonse de Neuville's *Isandhlwana 1879* showing two dead officers laid out beside a dead horse, discovered by a patrol in the aftermath of the disaster to British arms at the Battle of Isandhlwana, there is usually an element of nobility present that suggests the grandeur of the death and not the degradation of it—the above officers, for example, might well be sleeping, one clutching the regimental standard, having heroically performed their duty.[25] The battle scenes are full of life and action, and the presentation of death in the midst of all this is almost incidental to the exciting sweep of what was occurring on canvas. The paintings tended, therefore, to reinforce the comforting qualities of the novels—they are, after all, constructs just as much as the narrative presentations—and illustrated vividly, in more than living color, the qualities of heroism that writers presented in their works.

When battlefield photography was introduced in the second half of the nineteenth century, it is true that a different image was often forthcoming. Unlike in the paintings, the portrayals in the photographs were seldom larger than life; indeed, the unfortunate dead truly do appear to be unfortunate and, what is more, appear to be considerably diminished, with the stillness of the scene, frozen by a camera, emphasizing the consequences of an action that appears to have turned men into bundles of rags.[26] But the impression of reality is diminished because the images of both the living and the dead appear to be stiffly posed, unnatural. The photographs also are in black and white, and therefore while they are able to give some concept of the grotesqueness of death, they are free of blood, and it is the sight and the smell of blood that create a particularly disquieting image.

There is, of course, little romance in reality. Everyone of reasonably sound mind is subject to his or her own reality and instinctively knows that this particular bit of reality is not especially romantic. It is too close to home, and reality must often be seen through a distorting lens to gain a heightened glow; someone else's reality can gain a special aura when perceived from a distance, an aura that it does not necessarily hold to whoever directly possesses it. It is hard for ordinary people to live an entire day, let alone a lifetime, in a type of daydream, and the prosaic events of life will always threaten to swamp and to isolate those exceptional moments that can give a special meaning to existence. Imperial literature is a gathering of such moments, made to appear eternal, and directed to the presentation of a particular and slanted view of the political, economic, and social processes that the British were undergoing at a particular time in their history.

Just how effective such an imperial presentation can be in reinforcing a view of the imperial experience can be seen by looking at not one of the best of the novels of G. A. Henty, but one of his poorest, *Through Three Campaigns*.[27] The story line of this novel, which Henty cobbled together near the end of his life and which was published posthumously, is rudimentary. Out of a total of just under four hundred pages of text, two hundred deal with the adventures of the hero, Lisle Bullen; the rest is largely composed of long descriptions of military campaigns. At the age of fifteen, Lisle is about to be sent to England to attend a crammer that will prepare him for gaining a commission in the army, when his father, Captain Bullen, is mortally wounded in a frontier skirmish. Instead of returning to England, Lisle, desiring to participate in the expedition that is on the point of going to the relief of the border fort of Chitral, disguises himself as a native soldier and fights in the ranks. Indeed, he fights so well and kills so many of the enemy that he soon attracts attention, and his deception is discovered by the British officers, who subsequently conspire to get him a commission immediately, despite his age. He then participates in a campaign on the Northwest frontier, during which he is awarded a Victoria Cross, and the Ashanti campaign of 1900. At the end of this last campaign, still but twenty-one years of age, he holds the rank of captain, and has added a D.S.O. to his Victoria Cross.

Through Three Campaigns is really three almost totally different stories put together, with Lisle Bullen and the army as a connecting link, but with different elements of the imperial adventure epic dominating in each. The first is a typical boys' adventure story, with a fifteen-year-old disguising himself and going off on a dangerous and arduous campaign in relief of a besieged garrison. He deceives the officers and men of his regiment because he was raised among them and could speak the language of the native soldiers; disguise and language facility are stock-in-trade of such stories, though in this case the knowledge of the language was more realistically acquired over a long period of time, and not, as in so many other instances, in a matter of a few months. The second episode features a border campaign, and the personal element is largely concentrated on incidents of capture and escape,[28] in the second of which Lisle actually earns his release by taking part in an intertribal fight on the side of his captors and, typically, taking over the organization of the defense. The third episode is set in West Africa at a time when Lisle can be said to have reached young adulthood, and apart from the descriptions of the campaigns and a few minor adventures, it mainly features a great deal of fairly humorous repartee between Lisle and another subaltern, a Lieutenant Hallett who is a few years older than he.

As perfunctory as the novel mainly is, with very little effort at original construction, by relying on standard features of the genre, Henty has created a story that would hold the interest of young imperialists, at least to a certain point. It is full of reference to impetuous and courageous youth, performing deeds that would impress even adults, all essential qualities of the daydreams of the young. There are faithful natives willing to loyally defer to their European "superiors," and natives on the opposing side who, no matter how prodigious is their own fighting spirit, must always succumb to Europeans, certainly to fighting units composed of Europeans, but also to European-led natives. Throughout there is an insistence that the British especially stood for order and civilization.

Serious writers, who wrote on such topics as politics and economics, have for several centuries tried to explain why empires exist, and the proponents of empire, such as the mercantilists, tried to explain what empires are *for*. The fiction writers of the nineteenth and early twentieth centuries also had as their underlying theme the task of explaining the uses of empire. They seldom did this as directly as Buchan does in *A Lodge in the Wilderness*, where he notes that empire exists to "create opportunity for all."[29] Even Buchan's frankly economic motivations normally apply to individuals, or small groups of individuals; that the whole nation can benefit from such opportunity is only occasionally inferred. When he attempts to talk about more general benefits, he tends to slide off into philosophy or poetry which attempts to explain that empire is good for the soul of the British people. Most writers simply let the story line of their novels spell out the advantages of empire, and as with Buchan, these advantages were usually discussed in the context of the welfare of individuals. It is the hero, his companions, and his family who benefitted when the young man migrated and settled in the colonies, or found treasure of some sort, or was amply repaid for his heroic exploits in terms of worldly wealth. In less definitely stated ways, the young man thrown into adventures in the empire benefitted morally from the experience of serving his country.

That the fiction writers should stress the individual benefits of imperialism is entirely fitting and understandable. On the most practical level, the writers wrote as an economic activity, and it would not take a great deal of thought to figure out that adventure stories inundated with abstruse discussions of the economic and political benefits of empire to the nation would not be major sellers—even Buchan did not repeat the experiment of *A Lodge in the Wilderness*. The works of most writers, as, for example, imperial thrillers such as Buchan's *Prester John* and

Greenmantle, represented the personalization of the imperial philosophy, an illustration of how it worked best on the individual level. *Greenmantle*, for all its emphasis on Richard Hannay's insistence on doing his duty to his country in the midst of the first world war, concludes in a wild charge, a "mad *finale* of a dream,"[30] which emphasizes the personal satisfaction of the whole enterprise: "That was the great hour of my life, and to live through it was worth a dozen years of slavery."[31] This personalization is what made the imperial stories both memorable and popular for so long despite the fact that much of what was written was not "literature" of the type that would be featured in literature classes of schools and universities in the twentieth century.

In their own way these novels were also sentimental. At the end of *Kim* the lama finds the river he had been seeking; we know it is a river of his mind, and not likely the perhaps mythical river that had sprung up from the spot where landed the arrow shot by the Lord Buddha, but to him it is as physically real as it is metaphysically desirable. But the success of his quest is not the end of the story, because *Kim* is not only an adventure story, it is a novel about love. At the end of the book therefore, the lama "crossed his hands on his lap and smiled, as a man may who has won Salvation for himself and his beloved."[32] The conjunction of this sentimentality with a book of rousing adventure is a particularly happy one, because the adults who bought the books for their youngsters, and often read them themselves to ensure the appropriateness of their selections, would be more affected by the sentiment than the children who read them. They would be aware that proper sentiment, portraying the "human" emotions, is being linked with another sentiment, the sentiment that makes for emotional pride in the imperial achievements of a nation.

Surprisingly, not all the major authors dealt with this kind of sentimentality. Though some of W.H.G. Kingston's books have an element of familial love, it is usually subordinate to religious belief, and there is very little in the way of the creditable expression of love of any kind. On the other hand, G. A. Henty, perhaps the most popular writer of imperial fiction for the young, often includes sentimental passages, be it brotherly love that sends Rupert Clinton in disguise through the Sudan searching for his brother Edgar,[33] or mother love expressed by a mother who faints when she finds out that her sons are still alive,[34] or a young man's love, somewhat awkwardly expressed, for the young woman who has saved his life: "'Do you not know that I love you?'"[35] Passages like these, of course, are rare in books that mainly deal with action, but they add a human and ultimately satisfying element to the stories of the individuals who were so bravely creating or maintaining an empire for Britain. When all the elements of the imperial tales have been put together, what has been created is an image of imperialism with a very personal face.

In the Victorian period British imperialism, while certainly not young, since it had been in existence at least from the sixteenth century, was full of vigor. It had rejuvenated itself within the context of the new industrial and financial society that was operating with such confidence on a worldwide basis. Part of the articulation of this rejuvenation, and contributing to the extent of it, was the imperial literature of the period. This literature might not have been an exact description of what was, politically, actually happening in the British Empire and in the process of creating empire, but it was a good indication of the spirit with which the British undertook so many of their enterprises in what was still an age of optimism. The very fact that British adults not only read such literature themselves, but positively desired their young people to read it, is an indication of how in tune with the prevailing ethos it was. It is hard to image that if it were otherwise so many of these books would be given away as Sunday School prizes.

What the literature of imperialism added to the "reality" of the imperial experience was the impression that empire was more than something "useful" in economic-mercantilist terms, or "practical" or "impractical" as viewed by bankers and statesmen; on offer was the strong conviction that empire was exciting, something to be experienced at all levels with a great deal of pleasure. Empire was not only something to give intellectual homage to, or to extend realistic appraisals of the economic potentials of, but an experience to arouse passion, a swelling of pride, an incitement to honor and duty and the development of the kind of sense of purpose that embodied the best ideals of what it meant to be British. The strongest emphasis was placed on the virtue of all that was happening, and this conviction of virtue not only buoyed the feeling of hope that was integral to the optimism of the imperial age, but contributed essentially to the feeling of satisfaction with which the ordinary Briton viewed his or her world picture.

The fact that the literature of imperialism became so intertwined with the reality of empire in the minds of the general public helped make the process of imperialism more acceptable, at a fairly superficial level. People did not think deeply about what was happening, and if they could assume that what was happening was approximately like the writers were describing it, then all was well with the British world. This assumption in turn helped to reinforce the acceptability of imperial literature as an accurate reflection of a highly desirable state-of-affairs. The political realities of empire called forth a literature of empire because what was happening needed some explanation, or rationale, and the literature in turn made the realities of the empire more palatable than naked, unvarnished accounts would have. Since the political events would have occurred anyhow—the literature of imperialism did not cause empire—the literature could be accepted, consciously or unconsciously, as a true reflection of what was happening. It was also entertaining.

Unless they are involved in the creation of sheer fantasy, the writers of an age write about what is happening, or, at least, their version of what is happening. One of the many happenings of the Victorian period and later was the development and sometimes growth of the British Empire, a process that technological innovation and increasing literacy was making apparent to all sections of the British public, but primarily to its upper and middle classes. Writers about the empire may have started out to inform and to entertain in the same way as writers about any other facet of life and experience, but along the way, perhaps because imperialism was contentious, they developed a symbiotic relationship with their subject, and as they did so, they helped change and shape public perceptions of the empire. They believed in what they wrote about, and for a considerable period of time they created images compelling enough to persuade most of their readers that the rose-colored visions they were presenting were as solid as the real thing. As the twentieth century progressed, the physical reality of empire faded away, and it became more and more apparent that the reality behind the images left behind had been less than accurately portrayed; however, the images that had been created in the heyday of empire were vivid enough that they faded less quickly than the empire itself. Because the images dealt with so many basic human emotions, pride, courage, greed, and aggression to name a few, these images still have the power to stir if not to convince. They are, after all, fiction, and it is the prerogative of fiction to create enduring pictures in the mind.

NOTES

1. *Scholar Gypsies* (London: John Lane, 1896).

2. The best example is "The Finest Story in the World," but many of his stories have such passages.

3. G. W. Steevens, *With Kitchener to Khartum*, 126–28.

4. Page 244. Ignosi rejects contact with the rest of the "civilized world" as well.

5. Pages 318–19.

6. D. S. Higgins, *Rider Haggard*, 70–71.

7. Haggard, *King Solomon's Mines,* 253.

8. Allan Quatermain, Captain Good, and Sir Henry Curtis having refused to take a share, his brother George.

9. It is important that the witch, Gagool, their most implacable enemy, is here killed because of Foulata's action.

10. Ibid., 243.

11. *The Coral Island*, Preface.

12. Ibid., 196.

13. Ibid., 143.

14. Ibid., 232.

15. *Kim* was published in 1901, and *Lord Jim* as a book in 1900.

16. *Lord Jim*, 17.

17. See the master's thesis by Sean Stilwell, "'The Merry Dance of Death and Trade': Joseph Conrad and Imperialism" (University of Saskatchewan, 1993) for a discussion of Conrad's ideas.

18. *Something of Myself: For My Friends Known and Unknown* (London: Penguin Classics, 1987 [1936]), 116–17.

19. *Kim*, 96–99.

20. *Rudyard Kipling* (London: Macdonald: Queen Anne Press, 1989), 302. This book attempts to psychoanalyze Kipling and his works, and gets somewhat obsessive about the hidden sexuality in Kipling's writings.

21. Less fortunate because this phrase has tended to cloud the assessment of Kipling and his works by many critics, and not just those of a left-wing persuasion.

22. *Kim*, 237–39.

23. For a good discussion of the Henty heroes, see Guy Arnold, *Held Fast for England*, Chapter 3.

24. See Mark Girouard, *The Return to Camelot: Chivalry and the English Gentleman*.

25. See reproduction in Jan Morris, *The Spectacle of Empire: Style, Effect and the Pax Britannica* (London: Faber & Faber, 1982), 191.

26. Ibid., 161, showing Burmese dead after the action at Minhla in 1885.

27. *Through Three Campaigns: A Story of Chitral, Tirah, and Ashanti* (London: Blackie & Son, n.d. [1904]).

28. In the course of the second such episode, Lisle earned his Victoria Cross by giving up his horse to a wounded colonel, and then calmly surrendering to the charging tribesmen while the other officer made his escape. All other information about Lisle suggests that he would not surrender without a fight, but of course, this would not suit the dramatic purposes of Henty's plot.

29. *A Lodge*, 157.

30. John Buchan, *Greenmantle* (London: T. Nelson & Sons, 1945 [1916]), 375.

31. Ibid., 374.

32. Page 463.

33. In *The Dash for Khartoum*.

34. In *The Young Colonists: A Story of the Zulu and Boer Wars* (London: Blackie & Son, n.d. [1885]).

35. In *With Lee in Virginia*, 250.

Imperial Postscript

John Buchan's last imperial novel was *Sick Heart River*.[1] Published at the beginning of World War II, at a time when Buchan, now Lord Tweedsmuir, was Governor-General of Canada, it is almost unique as an imperialist work in that the personal element is emphasized almost to the point of the exclusion of the adventure elements. Sir Edward Leithen, one of the stable of main characters from Buchan's earlier thrillers, just as Britain's relationships with Nazi Germany were sliding into war, finds that he has tuberculosis, and that the illness will likely be fatal. It is with this death sentence hanging over him that Leithen launches into his final adventure.

Answering an appeal from a friend, and in the hope of taking his mind off his growing weakness, Leithen takes on the task of tracking down a French Canadian, Francis Galliard, who had made a name for himself as a financier in the United States, but had left his wife and associates and disappeared. Following clues found on a visit to the region of Quebec where Galliard had been born and raised, Leithen sets out for the Canadian North, here presented in such stark and vivid terms that it is almost personified. Leithen is accompanied by a Scots/Métis guide, Johnny Frizel, whose brother, coincidentally, was guiding for Galliard. They follow closely in the footsteps of the earlier party, until they are heading for Sick Heart River, flowing through an almost mythical valley with which Lew Frizel is obsessed, because of its supposed qualities of providing magical things, perhaps even cures for sick souls. And it is exactly a sick soul that Francis Galliard, afraid that he has betrayed his heritage, is suffering from. Leithen and Johnny Frizel ultimately rescue Galliard, who has been abandoned by the by-now half mad Lew, and Leithen, accompanied by an Indian, rescues Lew from the valley of the Sick Heart River, which is really a death trap. Then the whole party is snowbound in the wilderness; in the clear atmosphere of the North, nourished by wild game and nursed tenderly by Lew, Leithen eventually is on the road to restored health. Up to this point, apart from an excessive amount of introspective musing by the hero, this is a typical adventure story.

The novel does not end here. On the way back to civilization, Leithen, Galliard, and the Frizels pass through a village of the Hare Indians, where an illness, in large part psychological, is threatening to destroy the whole native population. Conscripted by the local missionary, and at the serious risk to the health of the barely recovering Leithen, the party sets to work to rescue the almost helpless natives. Leithen is in command—as what imperial hero would not be?—and he almost literally works himself to death in the service of a people that have been described in very unflattering terms as pitifully weak and almost irremediably superstitious. This is a serious departure from the adventure story, for imperial heroes seldom actually die. The insistence, however, on the leadership qualities of the British hero, and the weakness of the native population, which has physical bravery among its prime characteristics and a good deal of wilderness survival skill, but lacks the ability to pull itself out of a desperate situation without British help,[2] is absolutely standard adventure-novel fare.

Ultimately as an imperial adventure story, *Sick Heart River* is a failure because it has become too introspective; it asks too many questions about whether this or that action by Leithen is really worth doing, and though it does not ask such questions about the empire, it sets the stage for those questions to be asked after the immediate crisis of world war. Even though the imperial hero saves the Hares from the psychological death-trap in which they had become mired, it is all too easy to see that the civilization that the empire has brought to these people is in some way responsible for their dilemmas. The preWorld War I imperial novels would not have asked questions of these kinds, because the values expressed in these novels are as yet unchallenged by a major portion of the literate public. Therefore, *Sick Heart River* is more satisfying as literature than as a defense of the rationale of empire such as Buchan had expounded back in 1906 with *A Lodge in the Wilderness*.

What Buchan was making obvious in 1941 was that empire had its costs, and that these costs could be high. Buchan's hero in *Sick Heart River* spent most of the book being mortally weary, and this weariness could be a metaphor for imperialism in a period when Britain was facing a major war for the second time in a generation, and the outcome was not all that clear. The enthusiastic assurances of the earlier period no longer seemed to be appropriate; the emphasis had decidedly shifted from the invigorating action of the imperial epic to the deadly duty associated with the responsibility of empire. A poem published some ten years earlier than *Sick Heart River* in *Blackie's Boys' Annual* has much the same message as Kipling's "The White Man's Burden."[3] The last two stanzas are:

Old England's breed, they roam away
    Far from her island shore:
One glimpse of cliffs and clustered homes,
    Then out ... to Nevermore.

But when the last long role is called,
    And men are weighed and tried,
These ragged, tattered, unknown men
    God's hand will touch with pride.

Though the themes of the two poems are similar, the spirit is much different. Jackson's poem is not only more complacent, it is at the same time more melancholy. There is far less bounce to it than there had been in Kipling's poem. Already the imperial England that Jackson was writing about was "The Weary Titan," not old, but tired, with impulse for further imperial expansion considerably dimmed.

Imperial literature had a long run and only went into real decline after World War II. Not that the empire was no longer being written about. John Masters' books on India, though not motivated by the same pro-empire sentiment, certainly maintained the standard of rousing adventure.[4] Paul Scott's books on the decline of the Raj in India gave an excellent view of the splendor as well as the imperfections of the imperial structure.[5] The real successors of the imperial novels in the present period have been the essays in nostalgia, such as Jan Morris's *The Spectacle of Empire*,[6] and *Heroes for Victoria*,[7] by John Duncan and John Walton. Profusely illustrated, such books recall a bygone age when important things happened in Britain's relationship to the rest of the world, and these important happenings reflected a period of time when Britain counted in the world power structure. They are a perpetuation of the images of an imperial age that for a time gave a great deal of satisfaction, both in its real and in its fictional representations, to a great many people who could not escape the feeling that something special was going on, and that in some ways that special occurrence was creditable, and even heroic.

NOTES

1. John Buchan, *Sick Heart River* (Toronto: Musson Book Co., 1941). In the United States it was published as *Mountain Meadow*.

2. It required someone British to lead the rescue mission rather than just a European. In the village also were the missionary, who was French, Galliard, a French Canadian, and the Frizel brothers, who had a Scottish father but a Cree mother. Only the Scot, Leithen, really qualified for this leadership role.

3. P. Hoole Jackson,"Men," n.d. but probably 1930.

4. For example, *Night Runners of Bengal*, 1951, *The Deceivers*, 1952, and *Bhowani Junction*, 1954.

5. For example, *The Raj Quartet*, consisting of *The Jewel in the Crown*, 1966; *The Day of the Scorpion*, 1968; *The Towers of Silence*, 1971; and *A Division of Spoils*, 1975.

6. *The Spectacle of Empire: Style, Effect and the Pax Britannica* (London: Faber & Faber, 1982).

7. *Heroes for Victoria* (Tunbridge Wells, Kent: Spellmount, 1991).

Bibliography

PRIMARY SOURCES

Books

A.L.O.E. *War and Peace. A Tale of the Retreat from Caubul*. London: T. Nelson & Sons, 1879.

Avery, Harold. *Soldiers of the Queen*. London: T. Nelson & Sons, n.d.

Ballantyne, Robert M. *Black Ivory: A Tale of Adventure Among the Slavers of East Africa*. London: James Nisbet & Co., n.d. [1873].

———. *Blown to Bits, or The Lonely Man of Rakata: A Tale of the Malay Archipelago*. London: James Nisbet & Co., 1894.

———. *Blue Lights, or Hot Work in the Soudan*. London: James Nisbet & Co., n.d. [1888].

———. *The Buffalo Runners: A Tale of the Red River Plains*. London: James Nisbet & Co., n.d.

———. *The Coral Island*. London: T. Nelson & Sons, n.d. [1857].

———. *The Crew of the Water Wagtail: A Story of Newfoundland*. London: James Nisbet & Co., n.d.

———. *Deep Down: A Tale of the Cornish Mines*. London: T. Nelson & Sons, n.d. [1868].

———. *The Dog Crusoe*. London: Abbey Classics, 1970.

———. *Fighting the Flames: A Tale of the London Fire Brigade*. London: Ward, Lock & Co., n.d. [1867].

———. *Gascoyne: The Sandal-wood Trader, A Tale of the Pacific*. London: Blackie & Son, n.d.

———. *The Golden Dream: Adventures in the Far West*. London: James Nisbet & Co., n.d.

———. *The Gorilla Hunters: A Tale of the Wilds of Africa*. London: T. Nelson & Sons, 1897.

———. *Hudson's Bay, or Every-Day Life in the Wilds of North America During Six Years Residence in the Territories of the Honourable Hudson's Bay Company*. Rutland, Vt: C. E. Tuttle Co., 1972 [1848].

————. *The Iron Horse, or Life on the Line: A Tale of the Grand National Trunk Railway.* London: James Nisbet & Co., 1871.

————. *The Lifeboat: A Tale of Our Coast Heroes.* London: James Nisbet & Co., 1864.

————. *The Lighthouse: A Story of a Great Fight Between Man and the Sea.* London: Blackie & Son, n.d. [1865].

————. *The Madman and the Pirate.* London: James Nisbet & Co., n.d.

————. *Martin Rattler.* London: Collins, n.d.

————. *Philosopher Jack: A Tale of the Southern Seas.* London: James Nisbet & Co., 1879.

————. *The Pirate City: An Algerine Tale.* London: James Nisbet & Co., 1887.

————. *The Prairie Chief: A Tale.* London: James Nisbet & Co., 1886.

————. *The Settler and the Savage: A Tale of Peace and War in South Africa.* London: James Nisbet & Co., n.d. [1877].

————. *Six Months at the Cape, or Letters to Periwinkle from South Africa.* London: James Nisbet & Co., 1880.

————. *Ungava: A Tale of Esquimaux Land.* London: Ward, Lock & Co., n.d.

————. *The Young Fur Traders, or Snowflakes and Sunbeams: A Tale of the Far North.* London: Blackie & Son, n.d. [1856].

Barrie, James M. *Peter and Wendy.* London: Hodder & Stoughton, 1911.

Bowman, Anne. *The Boy Voyagers, or The Pirates of the East.* London: George Routledge & Sons, n.d.

————. *The Castaways.* London: George Routledge & Sons, n.d.

Brereton, Capt. Frederick S. *One of the Fighting Scouts: A Tale of Guerrilla Warfare in South Africa.* London: Blackie & Son, n.d.

————. *With Roberts to Candahar: A Tale of the Third Afghan War.* London: Blackie & Son, n.d.

————. *With Shield and Assegai: A Tale of the Zulu War.* London: Blackie & Son, n.d.

The British Empire Series. 5 Vols. London: Kegan Paul, Trubner & Co., 1899–1902.

Buchan, John. *The African Colony: Studies in the Reconstruction.* Edinburgh and London: William Blackwood & Sons, 1903.

————. *Greenmantle.* London: T. Nelson & Sons, 1945 [1916].

————. *The Half-Hearted.* London: Hodder & Stoughton, 1935 [1900].

————. *A Lodge in the Wilderness.* London: T. Nelson & Sons, 1916 [1906].

————. *Memory Hold-The-Door.* London: Hodder & Stoughton, 1945.

————. *Prester John.* London: T. Nelson & Sons, 1963 [1910].

————. *Scholar Gypsies.* London: John Lane, 1896.

————. *Sick Heart River.* Toronto: Musson Book Co., 1941.

Butler, William F. *The Great Lone Land: An Account of the Red River Expedition and other travels and adventures in Western Canada.* Edmonton: M. G. Hurtig, 1968 [1872].

————. *The Wild North Land: The Story of a winter journey, with dogs across Northern North America.* Edmonton: M. G. Hurtig, 1968 [1873].

Cameron, Verney Lovett. *In Savage Africa.* London: T. Nelson & Sons, n.d.

Campbell, Rev. William. *British India in its Relation to the Decline of Hindooism and the Progress of Christianity.* London: John Snow, 1839.

Carlyle, Thomas. *On Heroes, Hero-Worship, and the Heroic in History.* Berkeley: University of California Press, 1993 [1841].

Chalmers, J. *Fighting the Matabele.* London: Blackie & Son, 1898.

Childers, Erskine. *The Riddle of the Sands.* New York: Penguin Books, 1978 [1903].

Churchill, Lord Randolph. *Men, Mines and Animals in South Africa.* London: Sampson Low, Marston & Co., 1897.

Churchill, Winston. *The River War: An Account of the Reconquest of the Sudan.* New York:

Award Books, 1965 [1899].

————. *The Story of the Malakand Field Force: An Episode of Frontier War.* London and New York: Longmans, Green, 1898.

Cleland, E. Davenport. *The White Kangaroo. A Tale of Colonial Life. Founded on Fact.* London: Wells Gardner, Darton & Co.,1904.

Collingwood, Harry. *Across the Spanish Main: A Tale of the Sea in the Days of Queen Bess.* London: Blackie & Son, n.d.

————. *The Congo Rovers: A Story of the Slave Squadron.* New York: Worthington Co., n.d.

————. *The Pirate Island: A Story of the South Pacific.* London: Blackie & Son, n.d.

————. *A Pirate of the Caribees.* London: Henry Frowde, Hodder & Stoughton, n.d.

————. *The Rover's Secret: A Tale of the Pirate Cays and Lagoons of Cuba.* London: Blackie & Son, n.d.

Conrad, Joseph, *Heart of Darkness.* Robert Kimbrough, ed. 3rd ed. New York and London: W. W. Norton & Co., 1988 [1899].

————. *Lord Jim.* Oxford University Press, 1983 [1900].

Cooper, James Fenimore. *The Deerslayer.* New York: E. P. Dutton, 1906 [1841].

————. *The Last of the Mohicans.* New York: E. P. Dutton, 1906 [1826].

————. *The Pathfinder.* New York: E. P. Dutton, 1906 [1840].

Craig, G. M., ed. *Lord Durham's Report.* Toronto: McClelland & Stewart, 1963.

Cromer, The Earl of. *Modern Egypt.* 2 Vols. London: Macmillan & Co., 1908.

Curtin, Philip, ed. *Imperialism.* New York: Walker & Co., 1971.

Dalton, William. *The War Tiger: A Tale of the Conquest of China.* London: Griffith Farran Browne & Co., n.d.

Darwin, Charles. *The Voyage of the Beagle.* New York: Bantam Books, 1958 [1839].

Daunt, Achilles. *The Three Trappers. A Story of Adventure in the Wilds of Canada.* London: T. Nelson & Sons, 1889.

Dickens, Charles. *American Notes.* London: Chapman & Hall, 1907 [1842].

————. *Bleak House.* London: Oxford University Press, 1956 [1853].

————. *Martin Chuzzlewit.* Oxford: Clarendon Press, 1982 [1843–44].

Dilke, Charles. *Greater Britain.* London: Macmillan & Co.,1869.

Donkin, John George. *Trooper in the Far North-West: Reflections of Life in the North-West Mounted Police, Canada, 1884–1888.* Saskatoon, Sk.: Western Producer Books, 1987.

Doyle, Arthur Conan. *The White Company.* Toronto: Musson Book Co., 1945 [1891].

Drummond, Henry. *Tropical Africa.* London: Hodder & Stoughton, 1891.

Dufferin and Ava, Marchioness of. *My Canadian Journal, 1872–8.* London: John Murray, 1891.

Duncan, Sara Jeanette. *The Imperialist.* Toronto: McClelland & Stewart, 1968 [1904].

Eden, Charles H. *Jungle Jack, or To the East After Elephants.* London: S.P.C.K., n.d.

Eden, Emily. *Up the Country: Letters Written to her Sister from the Upper Provinces of India.* London: Oxford University Press, 1937 [1866].

Elton, Lord, ed. *General Gordon's Khartoum Journal.* New York: Vanguard Press, 1961.

Eyre, Edward John. *Autobiographical Narrative of Residence and Exploration in Australia, 1832–1839.* London: Caliban Books,1984.

Fenn, George Manville. *Begumbagh: A Tale Of the Indian Mutiny.* London: W. & R. Chambers, n.d.

————. *The Black Bar.* London: Sampson Low, Marston & Co., n.d.

————. *Bunyip Land, or Among the Blackfellows in New Guinea.* London: Blackie & Son, n.d.

————. *Ching, the Chinaman and His Middy Friends.* London: S.P.C.K., n.d.

————. *Diamond Dyke, or The Lone Farm on the Veldt. A Story of South African*

——— . *Adventure*. London: W. & R. Chambers, 1895.

——— . *Fire Island: Being the Adventures of Uncertain Naturalists in an Unknown Track*. London: Sampson Low, Marston & Co., n.d.

——— . *First in the Field: A Story of New South Wales*. London: S. W. Partridge & Co., n.d.

——— . *Gil the Gunner, or The Youngest Officer in the East*. London: S.P.C.K., n.d.

——— . *The Golden Magnet: A Tale of the Land of the Incas*. London: Blackie and Son Limited, n.d.

——— . *In the Mahdi's Grasp*. London: S. W. Partridge & Co., n.d.

——— . *Jungle and Stream, or The Adventures of Two Boys in Siam*. London: Dean & Son, n.d.

——— . *Mother Carey's Chicken: Her Voyage to the Unknown Isle*. London: Blackie & Son, n.d.

——— . *Nat the Naturalist, or A Boy's Adventures in the Eastern Seas*. London: Blackie & Son, 1905.

——— . *Off to the Wilds: The Adventures of Two Brothers*. London: Sampson Low, Marston & Co., n.d.

——— . *Rob Harlow's Adventures: A Story of the Grand Chaco*. London: S. W. Partridge & Co., n.d.

Fieldhouse, D. K. *The Theory of Capitalist Imperialism*. London: Longmans, 1969.

Froude, James A. *Oceana, or England and Her Colonies*. London: Longmans, Green & Co., 1886.

Galton, Francis. *Hereditary Genius: An inquiry into its laws and consequences*. London: Julian Freedmann, 1978 [1869].

Geddie, John. *Beyond the Himalayas: A Story of Travel and Adventure in the Wilds of Thibet*. London: T. Nelson & Sons, 1889.

Gilpatric, Guy. *The First Glencannon Omnibus*. New York: Dodd, Mead & Co., 1946.

——— . *The Second Glencannon Omnibus*. New York: Dodd, Mead & Co., 1946.

Gilson, Capt. Charles. *The Lost Island*. London: Henry Frowde Hodder & Stoughton, n.d.

Godley, John R. ed. *Letters from Early New Zealand by Charlotte Godley*. Christchurch: Whitcombe & Tombs, 1951.

Goldman, Charles Sydney, ed. *The Empire and the Century: A Series of Essays on Imperial Problems and Possibilities by Various Writers*. London: John Murray, 1906.

Grange, Herbert. *An English Farmer in Canada and a Visit to the States. Being Notes and Observations by a Practical Man and Commercial Man on Canada as a Field for British Capital and Labour*. London: Blackie & Son, 1904.

Haggard, H. Rider. *Allan Quatermain*. London: Cassell & Co., 1887.

——— . *Allan's Wife*. London: Hodder & Stoughton, 1907.

——— . *Ayesha: The Return of She*. London: Ward, Lock & Co., 1905.

——— . *Benita: An African Romance*. London: Macdonald, 1965 [1906].

——— . *Finished*. London: Macdonald, 1962 [1917].

——— . *The Ghost Kings*. London: Cassell & Co., 1908.

——— . *The Holy Flower*. London: Ward, Lock & Co., 1915.

——— . *The Ivory Child*. New York: Longmans, Green & Co., 1916.

——— . *Jess*. London: Smith, Elder & Co., 1887.

——— . *King Solomon's Mines*. London: Collins, 1965 [1885].

——— . *Maiwa's Revenge, or The War of the Little Hand*. London: Macdonald, 1965 [1888].

——— . *Marie*. London: Cassell & Co., 1912.

——— . *Nada the Lily*. London: Longmans, Green & Co., 1891.

——— . *Queen Sheba's Ring*. London: Eveleigh Nash, 1910.

——— . *She*. London: Cassell & Co., 1887.

————— . *The Witch's Head*. London: Spencer Blackett, n.d. [1885].

————— . *The Yellow God*. London: Cassell & Co., 1909.

Hall, Mrs. Cecil. *A Lady's Life on a Farm in Manitoba*. London: W. H. Allen & Co., 1884.

Hayens, Herbert. *Clevely Sahib: A Tale of the Khyber* Pass. London: T. Nelson & Sons, 1897.

————— . *In the Grip of the Spaniard*. London: T. Nelson & Sons, n.d.

————— . *Scouting for Buller*. London: T. Nelson & Sons, 1902.

Henty, George Alfred. *Among Malay Pirates: A Tale of Adventure and Peril*. New York: Hurst & Co., n.d. [1897].

————— . *At Aboukir and Acre: A Story of Napoleon's Invasion of Egypt*. London: Blackie & Son, 1899.

————— . *At the Point of the Bayonet: A Tale of the Mahratta War*. London: Blackie & Son, 1902.

————— . *By Sheer Pluck: A Tale of the Ashanti War*. London: Blackie & Son, n.d. [1884].

————— . *The Curse of Carne's Hold*. New York: Hurst & Co., n.d. [1889].

————— . *The Dash for Khartoum: A Tale of the Nile Expedition*. London: Blackie & Son, n.d. [1892].

————— . *Facing Death: A Tale of the Coal Mines*. London: Blackie & Son, n.d. [1882].

————— . *A Final Reckoning: A Tale of Bush Life in Australia*. Chicago: M. A. Donohue & Co., n.d. [1887].

————— . *For Name and Fame, or To Cabul with Roberts*. London: Blackie & Son, n.d. [1886].

————— . *The Golden Cañon*. Chicago: M. A. Donohue & Co., n.d. [1899].

————— . *In the Hands of the Cave Dwellers*. London: Blackie & Son, n.d. [1903].

————— . *In the Heart of the Rockies: A Story of Adventure in Colorado*. London: Blackie & Son, n.d. [1895].

————— . *A Hidden Foe*. New York: Hurst & Co., n.d.

————— . *In Times of Peril: A Tale of India*. Chicago: M. A. Donohue & Co., n.d. [1881].

————— . *Jack Archer: A Tale of the Crimea*. London: Sampson Low, Marston & Co., n.d. [1883].

————— . *Maori and Settler: A Story of the New Zealand War*. London: Blackie & Son, n.d. [1891].

————— . *The March to Coomassie*. London: Tinsley Brothers, 1874.

————— . *The March to Magdala*. London: Tinsley Brothers, 1868.

————— . *On the Irrawaddy: A Story of the First Burmese War*. London: Blackie & Son, n.d. [1897].

————— . *Orange and the Green: A Tale of the Boyne and Limerick*. London: Blackie & Son n.d. [1888].

————— . *Out on the Pampas: The Young Settlers*. London: Henry Frowde Hodder & Stoughton, n.d. [1871].

————— . *The Queen's Cup: A Novel*. Chicago: M. A. Donohue & Co., 1898.

————— . *Redskins and Cowboys*. London: Blackie & Son, n.d. [1892].

————— . *A Roving Commission, or Through the Black Insurrection of Hayti*. London: Blackie & Son, 1900.

————— . *Rujub, the Juggler*. New York: Hurst & Co., 1901.

————— . *Tales of Daring and Danger*. London: Blackie & Son, n.d. [1889].

————— . *Through Three Campaigns: A Story of Chitral, Tirah, and Ashanti*. London: Blackie & Son, n.d. [1904].

————— . *The Tiger of Mysore: A Story of the War with Tippoo Saib*. London: Blackie & Son, 1896.

————— . *The Treasure of the Incas: A Story of Adventure in Peru*. London: Blackie & Son, n.d. [1903].

————— . *True to the Old Flag: A Tale of the American War of Independence.* London: Blackie & Son, n.d. [1885].

————— . *With the Allies to Pekin: A Story of the Relief of the Legations.* London: Blackie & Son, 1904.

————— . *With Clive in India, Or The Beginnings of an Empire.* London: Blackie & Son, n.d. [1884].

————— . *With Cochrane the Dauntless: A Tale of the Exploits of Lord Cochrane in South American Waters.* London: Blackie & Son, 1909 [1897].

————— . *With Kitchener in the Soudan: A Story of Atbara and Omdurman.* London: Blackie & Son, 1903.

————— . *With Lee in Virginia: A Story of the American Civil War.* London: Blackie & Son, n.d. [1890].

————— . *With Roberts to Pretoria: A Tale of the South African War.* London: Blackie & Son, 1902.

————— . *With Wolfe in Canada, or The Winning of a Continent.* London: Blackie and Son, n.d. [1887].

————— . *The Young Colonists: A Story of the Zulu and Boer Wars.* London: Blackie & Son, n.d. [1885].

————— . *The Young Midshipman: A Story of the Bombardment of Alexandria.* Chicago: M.A. Donohue & Co., n.d. [1902].

Henty, G. A., G. M. Fenn, and E. Harcourt Burrage. *In Battle and Breeze: Sea Stories.* London: S. W. Partridge & Co., n.d. [1896].

Hobson, J.A. *Imperialism: A Study.* Ann Arbor: University of Michigan Press, 1967 [1902].

Hope, Ascott R. *The Wigwam and the Warpath, or Tales of the Red Indians.* London: Blackie & Son, n.d.

Horsley, Reginald. *In the Grip of the Hawk: A Story of the Maori Wars.* London: T. C. & E. C. Jack, 1907.

Hughes, Thomas. *Tom Brown's Schooldays.* London: George C. Harrap & Co., 1927 [1856].

Hutcheson, John C. *The Penang Pirate and the Lost Pinnace.* London: Blackie & Son, n.d.

Hutchinson, J. R. *Hal Hungerford, or The Strange Adventures of a Boy Emigrant.* London: Blackie & Son, n.d.

Hyne, C. J. *Stimson's Reef: A Tale of Adventure.* London: Blackie & Son, n.d. [1892].

Jackel, Susan, ed. *A Flannel Shirt and Liberty: British Emigrant Gentlewomen in the Canadian West, 1880–1914.* Vancouver and London: University of British Columbia Press, 1982.

Keppel, Sir Henry. *A Sailor's Life Under Four Sovereigns.* 3 Vols. London: Macmillan & Co., 1899.

Ker, David. *The Boy Slave in Bokhara.* London: Griffith, Farran, Okeden & Welsh, n.d. [1894].

————— . *Swept out to Sea.* London: W. & R. Chambers, n.d.

King, Major W. Ross. *The Sportsman and Naturalist in Canada.* Toronto: Coles Publishing Co., 1974 [1866].

Kingsley, Mary. *Travels in West Africa, Congo Francaise, Corisco and Cameroons.* London: Frank Cass & Co., 1965 [1897].

————— . *West African Studies.* London: Frank Cass & Co., 1964 [1899].

Kingston, William Henry Giles. *Adventures in India.* London: George Routledge & Sons, n.d.

————— . *Ben Burton, or Born and Bred at Sea.* London: Sampson Low, Marston & Co., 1892.

————— . *Dick Cheveley: His Adventures and Misadventures.* London: Sampson Low, Marston & Co., n.d.

————— . *The Frontier Fort, or Stirring Times in the North-West Territory of British*

America. London: Sheldon Press, n.d.

————— . *The Gilpins and Their Fortunes: An Australian Tale*. London: S.P.C.K., n.d.

————— . *Hendricks the Hunter, or The Border Farm: A Tale of Zululand*. New York: A. C. Armstrong & Son, 1880.

————— . *In the Eastern Seas, or The Regions of the Bird of Paradise. A Tale for Boys*. London: T. Nelson & Sons, 1893.

————— . *In the Rocky Mountains*. London: T. Nelson & Sons, n.d.

————— . *In the Wilds of Africa: A Tale for Boys*. London: T. Nelson & Sons, 1873.

————— . *James Braithwaite: The Supercargo. The Story of His Adventures Ashore and Afloat*. London: Humphrey Milford, Oxford University Press, n.d.

————— . *The Log House by the Lake: A Tale of Canada*. London: S.P.C.K., n.d.

————— . *Manco the Peruvian Chief, or An Englishman's Adventures in the Country of the Incas*. London: Collins' Clear-Type Press, n.d.

————— . *Mark Seaworth: A Tale of the Indian Ocean*. London: Henry Frowde, Hodder & Stoughton, 1912 [1852].

————— . *My First Voyage to the Southern Seas*. London: T. Nelson & Sons, n.d.

————— . *Ned Garth, or Made Prisoner in Africa: A Tale of the Slave Trade*. London: S.P.C.K., n.d.

————— . *Old Jack*. London: T. Nelson & Sons, n.d.

————— . *Peter the Whaler*. London: W. Foulsham & Co., n.d.

————— . *Snow-Shoes and Canoes, or The Early Days of a Fur-Trader in the Hudson's Bay Territory*. London: Sampson Low, Marston, Searle & Rivington, 1877.

————— . *The Three Commanders, or Active Service Afloat in Modern Days*. London: Griffith Farran & Co., 1876.

————— . *The Three Midshipmen*. London: J. M. Dent & Sons, 1920 [1862].

————— . *Twice Lost*. London: T. Nelson & Sons, n.d.

————— . *Very Far West Indeed, or The Adventures of Peter Burr*. London: Sunday School Union, n.d.

————— . *The Wanderers*. London: T. Nelson & Sons, n.d.

————— . *Western Wanderings, or A Pleasure Tour in the Canadas*. 2 Vols. London: Chapman & Hall, 1856.

————— . *The Young Llanero*, London: T. Nelson & Sons, n.d.

Kipling, Rudyard. *The Day's Work*. London: Macmillan & Co., 1964 [1898]

————— . *The Jungle Books*. New York: Penguin Books, 1987 [1894, 1895].

————— . *Kim*. New York: Doubleday, Page & Co., 1914 [1901].

————— . *Life's Handicap*. London: Macmillan & Co., 1964 [1891].

————— . *Many Inventions*. London: Macmillan & Co., 1964 [1893].

————— . *Plain Tales From the Hills*. London: Macmillan & Co., 1964 [1887].

————— . *Soldiers Three*. London: Macmillan & Co., 1964 [1895].

————— . *Something of Myself: For My Friends Known and Unknown*. New York: Penguin Classics, 1987 [1936].

————— . *Stalky & Co*. Oxford: Oxford University Press, 1987 [1899].

————— . *Wee Willie Winkie*. London: Macmillan & Co., 1964 [1895].

————— . *The Works of Rudyard Kipling*. Roslyn, N.Y.: Black's Readers Service Co., n.d.

————— . *The Works of Rudyard Kipling*. Ware, Hertfordshire, U. K.: The Wandsworth Poetry Library, 1994.

————— . *The Writings in Prose and Verse of Rudyard Kipling*. 32 Vols. New York: Charles Scribner's Sons, 1916.

Lenin, V. I. *Imperialism, The Highest Stage of Capitalism*. New York: International Publishers, 1970 [1917].

Liesching, L. F. *Through Peril To Fortune: A Story of Sport and Adventure by Land and Sea*. London: Cassell, Petter, Galpin & Co., n.d.

Livingstone, David. *Missionary Travels and Researches in South Africa*. London: John Murray, 1912 [1857].

Lowndes, E.E.K. *Everyday Life In South Africa*. London: S. W. Partridge & Co., 1900.

Macdonald, Alexander. *The Lost Explorers: A Story of the Trackless Desert*. London: Blackie & Son, 1907.

MacDonald, George. *Dealings With the Fairies*. London: Strahan, 1867.

Mahan, A. T. *The Influence of Seapower Upon History*. New York: Sagamore Press., 1957 [1890].

Marryat, Florence. *The Little Marine and the Japanese Lily, or The Land of the Rising Sun*. London: Hutchinson & Co., n.d.

Marryat, Captain Frederick. *The Children of the New Forest*. London: Abbey Classics, 1971 [1841].

——— . *Masterman Ready, or the Wreck of the "Pacific"*. London: T. Nelson & Sons, n.d. [1841–42].

——— . *The Mission, or Scenes in Africa*. Leipzig: Tauchnitz, 1845.

——— . *Mr. Midshipman Easy*. London and Birmingham: Rylee, n.d. [1836].

——— . *Peter Simple*. London: George Routledge & Sons, 1896 [1834].

——— . *The Pirate and The Three Cutters*. London: George Routledge & Sons, 1882 [1836].

——— . *The Settlers in Canada*. London: The Boy's Own Paper, n.d. [1844].

Masefield, John. *Selected Poems*. London: William Heinemann, 1922.

Mason, A.E.W. *The Four Feathers*. London: Macmillan Co., 1969 [1901].

Masters, John. *Bhowani Junction*. New York: Viking Press, 1954.

——— . *The Deceivers*. New York: Viking Press, 1952.

——— . *Night Runners of Bengal*. New York: Viking Press, 1951.

Maugham, W. Somerset. *Collected Short Stories*. New York: Penguin Books, 1961.

Metcalfe, W. Charles. *Blown Out To Sea*. London: S.P.C.K., n.d.

——— . *Undaunted. A Story of the Solomon Islands*. London: John F. Shaw & Co., n.d.

Milner, Viscount. *England in Egypt*. London: Edwin Arnold, 1920 [1892].

——— . *The Nation and the Empire*. London: Constable & Co., 1913.

Moodie, Susanna. *Roughing it in the Bush, or Forest Life in Canada*. Toronto: Coles Publishing Co., 1980 [1852].

Moore, F. Frankfort. *The "Great Orion"'*. London: S.P.C.K., n.d.

Mundy, Talbot. *King—of the Khyber Rifles: A Romance of Adventure*. New York: A. L. Burt Co., 1916.

Muter, Mrs. D. D. *My Recollections of the Sepoy Revolt (1857–58)*. London: John Long, 1911.

Newbolt, Henry. *Selected Poems of Henry Newbolt*. London: Hodder & Stoughton, 1981.

Norway, G. *Hussein the Hostage, Or A Boy's Adventures in Persia*. London: Blackie & Son, n.d.

Parker, Gilbert. *An Adventurer of the North: Being a Continuation of the Personal Histories of "Pierre and His People" and the Last Existing Records of Pretty Pierre*. London: George C. Harrap & Co., 1926 [1895].

——— . *Pierre and His People: A Tale of the Far North*. London: George C. Harrap & Co., 1926 [1892].

——— . *The Seats of the Mighty*. Toronto: Copp Clark Co., 1902 [1896].

——— . *The Trail of the Sword*. London: George C. Harrap & Co., 1926 [1894].

Percy-Groves, J. *Reefer and Rifleman: A Tale of Two Services*. London: Blackie & Son, n.d.

Reid, Capt. Mayne. *The Boy Slaves*. New York: James Miller, 1881 [1864].

——— . *The Bush-Boys or,The History and Adventures of a Cape Farmer and his Family in the Wild Karoos of Southern Africa*. London: Routledge, Warne & Routledge, 1861.

———— . *The Cliff-Climbers, or The Lone Home in the Himalayas*. London: Charles H. Clarke, n.d.

———— . *The Flag of Distress: A Tale of the South Seas*. New York: James Miller, 1876.

———— . *Gaspar, the Gaucho: A Tale of the Gran Chaco*. London: George Routledge & Sons, 1880.

———— . *The Giraffe Hunters*. London: C. H. Clarke, n.d.

———— . *The Young Yägers, or A Narrative of Hunting Adventure in Southern Africa*. London: Routledge, Warne & Routledge, 1862.

Richie, J. Ewing. *An Australian Ramble, or A Summer in Australia*. London: T. Fisher Unwin, 1890.

———— . *To Canada with Emigrants: A Record of Actual Experiences*. London: T. Fisher Unwin, 1885.

Scott, Paul. *The Day of the Scorpion*. New York: Morrow, 1968.

———— . *A Division of Spoils*. New York: Morrow, 1975.

———— . *The Jewel in the Crown*. New York: Morrow, 1966.

———— . *The Towers of Silence*. New York: Morrow, 1971.

Seeley, Sir John. *The Expansion of England*. Chicago: University of Chicago Press, 1971 [1884].

Selous, Frederick C. *A Hunter's Wandering in Africa*. London: Macmillan and Co., 1907 [1881].

———— . *Recent Hunting Trips in British North America*. London: Witherby & Co., 1907.

Smiles, Samuel. *Self-Help*. New York: Penguin Books, 1986 [1859].

Southesk, The Earl of. *Saskatchewan and the Rocky Mountains: A Diary and Narrative of Travel, Sport, and Adventure, During a Journey Through the Hudson's Bay Company's Territories in 1859 and 1860*. Edmonton: M. G. Hurtig, 1969 [1875].

Spry, Irene M. *The Palliser Expedition: An Account of John Palliser's British North American Exploring Expedition, 1857–1860*. Toronto: Macmillan Co., of Canada, 1963.

Stables, Gordon. *Captain Japp*. London: S.P.C.K., 1891.

———— . *The Cruise of the Snowbird*. London: Henry Frowde Hodder & Stoughton, n.d.

———— . *The Cruise of the "Vengeful": A Story of the Royal Navy*. London: Dean & Son, n.d.

———— . *Every Inch a Sailor*. London: T. Nelson & Sons, 1897.

———— . *A Fight for Freedom: A Story of the Land of the Tsar*. London: James Nisbet & Co., 1897.

———— . *The Hermit Hunter of the Wilds*. London: Blackie & Son, n.d.

———— . *In the Great White Land: A Tale of the Antarctic Ocean*. London: Blackie & Son, n.d.

———— . *The Island of Gold: A Sailor's Yarn*. London: T. Nelson & Sons, n.d.

———— . *The Ivory Hunters: A Story of Wild Adventure by Land and Sea*. London: Ward, Lock & Co., 1911.

———— . *The Naval Cadet: A Story of Adventure on Land and Sea*. London: Blackie & Son, n.d.

———— . *On Special Service: A Tale of Life at Sea*. London: Hodder & Stoughton, 1897.

———— . *Two Sailor Lads: A Story of Stirring Adventures on Sea and Land*. London: John F. Shaw & Co., n.d.

———— . *With Cutlass and Torch: A Story of the Great Slave Coast*. London: James Nisbet & Co., 1901.

Stanley, Henry M. *In Darkest Africa, or The Quest, Rescue and Retreat of Emin, Governor of Equatoria*. 2 Vols. New York: Charles Scribner's Sons, 1890.

———— . *Through the Dark Continent, or The Sources of the Nile Around the Great Lakes of Equatorial Africa and Down Livingstone's River To the Atlantic Ocean*. 2 Vols.

London: George Newnes, 1899 [1879].

Steel, Flora Annie. *On the Face of the Waters*. London: William Heinemann, 1897.

Steele, Col. S. B. *Forty Years in Canada*. Toronto: McLelland, Goodchild & Stewart, n.d. [1915].

Steevens, G. W. *With Kitchener to Khartum*. New York: Dodd, Mead & Co., 1898.

Stevenson, Robert Louis *In the South Seas: Being an Account of Experiences and Observations in The Marquesas, Paumotus and Gilbert Islands*. London: Chatto & Windus, 1900.

——— . *Treasure Island*. London: Dean & Son, n.d. [1883].

St. Johnston, Alfred. *Charlie Asgarde: The Story of a Friendship*. London: Macmillan & Co., 1884.

Strachey, Lytton. *Eminent Victorians*. London: Chatto & Windus, 1948 [1918].

Strang, Herbert. *Barclay of the Guides*. London: Humphrey Milford, Oxford University Press, 1908.

——— . *The Motor Scout: A Story of Adventure in South America*. London: Henry Frowde Hodder & Stoughton, 1913.

——— . *Samba: A Story of the Rubber Slaves of the Congo*. London: Hodder & Stoughton, 1906.

——— . *Settlers and Scouts: A Tale of the African Highlands*. London: Henry Frowde Hodder & Stoughton, 1910.

——— . *Tom Burnaby*. London: Oxford University Press, 1929.

Strickland, Samuel. *Twenty-Seven Years in Canada West, or The Experiences of an Early Settler*. Edmonton: M. G. Hurtig, 1972 [1853].

Swettenham, Sir Frank. *British Malaya: An Account of the Origin and Progress of British Influence in Malaya*. London: George Allen & Unwin, 1955 [1906].

Thomson, Joseph. *Through Masai Land*. London: Frank Cass & Co., 1968 [1885].

Traill, Catherine Parr. *The Backwoods of Canada, being Letters from the Wife of an Emigrant Officer, Illustrative of the Domestic Economy of British America*. Toronto: McClelland & Stewart,1929 [1836].

Trevelyan, Sir George. *The Competition Wallah*. London: Macmillan & Co., 1895.

Trollope, Anthony. *Australia and New Zealand*. Leipzig: Tauchnitz, 1873.

——— . *Harry Heathcote of Gangoil. A Tale of Australian Bush Life*. London: Sampson Low, Marston, Low, & Searle,1874.

——— . *North America*. Philadelphia: J. B. Lippincott & Co., 1863.

——— . *South Africa*. 2 Vols. London: Chapman & Hall, 1878.

——— . *The West Indies and the Spanish Main*. London: Dawson's of Pall Mall, 1968 [1859].

Verne, Jules. *Around the World in Eighty Days*. New York: William Morrow & Co., 1988 [1873].

Wakefield, Edward Gibbon. *A Letter from Sydney*. London, 1829.

——— . *A View of the Art of Colonization, in Letters Between a Statesman and a Colonist*. Oxford: At the Clarendon Press, 1914 [1849].

Wallace, Edgar. *Sanders of the River*. London: Ward, Lock & Co., n.d.

Wells, Ronald A., ed. *Letters from a Young Emigrant in Manitoba*. University of Manitoba Press, 1981.

Wilson, William R. A. *The King's Scouts*. London: S. W. Partridge & Co., 1910.

Winks, Robin W., ed. *The Age of Imperialism*. Englewood Cliffs, N.J.: Prentice-Hall., 1969.

Wyss, Johann David. *The Swiss Family Robinson*. New York: Grosset & Dunlop, 1949 [1812–13].

Younghusband, Francis E. *The Heart of a Continent: A Narrative of Travels in Manchuria, Across the Gobi Desert, Through the Himalayas, The Pamirs and Chitral, 1884–94*. London: John Murray, 1886.

Annuals

Blackie's Boys' Annual
The Boy's Own Annual
The Captain
The Empire Annual
The Girl's Own Annual

SECONDARY SOURCES

Books

Altick, Richard D. *Victorian Peoples and Ideas*. New York: W. W. Norton & Co., 1973.

Anene, J. C. *Southern Nigeria in Transition, 1885–1906*. Cambridge: At the University Press, 1966.

Arnold, Guy. *Held Fast for England: G. A. Henty, Imperialist Boy's Writer*. London: Hamish Hamilton, 1980.

Atwood, Margaret. *Survival: A Thematic Guide to Canadian Literature*. Toronto: Anansi, 1972.

August, Thomas G. *The Selling of the Empire: British and French Imperialist Propaganda, 1890–1940*. Westport, Conn.: Greenwood Press, 1985.

Avery, Gillian. *Childhood's Pattern*. London: Hodder & Stoughton, 1975.

Balfour, Michael. *Britain and Joseph Chamberlain*. London: George Allen & Unwin,1985.

Baucom, Ian. *Out of Place: Englishness, Empire, and The Location of Identity*. Princeton: Princeton University Press, 1999.

Beloff, Max. *Imperial Sunset: Britain's Liberal Empire 1897–1921*. London: Methuen & Co.,1969.

Benians, E. A., J. R. M. Butler, P N.S. Mansergh, and E. A. Walker, eds. *The Cambridge History of the British Empire*. Vol. 3. Cambridge: Cambridge University Press, 1959.

Bivona, Daniel. *Desire and Contradiction: Imperial Visions and Domestic Debates in Victorian Literature*. Manchester: Manchester University Press, 1990.

Blainey, Geoffrey. *A Land Half-Won*. Melbourne: Macmillan Co. of Australia, 1980.

Blake, Robert. *A History of Rhodesia*. London: Eyre Methuen, 1977.

Bloomfield, Paul. *Edward Gibbon Wakefield: Builder of the British Commonwealth*. London: Longmans, 1961.

Brander, Michael. *The Perfect Victorian Hero: The Life and Times of Sir Samuel White Baker*. Edinburgh: Mainstream Publishing Co., 1982.

Bratlinger, Patrick. *Rule of Darkness: British Literature and Imperialism,1830–1914*. Ithaca, N. Y.: Cornell University Press, 1988.

Bratton, J. S. *The Impact of Victorian Children's Fiction*. London: Croom Helm, 1980.

Brendon, Piers. *Thomas Cook: 150 Years of Popular Tourism*. London: Secker & Warburg, 1992.

Bristow, Joseph. *Empire Boys: Adventures in a Man's World*. New York: HarperCollinsAcademic, 1991.

Brown, Ford K. *Fathers of the Victorians: The Age of Wilberforce*. Cambridge: At the University Press, 1961.

Buchan, William. *John Buchan: A Memoir*. London: Buchan & Enright, Publishers, 1982.

Cain, P. J., and A. G. Hopkins. *British Imperialism: Innovation and Expansion, 1688–1914*. London: Longmans, 1993.

Cairns, H. Alan C. *Prelude to Imperialism: British Reactions to Central African Society, 1840–1890*. London: Routledge & Kegan Paul, 1965.

Carpenter, Humphrey, and Mari Prichard. *The Oxford Companion to Children's Literature*.

Oxford: Oxford University Press, 1984.

Carrington, Charles. *Rudyard Kipling: His Life and Work*. London: Penguin Books, 1970.

Christopher, A. J. *The British Empire at Its Zenith*. London: Croom Helm, 1988.

Cohen, Morton. *Rider Haggard: His Life and Works*. London: Hutchinson of London, 1960.

Curtin, Philip. *The Image of Africa: British Ideas and Action, 1780–1850*. London: Macmillan & Co., 1965.

Curtis, L. P. *Anglo-Saxons and Celts: A Study of Anti-Irish Prejudice in Victorian England*. Bridgeport, Conn.: University of Bridgeport,, 1968.

Daniell, David. *The Interpreter's House: A Critical Assessment of John Buchan*. London: Nelson, 1975.

David, Hugh. *Heroes, Mavericks and Bounders: The English Gentleman from Lord Curzon to James Bond*. London: Michael Joseph, 1991.

Desmond, Adrian, and James Moore. *Darwin*. New York: Warner Books, 1992.

Doyle, Brian, ed. *The Who's Who of Children's Literature*. London: Hugh Evelyn, 1971.

Doyle, Michael W. *Empires*. Ithaca, N.Y.: Cornell University Press, 1986.

Dunae, Patrick A. *Gentlemen Emigrants: From the British Public Schools to the Canadian Frontier*. Vancouver and Toronto: Douglas & McIntyre, 1981.

Duncan, John, and John Walton. *Heroes for Victoria*. Tunbridge Wells, Kent: Spellmount, 1991.

Dutton, Geoffrey. *The Hero as Murderer: The Life of Edward John Eyre, Australian Explorer and Governor of Jamaica, 1815–1901*. Sydney: Collins, 1967.

Dyson, K. K. *A Various Universe: A Study of the Journals and Memoirs of British Men and Women in the Indian Subcontinent, 1765–1856*. Delhi: Oxford University Press, 1978.

Edwardes, Michael. *The Nabobs at Home*. London: Constable, 1991.

Eldridge, C. C. *England's Mission: The Imperial Idea in the Age of Gladstone and Disraeli, 1868–1880*. London: Macmillan, 1973.

———. *The Imperial Experience: From Carlyle to Forster*. London: Macmillan Press, 1996.

Ellis, Peter Beresford. *H. Rider Haggard: A Voice from the Infinite*. London: Routledge & Kegan Paul, 1978.

Etherington, Norman. *Theories of Imperialism: War, Conquest and Capital*. London: Croom Helm, 1984.

Farwell, Byron. *For Queen and Country: A Social History of the Victorian and Edwardian Army*. London: Allen Lane,1981.

———. *Queen Victoria's Little Wars*. New York: W. W. Norton & Co., 1972.

Field, H. John. *Toward a Programme of Imperial Life: The British Empire at the Turn of the Century*. Westport, Conn.: Greenwood Press, 1982.

Fieldhouse, D. K. *Colonialism, 1870–1945*. London: Weidenfeld & Nicolson, 1981.

———. *Economics and Empire, 1830–1914*. London: Weidenfeld & Nicolson, 1973.

Flint, John.*Cecil Rhodes*. Boston: Little, Brown & Co., 1974.

———. *Sir George Goldie and the Making of Nigeria*. London: Oxford University Press, 1960.

Fraser, Peter. *Lord Esher: A Political Biography*. London: Hart-Davis, MacGibbon, 1973.

Galbraith, John S. *Mackinnon and East Africa, 1878–1895: A Study in the "New Imperialism."* London: Cambridge University Press, 1972.

Gann, L. H., and Peter Duignan, eds. *Colonialism in Africa, 1870–1960*. 2 Vols. Cambridge: Cambridge University Press, 1981.

Garvin, J.L. *The Life of Joseph Chamberlain*. Vol. 3. London: Macmillan & Co., 1932.

Giddings, Robert, ed. *Literature and Imperialism*. New York: St. Martin's Press, 1991.

Girouard, Mark. *Life in the English Country House: A Social and Architectural History*.

New Haven and London: Yale University Press, 1979.

——— . *The Return to Camelot: Chivalry and the English Gentleman*. New Haven: Yale University Press, 1981.

Goonetilleke, D.C.R.A. *Developing Countries in British Fiction*. London: Macmillan Press, 1977.

Green, Martin. *Dreams of Adventure, Deeds of Empire*. London and Henley: Routledge & Kegan Paul, 1980.

Greenberger, Allen J. *The British Image of India: A Study in the Literature of Imperialism*. London: Oxford University Press, 1969.

Grenville, J.A.S. *Lord Salisbury and Foreign Policy: The Close of the Nineteenth Century*. London: Athlone Press, 1964.

Hall, D.G.E. *Henry Burney: A Political Biography*. London: Oxford University Press, 1974.

Headrick, Daniel R. *The Tentacles of Progress: Technology Transfer in the Age of Imperialism, 1850–1940*. Oxford: Oxford University Press, 1988.

——— . *The Tools of Empire: Technology and European Imperialism in the Nineteenth Century*. New York and Oxford: Oxford University Press, 1981.

Higgins, D. S. *Rider Haggard: The Great Storyteller*. London: Cassell, 1981.

Hough, Richard. *Captain Bligh and Mr. Christian: The Men and the Mutiny*. New York: E. P. Dutton & Co., 1973.

House, Humphrey. *The Dickens World*. London: Oxford University Press, 1941.

Howarth, David. *Tahiti: A Paradise Lost*. London: Harvill Press, 1983.

Hughes, Robert. *The Fatal Shore: The Epic of Australia's Founding*. New York: Alfred A. Knopf, 1987.

Hutchins, Francis G. *The Illusion of Permanence: British Imperialism in India*. Princeton, N.J.: Princeton University Press, 1967.

Hynes, Samuel. *The Edwardian Turn of Mind*. Princeton, N.J.: Princeton University Press, 1968.

Ingham, Kenneth. *Reformers in India, 1793–1833*. Cambridge: At the University Press, 1956.

Ingram, Edward. *Beginning of the Great Game in India, 1828–1834*. Oxford: Clarendon Press, 1979.

Islam, Shamsul. *Kipling's "Law": A Study of His Philosophy of Life*. London: Macmillan Press, 1975.

James, Robert Rhodes. *The British Revolution: British Politics, 1880–1939*. London: Methuen & Co., 1978.

Jarrett, Derek. *The Sleep of Reason: Fantasy and Reality from the Victorian Age to the First World War*. London: Weidenfeld & Nicolson, 1988.

Jeal, Tim. *Livingstone*. London: Heinemann, 1973.

Katz, Wendy R. *Rider Haggard and the Fiction of Empire: A Critical Study of British Imperial Fiction*. Cambridge: Cambridge University Press, 1991.

Kent, Marian. *Oil and Empire: British Policy and Mesopotamian Oil, 1900–1920*. New York: Harper & Row Publishers, 1976.

Keppel-Jones, Arthur. *Rhodes and Rhodesia: The White Conquest of Zimbabwe, 1884–1902*. Kingston and Montreal: McGill-Queen's University Press, 1983.

——— . *South Africa: A Short History*. London: Hutchinson University Library, 1975.

Kingsford, Rev. Maurice R. *The Life, Work and Influence of William Henry Giles Kingston*. Toronto: Ryerson Press, 1947.

Knightley, Philip. *The First Casualty: From the Crimea to Vietnam: The War Correspondent as Hero, Propagandist, and Myth Maker*. New York and London: Harcourt Brace Jovanovich, 1975.

Knorr, Klaus E. *British Colonial Theories, 1570–1850*. Toronto: University of Toronto Press, 1964.

Kruse, Juanita. *John Buchan (1875–1940) and the Idea of Empire: Popular Literature and Political Ideology*. Lewiston, N.Y.: Edwin Mellen Press, 1989.

Kunitz, Stanley J., and Howard Haycroft, eds. *British Authors of the Nineteenth Century*. New York: H. W. Wilson Co., 1936.

Limb, Sue, and Patrick Cordingley. *Captain Oates: Soldier and Explorer*. London: B. T. Batsford, 1983.

Lofts, W.O.G., and D. J. Adley. *The Men Behind Boy's Fiction*. London: Howard Baker, 1970.

Long, Roger D. *The Man on the Spot: Essays on British Empire History*. Westport, Conn.: Greenwood Press, 1995.

Longford, Elizabeth. A *Pilgrimage of Passion: The Life of Wilfrid Scawen Blunt*. New York: Alfred A. Knopf, 1980.

Mackenzie, John M., ed. *Imperialism and Popular Culture*. Manchester: Manchester University Press, 1985.

——— . *Popular Imperialism and the Military*. Manchester: Manchester University Press, 1992.

MacLaren, Roy. *Canadians on the Nile, 1882–1898*. Vancouver: University of British Columbia Press, 1978.

McClintock, Anne. *Imperial Leather: Race, Gender and Sexuality in the Colonial Conquest*. New York: Routledge, 1995.

McClure, John A. *Kipling and Conrad: The Colonial Fiction*. Cambridge, Mass.: Harvard University Press, 1981.

McCourt, Edward. *Remember Butler: The Story of Sir William Butler*. London: Routledge & Kegan Paul, 1967.

McLynn, Frank. *Hearts of Darkness: The European Exploration of Africa*. London: Pimlico, 1993.

——— . *Stanley: The Making of an African Explorer*. London: Constable, 1989.

——— . *Stanley: Sorcerer's Apprentice*. London: Constable, 1991.

Mangan, J. A. *"Benefits Bestowed"? Education and British Imperialism*. Manchester: Manchester University Press, 1988.

——— . *The Games Ethic and Imperialism: Aspects of the Diffusion of an Ideal*. New York: Viking, 1986.

——— . *Making Imperial Mentalities: Socialisation and British Imperialism*. Manchester: Manchester University Press, 1990.

Martin, Sandra, and Roger Hall, eds. *Rupert Brooke in Canada*. Toronto: PMA. Books, 1978.

Mason, Philip. *Kipling: The Glass, the Shadow and the Fire*. London: Jonathan Cape, 1975.

——— . *A Matter of Honour*. New York: Holt, Rinehart & Winston, 1974.

Matthew, H.G.C. *The Liberal Imperialists*. London: Oxford University Press, 1973.

Miller, Carman. *Painting the Map Red: Canada and the South African War, 1899–1902*. Montreal and Kingston: Canadian War Museum and McGill-Queen's University Press, 1993.

Milne, James Lees. *The Enigmatic Edwardian: The Life of Reginald, 2nd Viscount Esher*. London: Sidgwick & Jackson, 1968.

Moorehead, Alan. *Cooper's Creek*. London: Hamish Hamilton, 1963.

——— . *The Fatal Impact: The Invasion of the South Pacific, 1767–1840*. New York: Harper & Row, 1987 [1966].

Moorhouse, Geoffrey. *The Missionaries*. London: Eyre Methuen, 1973.

Morley, John. *Death, Heaven and the Victorians*. Pittsburgh: University of Pittsburgh Press, 1971.

Morrell, W. P. *Britain in the Pacific Islands*. Oxford: Clarendon Press, 1960.

Morris, Jan. *The Spectacle of Empire: Style, Effect and the Pax Britannica*. London: Faber

& Faber, 1982.

Moss, Robert F. *Rudyard Kipling and the Fiction of Adolescence.* London: Macmillan Press 1982.

Mostert, Noël. *Frontiers: The Epic of South Africa's Creation and the Tragedy of the Xhosa People.* New York: Alfred A. Knopf, 1992.

Musgrave, P. W. *From Brown to Bunter: The Life and Death of the School Story.* London: Routledge & Kegan Paul, 1985.

Oliver, Roland. *Sir Harry Johnston and the Scramble for Africa.* London: Chatto & Windus, 1957.

Pakenham, Thomas. *The Boer War.* London: Weidenfeld & Nicolson, 1979.

———. *The Scramble for Africa: White Man's Conquest of the Dark Continent from 1876 to 1912.* New York: Avon Books, 1991.

Parr, Joy. *Labouring Children: British Immigrant Apprentices to Canada, 1869–1924.* London: Croom Helm, 1980.

Parsons, Neil. *King Khama, Emperor Joe, and the Great White Queen: Victorian Britain through African Eyes.* Chicago and London: University of Chicago Press, 1998.

Perham, Margery. *Lugard.* 2 Vols. London: Collins, 1968.

Pocock, Tom. *Rider Haggard and the Lost Empire.* London: Weidenfeld & Nicolson, 1993.

Pottinger, George. *The Afghan Connection: The Extraordinary Adventures of Major Eldred Pottinger.* Edinburgh: Scottish Academic Press, 1983.

Potts, E. Daniel. *British Baptist Missionaries in India, 1793–1837.* Cambridge: At the University Press, 1967.

Powell, Violet. *Flora Annie Steel.* London: Heinemann, 1981.

Preston, Anthony, and John Major. *Send a Gunboat! A Study of the Gunboat and Its Role in British Policy, 1854–1905.* London: Longmans, 1967.

Price, Richard. *An Imperial War and the British Working Class: Working Class Attitudes to the Boer War, 1899–1902.* London: Routledge & Kegan Paul, 1972.

Quayle, Eric. *Ballantyne the Brave: A Victorian Writer and His Family.* Chester Springs, Pa.: Dufour Editions, 1967.

Reader, W. J. *"At Duty's Call": A Study in Obsolete Patriotism.* Manchester: Manchester University Press, 1988.

Richards, Jeffery, ed. *Imperialism and Juvenile Literature.* Manchester: Manchester University Press, 1988.

Richardson, Alan, and Sonia Hofkosh, eds. *Romanticism, Race, and Imperial Culture, 1780–1834.* Bloomington: Indiana University Press, 1996.

Ridley, Hugh. *Images of Imperial Rule.* London: Croom Helm, 1983.

Rose, Kenneth. *Superior Person: A Portrait of Curzon and His Circle in Late Victorian England.* New York: Weybright & Talley, 1969.

Rosenthal, Michael. *The Character Factory: Baden Powell and the Origins of the Boy Scout Movement.* London: Collins, 1986.

Rotberg, Robert I. *The Founder: Cecil Rhodes and the Pursuit of Power.* New York and Oxford: Oxford University Press, 1988.

Russell, A. K. *Liberal Landslide: The General Election of 1906.* Newton Abbott: David & Charles, 1973.

Rutherford, J. *Sir George Grey K.C.B., 1812–1898: A Study in Colonial Government.* London: Cassell, 1961.

Said, Edward W. *Culture and Imperialism.* New York: Alfred A. Knopf, 1993.

———. *Orientalism.* New York: Pantheon Books, 1978.

Sandison, Alan. *The Wheel of Empire.* New York: St. Martin's Press, 1967.

Seaver, George. *Francis Younghusband: Explorer and Mystic.* London: John Murray, 1952.

Semmel, Bernard. *The Governor Eyre Controversy.* London: Macgibbon & Kee, 1962.

———. *The Liberal Ideal and the Demons of Empire.* Baltimore: Johns Hopkins

University Press, 1993.

Sen, Surendra Nath. *Eighteen Fifty-Seven*. The Publications Division, Ministry of Information & Broadcasting, Government of India, 1957.

Seymour-Smith, Martin. *Rudyard Kipling*. London: Macdonald: Queen Anne Press, 1989.

Simpson, Donald. *Dark Companions: The African Contribution to the European Exploration of East Africa*. London: Paul Elek, 1975.

Smith, Janet Adam. *John Buchan: A Biography*. London: Rupert Hart Davis, 1965.

Smith, M. Van Wyck. *Drummer Hodge: The Poetry of the Anglo-Boer War (1899–1902)*. Oxford: Clarendon Press, 1978.

Smith, Robert S. *The Lagos Consulate, 1851–1861*. London: Macmillan Press, 1973.

Southgate, Donald. *The Most English Minister: The Politics of Lord Palmerston*. New York: St. Martin's Press, 1966.

Springhall, John. *Youth, Empire and Society: British Youth Movements, 1833–1940*. London: Croom Helm, 1977.

Steele, Joan. *Captain Mayne Reid*. Boston: Twayne Publishers, 1978.

Steiner, Zara. *Britain and the Origins of the First World War*. London: Macmillan Press, 1977.

Stepan, Nancy. *The Idea of Race in Science: Great Britain, 1800–1960*. London: Macmillan Press, 1982.

Stewart, A.T.Q. *The Pagoda War: Lord Dufferin and the Fall of the Kingdom of Ava, 1885–6*. Newton Abbey: Victorian (& Modern History) Book Club, 1973.

Street, Brian V. *The Savage in Literature: Representations of "Primitive" Society in English Fiction, 1858–1920*. London: Routledge & Kegan Paul, 1975.

Sullivan, Z. T. *Narratives of Empire: The Fictions of Rudyard Kipling*. Cambridge University Press, 1993.

Swinglehurst, Edmund. *Cook's Tours: The Story of Popular Travel*. Poole, Dorset: Blandford Press, 1982.

———— . *The Romantic Journey*. London: Pica Editions, 1974.

Taylor, Robert. *Lord Salisbury*. London: Allen Lane, 1975.

Thompson, F.M.L. *The Rise of Respectable Society: A Social History of Victorian Britain, 1830–1900*. London: Fontana Press, 1988.

Thompson, Roger C. *Australian Imperialism in the Pacific: The Expansionist Era, 1820–1920*. Melbourne: Melbourne University Press, 1980.

Thomson, George Malcolm. *The North-West Passage*. London: Secker & Warburg, 1975.

Thornton, A. P. *For the File on Empire*. London: Macmillan,1968.

———— . *The Imperial Idea and its Enemies: A Study in British Power*. London: Macmillan & Co., 1963.

Tidrick, Kathleen. *Empire and the English Character*. London: I. B. Taurus & Co., 1990.

———— . *Heart Beguiling Araby: The English Romance with Arabia*. London: I. B. Taurus & Co., 1989.

Tingsten, Herbert. *Victoria and the Victorians*. London: George Allen & Unwin, 1972.

Trotter, L. J. *The Life of John Nicholson: Soldier and Administrator*. London: John Murray, 1904.

Usborne, Richard. *Clubland Heroes*. London: Constable, 1953.

Walker, Eric. *The Great Trek*. London: Adam & Charles Black, 1965.

Ward, Alan. *A Show of Justice: Racial "Amalgamation" in Nineteenth Century New Zealand*. Toronto: University of Toronto Press, 1973.

Ward, Russel. *The Australian Legend*. Melbourne: Oxford University Press, 1977.

Warner, Oliver. *Captain Marryat: A Rediscovery*. London: Constable, 1953.

Waterston, Elizabeth. *Gilbert Parker and His Works*. Toronto: ECW. Press, 1989.

Weiner, Martin J. *English Culture and the Decline of the Industrial Spirit*. Cambridge: Cambridge University Press, 1982.

Wilson, Angus. *The Strange Ride of Rudyard Kipling: His Life and Works.* London: Panther, Granada Publishing, 1979.

Windschuttle, Keith. *The Killing of History: How a Discipline Is Being Murdered by Literary Critics and Social Theorists.* Paddington, N.S.W.: Macleay Press, 1996.

Woodruff, Philip. *The Men Who Ruled India.* 2 Vols. London: Jonathan Cape, 1963.

Wright, Harrison M. *New Zealand, 1769–1840: Early Years of Western Contact.* Cambridge, Mass.: Harvard University Press, 1959.

Wurgraft, Lewis. *The Imperial Imagination: Magic and Myth in Kipling's India.* Middletown, Conn.: Wesleyan University Press, 1983.

Theses

Bennett, David. "Trollope and Greater Britain: The Development of Anthony Trollope's Ideas on Imperialism." Master's thesis, University of Saskatchewan, 1993.

Charabin, Craig. "Voyages to the Gates of Dawn: Official Exploring Expeditions to the South Pacific, 1776–1857." Master's thesis, University of Saskatchewan, 1999.

Fedorowich, Kent. "H. Rider Haggard: The Spirit of Empire."   Master's thesis, University of Saskatchewan, 1983.

Ferguson, Derek. "Robert Louis Stevenson and Samoa: A Reinterpretation." Master's thesis, University of Saskatchewan, 1980.

Labach, Jennifer. "Responding to Adversity: British Women in India, 1813–1914." Master's thesis, University of Saskatchewan, 1991.

Stilwell, Sean. "'The Merry Dance of Death and Trade': Joseph Conrad and Imperialism, 1895–1905." Master's thesis, University of Saskatchewan, 1993.

Vanderhaeghe, Guy. "John Buchan: Conservatism, Imperialism, and Social Reconstruction." Master's thesis, University of Saskatchewan, 1975.

Index

About the Author

LAURENCE KITZAN is an Associate Professor in the Department of History, University of Saskatchewan, where he lectures on British and British Imperial History. He has published in the area of Christian missions to India and China and on the First Burmese War.